PRAISE FOR
ONE MOUNTAIN THOUSAND SUMMITS

"In a single two-day period, eleven climbers lost their lives on K2. In a mystery clouded by the haze of exhaustion, thin air, and poor communication we are left to wonder: What happened on August 1–2, 2008? With an insider's knowledge of Himalayan climbing, Wilkinson goes deep into the lives of the climbers and particularly the Sherpas on this fateful climb to produce a book that should be essential reading for those wanting to understand the disaster. From the very start, I found *One Mountain Thousand Summits* riveting."

—Conrad Anker, coauthor of *The Last Explorer: Finding Mallory on Mt. Everest*

"Interviewing not only the survivors and the families of the victims but the heroic Sherpa guides in Nepal, [Wilkinson] gives the daunting legacy of the challenging terrain and a blow-by-blow account, with clinical accuracy and detail, of the disaster that nearly wiped out the international climbing team." —*Publishers Weekly*

"The book is moving and it succeeds thematically. *One Mountain Thousand Summits* finally offers hope that human dignity can prevail in the rarefied air above eight thousand meters." —*Rock and Ice*

"Wilkinson is a talented alpinist himself, as well as an enquiring writer, and he takes nothing for granted. . . shrewdly structured to take full account of the Nepali climbers' and Sherpas' stories."

—Ed Douglas, author of *Tenzing: Hero of Everest*

"Wilkinson focuses on the generally unsung guides and porters employed by the ill-fated 2008 expeditions, including a potted history of the Sherpas." —*Financial Times*

continued. . .

"*One Mountain Thousand Summits* is both a high-altitude thrill ride and an eloquent meditation on our infatuation with—and frequent misunderstandings of—individuals driven to climb to the highest places on earth. Thanks to Wilkinson's tenacious investigation, narrated with uncommon skill and grace, he has produced the definitive account of the much-debated 2008 disaster on K2."

—Nick Heil, author of *Dark Summit: The True Story of Everest's Most Controversial Season*

"Freddie Wilkinson is one of his generation's best and most articulate mountaineers. K2 can be a savage mountain. Imagine yourself above 28,000 feet, in a storm, in the dark, and an avalanche has swept away your fixed ropes. Survival is on the line. Is it every man for himself or do you risk it all to help another? There is no one better to search for answers and relive the greatest drama on the world's most dramatic mountain than Freddie. This is a must read for climbers or for anyone who wants to know what it feels like to push yourself to the very edge and the lessons we can learn about ourselves and humanity from extreme adventure."

—Geoff Tabin, author of *Blind Corners: Adventures on Seven Continents*

"In his *One Mountain Thousand Summits*, Freddie Wilkinson tells us what really happened high on K2 in August 2008 when eleven climbers lost their lives. . . . Especially compelling is the credence Wilkinson gives to the surviving Sherpas' version of events and the way he weaves the affected families and loved ones into this amazing story of survivors and heroes. This is a must read because it illuminates the most complex and tragic two days in the mountain's history."

—Jim Wickwire, coauthor of *Addicted to Danger* and the first American (with Lou Reichardt) to summit K2

ONE MOUNTAIN THOUSAND SUMMITS

THE UNTOLD STORY OF TRAGEDY AND TRUE HEROISM ON K2

FREDDIE WILKINSON

NEW AMERICAN LIBRARY

NEW AMERICAN LIBRARY
Published by New American Library, a division of
Penguin Group (USA) Inc., 375 Hudson Street,
New York, New York 10014, USA
Penguin Group (Canada), 90 Eglinton Avenue East, Suite 700, Toronto,
Ontario M4P 2Y3, Canada (a division of Pearson Penguin Canada Inc.)
Penguin Books Ltd., 80 Strand, London WC2R 0RL, England
Penguin Ireland, 25 St. Stephen's Green, Dublin 2,
Ireland (a division of Penguin Books Ltd.)
Penguin Group (Australia), 250 Camberwell Road, Camberwell, Victoria 3124,
Australia (a division of Pearson Australia Group Pty. Ltd.)
Penguin Books India Pvt. Ltd., 11 Community Centre, Panchsheel Park,
New Delhi - 110 017, India
Penguin Group (NZ), 67 Apollo Drive, Rosedale, Auckland 0632,
New Zealand (a division of Pearson New Zealand Ltd.)
Penguin Books (South Africa) (Pty.) Ltd., 24 Sturdee Avenue,
Rosebank, Johannesburg 2196, South Africa

Penguin Books Ltd., Registered Offices:
80 Strand, London WC2R 0RL, England

Published by New American Library, a division of Penguin Group (USA) Inc. Previously published in a New
American Library hardcover edition.

First New American Library Trade Paperback Printing, July 2011
10 9 8 7 6 5 4 3 2 1

Copyright © Freddie Wilkinson, 2010
Maps by Emilie Lee
All rights reserved

 REGISTERED TRADEMARK—MARCA REGISTRADA

New American Library Trade Paperback ISBN: 978-0-451-23331-8

The Library of Congress has cataloged the hardcover edition of this title as follows:

Wilkinson, Freddie.
    One mountain thousand summits: the untold story of tragedy and true heroism on K2/Freddie Wilkinson.
      p.   cm.
    ISBN 978-0-451-23119-2
1. Mountaineering—Pakistan—K2 (Mountian) 2. Mountaineers—Pakistan—K2 (Mountain)
3. Mountaineering accidents—Pakistan—K2 (Moutain)   4. K2 (Pakistan: Mountain)   I. Title.
    GV199.44.P182W55 2010
    796.522095491—dc22   2010009215

Set in Fairfield
Designed by Ginger Legato

Printed in the United States of America

PUBLISHER'S NOTE
Penguin is committed to publishing works of quality and integrity. In that spirit, we are proud to offer this book
to our readers; however the story, the experiences and the words are the author's alone.
    While the author has made every effort to provide accurate telephone numbers and Internet addresses at
the time of publication, neither the publisher nor the author assumes any responsibility for errors, or for
changes that occur after publication. Further, publisher does not have any control over and does not assume
any responsibility for author or third-party Web sites or their content.

CONTENTS

PART THREE

For Janet Bergman

ONE MOUNTAIN
THOUSAND SUMMITS

PROLOGUE

Four voices spoke in the night.

The mountain around them was windless and still. No moon showed. Breathing the air felt like breathing shards of glass. The voices spoke in anxious staccato bursts, the speech pushed from somewhere deep within the gut of each man, forced up out of the lungs and through their cracked lips to dissipate into darkness. It was a strange language, mixed with the occasional English word, but if you listened carefully there was a melody lost in the indecipherable cadences:

"Hamile pahila *fixed lines* ko tupo khuchnu parcha."

We have to find the top of the fixed lines.

"Yo ta derai naramro *avalanche* aucha jasto cha."

These are very bad avalanche conditions. This is a wind slab.

"La! Batoi chaina."

Whoa! There's no trail.

"Sabai jana eutai route ma janu parcha *avalanche*."

Keep everyone together on one path or it will trigger an avalanche.

As the four conferred in terse declarations, the others were mostly silent. A few were sitting down, their heads drooping toward the ground,

1

the beams of their headlamps focusing tighter on the small patch of snow at their feet. One or two might have already fallen asleep. The rest coughed and wheezed in the biting cold of the night sky at eighty-five hundred meters, but no one had the energy to speak.

"We need to keep descending," Pemba said, switching to slightly clipped English. "Everyone stand up!" Two more headlamps bobbed down toward them, jumping a small crevasse and splashing into their collective pool of light. It was Cas and Marco. The last two to leave the summit. No one else moved.

Pemba looked around him, trying to focus on each individual beam. There were his three teammates, Cas, Wilco, and Gerard; the Italian, Marco; the Korean leader, Mr. Kim, his partner Ms. Go, and three more of their teammates; the Frenchman, Hugues, and his Pakistani guide, Karim. Eleven climbers, Pemba thought, plus Pasang Lama, Chhiring Dorje, Jumik Bhote, and himself. Fifteen people, and every one of them was wrecked from the struggle to stand on top of the mountain.

Somewhere in the darkness below, Pemba knew, was the top anchor of the lines they had fixed earlier that day, on their ascent to the summit. Now, those ropes were quite literally their lifeline back to Camp IV, another five hundred meters in elevation below on the Shoulder of the Abruzzi Ridge. Without them, they would have to descend the exposed sections of water-ice in the Diagonal snowfield and the Bottleneck couloir unroped. It would be every man for himself. Pemba glanced at the exhausted men around him one more time. If they didn't get to the fixed lines, he knew, the weaker ones were surely lost. They had to navigate precisely down the interminable thirty-degree slope, searching for the highest anchor, an old hunk of spectra line that emerged from the surface of the mountain at the very edge of the serac. Pemba knew it was somewhere in the darkness, perhaps another hundred and fifty vertical meters below. Scarcely a hundred meters above them, resting peacefully in the eerie calm of that night, was the summit of K2.

They keep falling asleep, Chhiring responded, switching back to Nepali. *And they can't walk in a straight line either.*

At a lower elevation, the terrain separating them from the security of the fixed lines would not be considered excessively challenging; it wasn't much steeper than an expert ski trail. But the mountain was in unforgiving conditions, stripped bare by weeks of hurricane winds. Anyone who fell would not stop.

The others were looking at Pemba. Pemba spoke.

"Sabai jana eutai *rope* ma bandnu," he said. "Everyone should tie together on a rope," Pemba repeated in English. "We need to make belay, to find the proper route to the top of the fixed lines."

Only one voice responded. "Yes," Marco Confortola said, "I agree with what you propose to do." The strain of the previous eighteen hours crept into his voice.

The four climbing Sherpas looked at one another. Each man's visage was hidden behind stretch balaclavas and the thick hoods of their down parkas. But in the shadows cast by their headlamps one could faintly see the general contours of their faces, the flat noses and broad sweep of Asiatic features. They nodded in agreement.

Loose turns of rope lay stacked at the feet of Jumik Bhote, the sirdar of the Korean expedition. The five-millimeter Kevlar line was thin and light compared to other climbing ropes, but with a breaking strength of more than five thousand pounds. It was more than sixty meters long—the last of the approximately six hundred meters of line that had left camp that morning. They had almost fixed it as well, but at the last moment Pemba and Jumik decided to use a section of old line they found in place from the previous season, and carry the length of new rope to the summit in case of an emergency.

Jumik and Pasang Lama had left the summit with their Korean clients an hour ahead of the others. They started using the rope almost immediately: Jumik hastily built an anchor by stabbing his ice ax into the hardened snow and attached one end to it. Pasang Lama descended first to anchor the bottom end of the line with his ax as well. Then their five clients shuffled down, holding the line for balance, keeping slight tension on it in case they slipped. Once all had joined Pasang Lama at the lower anchor, Jumik removed his ax and down-climbed with the other end of the rope. They managed a couple of pitches of descent in this manner. Then the other summiteers began to catch up with them.

By the fourth—or was it the fifth?—pitch, Pasang Lama noticed more headlamps on their rope, one by one, descending toward him. He waited for Jumik to appear with the end of the rope, but other lights kept arriving instead, more climbers joining him at his stance until they were one connected constellation of fifteen lights. Individual teams and clients and responsibilities dissolved in the empty night air as the four Nepalis discussed what to do next—the choice seemed mostly made for them. They had become one entity, descending together.

And so they began again.

Jumik Bhote went first on the rope to build the low anchor, with Pasang Lama, who had fixed the final section of ropes that morning. Chhiring went in the middle to make sure everyone stayed on the trail and to keep the weakest from sitting down. Pemba went last. Any mistakes, a simple trip over his crampons or a misjudged step—and there would be nothing to stop him.

They moved at a stuttering pace, Chhiring often tugging the rope this way and that to keep the men moving in a straight line. In front, Jumik and Pasang stopped frequently to peer down the mountain slope, looking for the top of the fixed lines. The beams of their headlamps showed nothing but the icy skin of the mountain falling into blackness, and the occasional cookie-cutter imprint of a crampon track. They had to be careful: just below the top anchor, Pasang remembered, there was a ten-meter slope of exposed glacial ice that waited like a fatal trap. They had to be on the ropes.

After several more pitches of descent, Pasang Lama plunged his ax into the snow to make another anchor. The mountain was less steep than before. He couldn't see any ropes. One by one, the antiseptic halogen lights arrived at the anchor behind him. A biting wind began to blow. It blew a stream of snow crystals that sifted down the mountain and sounded like rain. Pasang Lama noticed that Little Kim, the one he had given the rest of his oxygen to just below the summit, was shivering badly. Pasang called to the others. He was beginning to feel very cold himself. Pemba appeared.

I can't see the ropes. Can you go first to find them?

Pemba untied from the rope and continued down, searching for the anchor. He traced a diagonal line to his left, trying to follow the switchback that the Basque climber Alberto had made that morning. He knew that if he went too far to the left he would be on top of the big serac; too far to the right, toward the south face, was an ever-steepening snowfield ending in a line of vertical cliffs. Beyond that, the void stretched nearly two vertical miles to the Godwin Austen Glacier far below.

Pasang Lama untied as well. Some of the others were sitting down, resting. He turned to his leader, Mr. Kim. "There is a little flat area, then the top anchor of fixed lines," he said.

"Okay," Kim responded.

Pasang Lama turned and continued searching for the anchor. But unlike Pemba, he skipped the switchback and followed a more direct course down. As a result he lost elevation quicker. He inched forward, stopping every few steps to scan the limit of his field of vision, his light probing the amorphous gloom. Then he saw it: a thin shadow streaking out of sight—the fixed line.

A light joined him a few moments later. It was Pemba. They turned around and looked back at the rest of the group. They could see their headlamps, still stopped at the last anchor. They were not far. "I found them! The fixed lines are here! Come here!" Pemba called in English to the others.

Jumik Bhote's voice called out from above. "Okay, we see you!" But none of the headlamps moved. Despite themselves, both Pemba Gyalje and Pasang Lama began to shiver.

"Yekchin, ma pahila *anchors* cha ki herchu," Pemba told Pasang. *I'm going to keep descending first to check the anchors.*

Pasang Lama nodded in agreement. He clipped into the top of the fixed rope. The ice just below the anchor was rock hard and smooth, its surface withered by gale-force winds and the sun's anemic powers at that altitude. He wrapped the rope around his upper wrist once, then twice for added friction and began to descend. When Pasang Lama had cleared the rope at the lower anchor, Pemba clipped and followed.

Chhiring Dorje shook suddenly. He must have momentarily fallen asleep.

He had seen the two headlamps flashing below, and heard Pemba's voice calling to them. There it was! That was the top anchor of the fixed lines! "Come on, guys!" Chhiring said in English to the others. He felt a momentary panic flare inside of him, the sudden feeling that this was his chance and he had to keep moving. The anchor was all that mattered. They had to get to the anchor; they had to keep descending.

He started down-climbing in the direction of the two lights. No one else followed. "Everyone keep moving. Stand up! Let's go down; we need to go down now!" Chhiring shouted back into the darkness.

"Okay, okay . . ." one feeble voice responded. But no one stirred.

"You need to keep moving down. No stopping!" Chhiring pleaded once more into the night. He waited, catching his breath after yelling, looking at the headlamps behind him. A few moved slowly forward. Others were stationary. *This is bad*, the Sherpa thought to himself. *This is a bad situation.* The realization cut through him. They would not all make it down. Some were going to spend the night sitting right there.

Chhiring looked downhill again and saw that Pasang Lama and Pemba Gyalje's headlamps had disappeared. They had started down the fixed lines. He felt a sudden dread that he wouldn't find the ropes, that they were leaving him. He stared ahead, trying to fix the location of the top anchor in his memory, where they had signaled from only a few moments before. Chhiring hesitated, caught between his desire to wait for the others and his urge to go down. It was completely dark. There were bad avalanche conditions and he had to get to the fixed lines to descend the steep snow below. Somewhere in his subconscious, he knew it was time to make a decision.

And then in the darkness the Sherpa's thoughts turned eastward, to home. He saw his two daughters, Namdu and Tenzing, sitting around the warm bench seat of their kitchen table doing homework while his wife, Dawa, prepared dinner. What would they do if he died? How would they survive without him? The decision came very quickly to Chhiring.

Okay, he thought, *I must live for them. I must go down.*

A long second passed. Chhiring called once more. Then he turned his back away from the summit, away from the tiny constellation of lights above him. He began down-climbing again, moving toward the fixed lines.

There was a new line just beyond the cache of empty oxygen bottles Pasang Lama had left that morning. It was another section of thin five-millimeter cord, different from what Pasang Lama remembered being there that morning. The old line was gone. The light from his headlamp flickered on the serac wall above him, a massive bulwark of ice a hundred meters high. It was overhung, and it loomed directly above him in the colorless glow of his LED light. The surface of the frozen cliff was shattered and freshly scarred, a truck-size piece of ice missing from its base. Small pieces of debris trickled from the bottom. Like a festering wound in the side of the mountain that refused to clot.

The route they had climbed that morning continued a few meters farther to the left, to reach the top of the Bottleneck couloir, which it followed straight down toward the top of the Shoulder, another two hundred and fifty meters below.

But the final few meters of the traverse, a pitch they had carefully fixed that morning, was now nothing but a swath of barren, fifty-degree névé, and the strange new rope dropped plumb-line directly into the void—Pasang Lama hoped it stretched far enough to reach into the Bottleneck somewhere below. He could hear small pieces of ice trickling down the mountain.

Pemba joined him at the anchor. He surveyed the scene, then removed his radio from an inner pocket of his down suit. *Jumik, Jumik*, he called. *We have a problem down here. Jumik, are you there? Jumik?* Jumik didn't answer. Pemba put the radio away and looked at Pasang Lama. *Do you want to go first or me?*

Pemba went first. Slowly, deliberately, he rappelled down the thin line, keeping his figure-eight device firmly braked with both hands. He could feel the line dangling untethered beneath him. Pasang Lama waited at the top anchor, and then the thin line bearing Pemba's weight suddenly pendulumed to the right, as if Pemba had just swung off the edge of something. Pasang Lama was momentarily wrenched off his stance and slammed against a rock. Inside his gloves, he felt warm fluid. A trickle of blood. Somewhere in the night, he heard more pieces of ice tinkling down the mountain, rushing and skipping, draining away.

Pemba's voice called out from below. *The ropes are gone. There is no more rope down here.* The line went slack. *Pasang! Let's hurry up—this is very dangerous here.* Pemba was crouched beneath a rock island on the right side of the couloir when Pasang Lama joined him at the end of the new rope. *We go quickly now. Let's go.*

Then they heard a cry from above. The voice called out in Nepali and they could tell it was Chhiring Dorje.

What has happened here? Wait for me.

Pasang and Pemba waited. More ice came down. There was a constant stream of small pieces down the couloir, surging and flowing like a turbulent small river. Larger pieces bounced and ricocheted out of the darkness.

Pemba started down almost as soon as Chhiring Dorje reached them. There were no ropes beneath them, nothing to clip into—each man was frightfully alone in the night, knowing that his fate rested on the front points of his crampons and the sturdy swing of his ice ax. An inch of steel, no more, was all that would hold them to the mountainside. Chhiring moved to follow. Then he noticed Pasang Lama, standing still.

Come on, Pasang Lama. We have to get out of here.

Pasang Lama was quiet. Chhiring looked at him.

Pasang Lama's mind raced back over the series of pitches they had rigged as a hand line above. He had gone first. He used his ax to make the anchor. His ax. He had left it at the bottom anchor for the others when he and Pemba untied and continued on to find the top of the fixed lines.

I don't have my ice ax, Pasang Lama said. *I lost it.*

What are you going to do? Chhiring asked. He kicked one foot sideways against the slope, rolling his ankle so he could stand flat-footed and rest. There were no more fixed ropes in the Bottleneck, no more safety lines to aid their descent. Each knew they had to down-climb alone to safety. Without an ice ax, there was no down-climbing. Pasang Lama might as well have been stuck on the far side of the moon.

I don't know. . . .

Chhiring looked at Pasang. His face had a blankness to it. His eyes were wide and slightly unfocused. A single tear trickled out of one of them. It ran down toward his nostril before it froze. Pasang Lama stood very still, with nothing more to say.

Chhiring Dorje took another breath and then he spoke.

"Ki hami dubai baichcha ki dubai marcha, jam."

We will live together, or die together.

Pemba stayed in front of Chhiring and Pasang Lama. He stopped frequently and leaned out from the mountain, peering down the slopes below him. His instinct told him to move to his left, toward the north, away from the danger of the avalanches. There were several small bands of exposed rocks in the way, but there were also remnants of old fixed line to help. He scouted ahead, finding the best path through the intermittent terrain, occasionally flashing his light backward at Chhiring and Pasang to guide them forward.

A short section of cutoff line bound them together. Chhiring leaned in over his crampon points, overdriving each step and planting the shaft of his mountaineering tool through the hardened snow; Pasang Lama down-climbed just beneath him, doing his best to keep his weight over his crampons. Both his mittens desperately held on to the mountain, pounding against its surface like some primitive instrument. The rope between them stayed taut.

By the way Pasang Lama kicked, Chhiring could tell how hard the snow was. He could feel how big the next step would be, whether the slope was getting steeper, or if there was a bit of fixed line to hold on to. Chhiring knew everything. His concentration was total. He felt Pasang Lama's weight and knew that his friend would not pull him unexpectedly. For forty-five minutes, the two men worked down the slopes of K2 together, their survival resting on Chhiring's legs, the sturdy, indefatigable legs of a Rolwaling potato farmer.

Below eighty-one hundred meters, the angle of the slope began to moderate. The rocks disappeared. Nothing shone in Pemba's headlight but a broad slope of windblown snow. It squeaked underfoot. Then the wreckage began to appear out of the darkness, ghostly blocks of ice and debris that lay scattered about. Pemba finally stepped into the safe zone, beyond the farthest reaches of the serac fall. As he waited for Chhiring and Pasang to join him, he again removed the radio.

Jumik, Jumik . . . are you there? There was no answer.

Below, several hundred meters distant, two headlamps inched through the darkness toward them. The threesome continued down, letting gravity pull them lower, toward the pinpricks of light. Pemba felt his shoulders sag, and realized how tired he was.

Pasang Bhote and Tsering Bhote had a thermos of hot tea and some food. They met them just below eight thousand meters. They had come up to Camp IV with the second team of Koreans that day. Pemba drank from the thermos. A short while later, Chhiring and Pasang Lama's headlamps appeared out of the darkness. They all drank.

Where are they? Why did you let them go to the summit that late in the day? Pasang Bhote asked.

Pemba looked down at the cup of tea he held in his mitten-clad hand. The steam rose and disappeared into the dry, frigid air around them. It was the first thing he had had to drink in six hours. He had nothing to say.

Where are Jumik and the Koreans? Why did you leave the others? Pasang Bhote was angry. He anxiously eyed the mountain above for more headlamps descending. He saw none, other than a distant smudge of light at the top of the fixed lines. It was right where the three Sherpas had left the others. They hadn't moved.

They wouldn't move. They were too tired. They were sick from the air. Pemba raised his gaze, looking at the thin glow at the top of the fixed lines, where he knew a dozen people lay. Were they all still alive? What was happening up there?

A new constellation of lights flashed yellow and red. The men in camp heard the crunch of footsteps approaching. They sat up in their sleeping bags. More headlamps turned on, lighting the colored fabric of the small cluster of tents from within. A few hoarse voices called out. "We have water for you, come inside," an American voice called from Chhiring's tent.

Pemba's tent was empty. Jelle had descended to Camp III that afternoon; Wilco, Cas, and Gerard were somewhere above. Pemba crawled inside and lit the stove.

Pemba had the satellite phone with him. The phone was not his; it belonged to Gerard. As he melted snow above the incandescent blue flame, he patiently warmed the battery for the phone in his sleeping bag. Sometime later, he removed the plastic device from between his legs, cupping his hands around it as if to check the temperature of its circuitry, extended the antenna, and pressed the power button.

It took a long minute to connect to the satellite network. Suddenly the phone let out a beep, and a message flashed onto the screen. YOU HAVE NEW TEXT MESSAGES, the display read.

Pemba didn't check the messages. Instead, he pressed the green dial button, and then began to type in a phone number.

PART ONE

*T*he general public is inevitably drawn to Mount Everest. It's the most famous, the most important, the tallest mountain on the planet. But my own
imagination, the imagination of a twelve-year-old pimple-faced boy, latched onto
the mountain that is the most difficult, the most dangerous, and the cruelest.

Sometime in the middle of sixth grade, I acquired a copy of Jim Curran's
account of the 1986 season, K2: Triumph and Tragedy. It was a paperback
version, the pages creased and folded, but it was the first mountaineering
book I ever read. Next, I devoured Rick Ridgeway's story of the 1978 American expedition, The Last Step. More books followed, with names like In
the Throne Room of the Mountain Gods, The Endless Knot, and K2:
The Savage Mountain.

Each story of the second-highest mountain in the world was an intox-
icating mix of real-life adventure and peril. As long as men had tried to
climb K2, I learned, the mountain had a beguiling power not only to push
climbers to the very brink of their capabilities, but also to sow confusion and
disorder on its flanks. Major disasters occurred on the mountain in 1939,
when four climbers were killed, and in 1986, when thirteen climbers perished in a single season.

With every new expedition tome I read, the mountain seemed less like an inanimate object to be conquered, and more like a living, breathing thing. K2 was a violent creature, with steep, avalanche-prone faces, devastating rockfalls, and quick-striking storms. It seemed to strike with perfect, malevolent timing, like when Art Gilkey's stretcher was swept away in a fatal avalanche in the midst of a heroic rescue attempt in 1953, or when Renato Casaratto's life was swallowed into a crevasse in 1986, when he was only minutes from safety.

The quality that made K2 uniquely lethal was the fact that it forced climbers to negotiate steep, hazardous terrain while under the extreme psychological and cognitive duress of climbing at high altitude. Climbers went to Everest, I thought, to conquer themselves. But on K2, climbers were very much at war with a greater power.

The violence of this brooding colossus was best summed up in the manner in which the two mountains disposed of their victims. On Everest, the bodies of dead climbers often lay high on the mountain for years, calmly desiccating and withering away in the same location where they took their final breaths. Indeed, several frozen bodies serve as important landmarks to this day high on the mountain's two most popular routes to the summit, and in 1999, the body of George Mallory was found at an altitude of eight thousand meters, seventy-five years after he disappeared.

On K2, the bodies of the deceased rarely rest where they fall. The mountain is too steep. Gravity cleanses its flanks, flushing the human remains with myriad avalanches and windstorms down thousands of feet of snow slopes, rocky cliffs, and serac bands. Only once the corpse finally reaches the talus of the Godwin Austen Glacier at the base of the mountain, a process of years or decades, will it finally come to rest. By then, all that is most often left are a few shattered bones, perhaps a bit of flesh, and pieces of tattered clothing and tarnished gear.

Two years after I first read about K2, the summer before my freshman year in high school, I was on vacation in Maine when one of my parents pointed out an article about six pages deep in the A section of the Boston Globe. The British climber Alison Hargreaves and six other mountaineers *had been caught in a severe windstorm on the summit of K2. They were all missing and presumed dead.*

That same year I had just learned to climb myself, on the short rock cliffs and stubby mountains of New England. K2 became a symbol of everything climbing meant to me. It represented what the addiction was all about, distilled down to its most basic, primal form. K2 was a mountain of overwhelming beauty, a thing that irreversibly attracted climbers, and killed them with indiscriminate violence.

By then I knew the names and elevations of obscure features on the mountain, the different routes to the summit, and the locations of each camp. Many of the heavyweights in the history of Himalayan climbers have written extensively about the mountain, including Charlie Houston and Bob Bates, Galen Rowell, Rick Ridgeway, Reinhold Messner, Kurt Diemberger, and Greg Child. I knew all their stories. Despite the fact that I had never been to Pakistan, the mountain became a fundamental part of who I was as a climber.

When I absently turned on a TV in a hotel room one morning in August, I felt the presence of the imaginary dragon of my youth suddenly return.

It was happening again. . . .

K2: 8611 meters

View from the Southeast

Abruzzi ridge: L. Lacadelli & A. Compagnoni
  July 31 st, 1954 (1st ascent)

South Southeast Spur: J. Oiarzabal,
J. Gutierrez, A. Inurrategui, F. Inurrategui,
& J. Pablo, June 24, 1994

marked locations indicate the modern
positions of camps used during the 2008
season.

ELee 2010

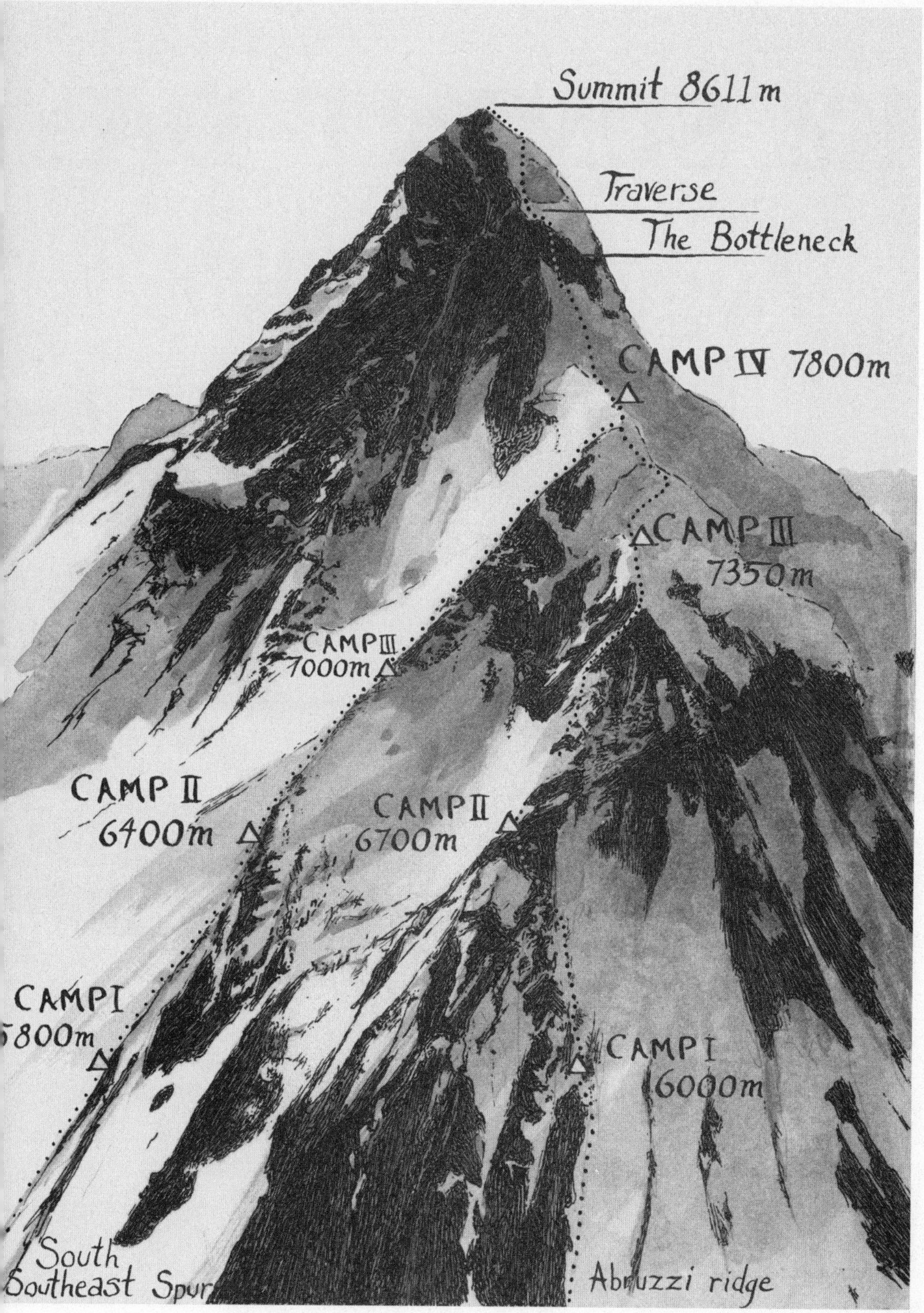

Summit 8611 m

Traverse
The Bottleneck

CAMP IV 7800m
△

△ CAMP III
7350 m

CAMP III
7000 m △

CAMP II
6400 m △

CAMP II
6700 m △

CAMP I
5800 m
△

CAMP I
6000 m △

South
Southeast Spur

Abruzzi ridge

K2 SUMMIT DAY

August 1 2008

Elee 2010

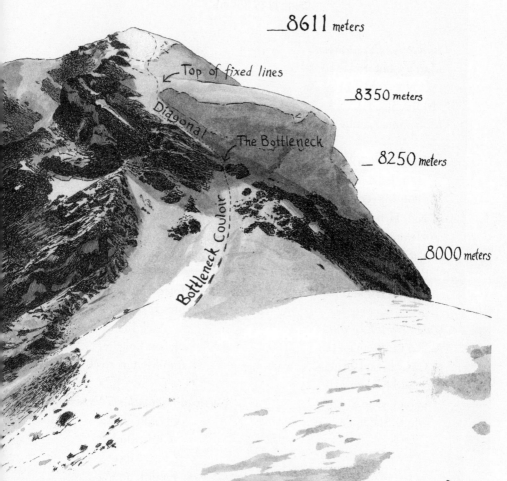

_8611 meters

Top of fixed lines

_8350 meters

Diagonal

The Bottleneck

_8250 meters

Bottleneck Couloir

_8000 meters

view from camp IV at 7,800 meters on the shoulder of the Abruzzi ridge

DRAMATIS PERSONAE

As of ten p.m. on July 31, 2008, the following are the best-known locations for the forty-seven climbers believed to be on the flanks of K2.

Camp IV (7,800m)

Italian K2 Expedition
Marco Confortola (L)
Roberto Manni
Mohammad Ali (P)
Mohammad Amin (P)

Korean Flying Jump K2 Expedition
Kim Jae-su (L)
Go Mi-yeong
Kim Hyo-gyeong
Hwang Dong-jin
Park Kyeong-hyo
Jumik Bhote (P)
Pasang Lama (P)

Dutch Norit Expedition
Wilco van Rooijen (L)
Cas van de Gevel
Gerard McDonnell
Pemba Gyalje Sherpa
Jelle Staleman

Serbian K2 Expedition
Dren Mandic
Iso Planic
Predrag (Pedja) Zagorac
Muhammad Hussain (P)
Muhammad Khan (P)

Norwegian K2 Expedition
Cecilie Skog (L)
Rolf Bae
Lars Nessa
Oystein Stangeland

French International Expedition
Hugues D'Aubarède (L)
Nick Rice
Jehan Baig (P)
Karim Meherban (P)

American International Expedition
Chhiring Dorje
Chris Klinke
Eric Meyer
Fredrik Sträng

(L) Expedition Leader
(P) Professional High-mountain Worker
(LO) Liaison Officer

South-southeast Spur	Abruzzi Ridge
Camp III (7,000m)	**Camp III (7,350m)**

<table>
<tr><td valign="top">

Dutch Norit Expedition
Mark Sheen

Camp II (6,400m)

Camp I (5,800m)

</td><td valign="top">

Korean Flying Jump Expedition
Kim Sueng-sang
Son Byung-woo
Lee Sung-rok
Kim Tae-gui
"Big" Pasang Bhote (P)
Tsering Bhote (P)

Singapore Expedition
Robert Goh EE Kiat (L)
Edwin Siew Cheok Wai
Ang Chhiring Sherpa (P)
Jamling Bhote (P)

Spanish Broad Peak Expedition
Alberto Zerain

American International Team
Paul Walters

Camp II (6,700m)

American International Team
Mike Farris (L)

Camp I (6,000m)

</td></tr>
</table>

Base Camp (5,000m)
Not everyone present at K2 base camp is listed.

Roeland van Oss (Dutch Norit Expedition); Nawang Sherpa (cook), Captain Azimullah Beg (LO) (Korean Flying Jump Expedition); Milivoj Erdeljan (L), Captain Sabir Ali Changazi (LO) (Serbian K2 Expedition); Hoselito Bite (Serbian Solo K2 Expedition)

1

LIGHT A CANDLE

At a little past midnight, on August 1, 2008, a small company of men and women roused in their high camp at seventy-eight hundred meters on a snow-laden ridge deep in the crinkled topography of the Karakoram mountain range, in northeast Pakistan. Outside, the night sky was cold and quiet and clear of cloud cover. Stars shone overhead, and the twinkling lights of the trailbreaking party could be faintly seen, already moving upward, bound for the 8,611-meter summit of K2, the second-highest point on planet Earth.

Their tents were clustered together, pitched so closely that it was hard to maneuver in and out of the vestibule entrance of one shelter without brushing against the adjacent dwelling or tripping over an unseen cord that guyed the structure to the mountain. The thin fabric walls did nothing to suppress the chorus of hollow coughs and isobutane stoves that sputtered and hacked in the darkness, punctuated by the occasional sound of a sleeping bag zipper or the rustle of nylon.

It was to be one of the single largest blitzes in the history of the mountain, and a more pluralistic group of modern climbers could hardly be imagined. They came from France, Italy, Ireland, Sweden, Serbia,

Norway, the Netherlands, the United States, South Korea, Pakistan, and Nepal: More than thirty individuals from seven separately permitted expeditions occupied the final bivouac, only a day's climb from the summit. They had invested months of time, thousands of dollars, and made untold personal sacrifices just to be there, to have this chance. With few exceptions, they were ambitious, successful men in the prime of their lives.

Some, like Wilco van Rooijen, the outspoken, prematurely gray leader of the Dutch Norit team, and Kim Jae-su, the taciturn, no-nonsense head of the Korean expedition, were devoted professionals with large corporate sponsors backing their climbs. But others, like Lars Nessa, a lanky nurse from Norway, Cas van de Gevel, a mild-mannered carpenter from Holland, and Gerard McDonnell, a barrel-chested Irish electronic engineer, were skilled amateurs who had worked long months to save enough money to attempt K2. Hugues D'Aubarède, a compact insurance agent from Lyons, France, had changed his travel arrangements at the last possible moment, delaying his plane flight home to have one more crack at the summit. Two women joined the otherwise male-dominated summit push. Cecilie Skog, an attractive professional adventurer with a shock of curly, sandy-blond hair, climbed with her husband, Rolf Bae, as part of the Norwegian team. Go Mi-yeong, from South Korea, was an accomplished competition rock climber who had recently turned her attention to high-altitude climbing. Partnered with Kim Jae-su, she had summited four different eight-thousand-meter peaks in just over a year: Everest, Broad Peak, Shishapangma, and Lhotse.

Inside each shelter, all was covered in a glittering universe of ice crystals, formed as the climbers' moist breath condensed and froze in the arctic temperatures. Most climbers sat facing one another, their backs leaning against the taut tent cloth, a lit stove between them. A carpet of Ensolite foam pads covered the floor; equipment and clothing littered almost every available space. The cramped environs were impossible to keep organized, and if one climber needed to stretch his legs, or change position, it had to be carefully choreographed with his tentmates so as not to inadvertently kick anyone or knock over the stove.

In slow, uncoordinated movements, they dressed in thick one-piece down suits with balaclavas, hats, hoods, and headlamps. Spare mittens, ski goggles, sunblock, and a few packets of energy gel were placed near the door. Perhaps a folded flag or small memento was added to the pile. Then all that remained to be done was to top off the last of the insulated bottles with lukewarm water, poured ever so carefully from small titanium pans.

They came from all walks of life, and all corners of the globe, and were motivated by a varying mix of personal challenge and professional gain—just as the challenge of the world's highest mountains has always attracted complex and compulsive personalities. Indeed, the only thing that could be said without hesitation about all of them was this: They were obsessed. And each climber knew the final challenge—summit day—would be the most severe.

Viewed from the south, K2 is a wonder of geologic architecture, a giant sculpture of steep snowfields and rocky cliffs cleaved in near-perfect symmetry, a pyramid pointing directly to the heavens. For six weeks, teams of climbers had prepared for this day, methodically fixing rope and establishing camps on two variant paths up the mountain's southeastern flank, the South-southeast (SSE) Spur and the Abruzzi Ridge.* From the Godwin Austen Glacier, the two lines follow separate ridgelines that slowly taper to converge on the Shoulder, a broad section of snow ridge at just under eight thousand meters where Camp IV, the highest camp, is located. From there, everyone would share one route to the top.

In a marathon effort, they would race to the summit and back, covering eight hundred vertical meters of terrain, pushing their bodies—and the limits of human physiology itself—to reach the 8,611-meter apex of the mountain. Above Camp IV, the final challenge guarding the summit of K2 is brutally obvious. But it also has an aesthetic quality, some intangible value that perhaps only a true mountaineer can appreciate. Something approaching *elegance*. Beyond the Shoulder, the upper mountain

---

* The SSE Spur is also commonly called the Cesen Route, after the Slovenian climber Tomo Cesen, who claimed a partial ascent of the line in 1986.

is defined by one massive feature: a gigantic, overhanging, otherworldly ice cliff known to mountaineers as a serac. The impassible barrier continues far to the east, while rock slabs and cliff bands wrap in underneath it from the south. To get to the summit, you have to get around the serac.

Seracs are inherently unstable structures; occasionally pieces of ice will cleave off and fall, exfoliating like layers of an onion. From a route-finding standpoint, there are two possible choices to get to the top of K2. The only way to avoid the danger of climbing beneath the serac is to climb the technical and time-consuming rocky terrain to the south. Or one could choose to race under the serac, threading a needle up a slender snow couloir known as the Bottleneck, then jogging left across a diagonal snowfield between the bottom of the serac and the top of the rock cliffs, to reach the easier summit slopes. Several hundred mountaineers have reached the summit via the latter option; to date no climber has succeeded on the former. It is a classic case study in risk management: a harder route that is safer from objective hazards, or an easier route that takes more chances. The fact that the objectively dangerous option has grown to be considered the normal route on the mountain proves one thing.

Climbing K2 is not, by its very nature, conservative mountaineering.

The men and women setting out from Camp IV to the summit of K2 knew they would be climbing over fabled ground. Mountaineering literature is filled with seventy years of human drama that has occurred on this very section of mountain. It has been the scene of great epics and courageous efforts, and comparatively few unmitigated victories. While the particulars of each mishap vary, one pattern clearly emerges: The closer a climber gets to the summit of K2, the more willing he or she is to hang it out there—just a little bit further—to finish the job. Time and time again, climbers have found themselves on the summit having overextended their physical reserves and losing mental awareness with each passing second. Throw in one more factor—nightfall, an approaching storm, a sick climber, or a moonless night—and the descent can quickly become an all-out fight for survival.

Sometime around two a.m., local time, individual teams began to exit their shelters, staring for a moment at the darkened peak above them. Then they dropped to one knee, painstakingly attaching a spiked crampon to each boot. Packs were shouldered and bulky mittens pulled over thin liner gloves. The thick down suits and protective garb hid each person's true identity, making it sometimes difficult even for teammates to recognize one another.

Nevertheless, there was an anonymous camaraderie in the night as slowly, in ones or twos, the climbers left Camp IV and began trudging forward in slow, measured steps. It was a sign of just how close-knit their community was, the world of modern high-altitude climbing, that most everybody on the mountain knew at least one other person from a previous Himalayan expedition. Many more knew one another by reputation, or shared mutual friends. For the better part of the summer, they had lived as neighbors at the foot of the great mountain. They had crowded together to watch movies on tiny laptop screens, shared laughs in broken English, and slowly become friends. And as they whiled away the hours, one subject came up over and over again: summit day. Which teams would be in position when the weather window came? What would the conditions be like? How long would it take? Clasping steaming mugs of coffee and tea in the mess tent, or standing in a small knot outside, they had gone over the variables, calculating every possible iteration of events.

To a person, they should have been experienced enough to understand the dangers of the mountain they chose to climb. But how much they truly knew and trusted one another is impossible to say. And so, to understand the events that were soon to follow, we must first understand these men and women and their world, and the culture of modern high-altitude mountaineering. An unchartable cascade of events and circumstances had led them all to the same place, at the same time. For all their differences, the climbers who crawled out of their tents at Camp IV in the early morning hours of August 1, 2008 and set foot toward the top of K2 were bound together by one inescapable fact: No one team would have the luxury of complete independence, of being alone. They would have to work together, and share the same path on the same mountain.

———

A brisk, metronomic beat shattered the silence.

It was eleven p.m. in the city of Utrecht, the Netherlands, and Maarten van Eck's telephone was ringing. Maarten sat at a tastefully modern wood table in his darkened kitchen, three phones and a laptop computer neatly arranged in front of him. The sterile glow from the screen reflected off a large plate-glass window, casting a blurred image of the room back at him.

Maarten picked up the phone. He listened for a moment, uttered a few terse words in reply, and then ended the conversation. Pushing his wire-rimmed glasses back to the bridge of his nose, Maarten felt a twinge of excitement in his fingers as he tapped a new dispatch:

The telephone is ringing! The Norit K2 team is on its way to the summit of K2. The longest day has begun. . . .

Among the rare subset of climbers dedicated to the craft of reaching the planet's highest summits, one number counts above all others: eight thousand meters. Only fourteen of the world's mountains are higher than that elevation, and all of them are located in Central Asia, either part of the Himalayas, or its twin range to the northwest, the Karakoram. By sheer statistical coincidence, that altitude has become the yardstick that defines the true alpine heavyweights, the playing field of the game.

By the mid-1950s, after thirty years of trial and error, mountaineers perfected a well-proven method for reaching the top of these Himalayan giants and getting back down alive. Beginning with the French on Annapurna in 1950, and ending with the Chinese on Shishapangma in 1964, all of the fourteen eight-thousanders were first climbed in a watershed golden age of high-altitude mountaineering. The key to success revolved around having two things in abundance: rope and manpower. By equipping the climbing route with miles of line permanently anchored to the mountain, expeditions made traveling between camps quicker, easier, and safer. Once the route was equipped, it was relatively easy for the manpower—typically a full complement of foreign climbers and hired local labor, sometimes totaling more than fifty people—to transport provisions upward, building a supply pyramid that hopefully, by the end of the expedition, would catapult a few team members all the way to the summit.

This siege-style climbing prevailed until the mid-1970s, when an ambitious young alpinist from the Tyrol region of the Italian Alps, Reinhold Messner, staged a series of lightning raids on the Himalayan monsters. First to fall was Hidden Peak, at 8,068 meters, the eleventh-highest mountain in the world. Messner, partnered with Austrian Peter Habeler, sprinted up the peak, summiting and returning to base camp in a gob-smacking three days round-trip. In one stroke, they blithely dispensed with fixed ropes, load carrying, and permanent camps—the whole concept of the supply pyramid. It was the first time in history an eight-thousander was climbed alpine style. Three years later, Messner and Habeler produced an even more extraordinary feat, becoming the first two men to summit Everest without the use of supplemental oxygen. Though the pair relied on some elements of the traditional siege infrastructure to complete their ascent of the South Col route, Messner produced a second, equally stunning achievement later that same year in unimpeachable style, by establishing a new route, solo, on Nanga Parbat, at 8,125 meters the ninth-highest mountain in the world. Two years after that, in 1980, he returned to Everest and blitzed the mountain in similar fashion.

With a mane of fashionably shaggy brown hair, steel blue eyes, and the slight physique of a long-distance runner, Messner cast an iconographic shadow across the sport of Himalayan climbing. He possessed topflight technical skills, finely honed on the hardest climbs in the Alps, legendary endurance at altitude, and a staggering amount of mental fortitude. In public, he cultivated the whimsical mystique of a modern pilgrim, at once impossibly strong in the mountains, yet also prone to moments of self-doubt, megalomania, and emotional insecurity.

Messner's own ascent of K2, via the Abruzzi Ridge in 1979, was a surprisingly conventional climb compared to his bold solo efforts and imaginative traverses and enchainments. With a team of five, he established three camps and fixed lines to seventy-four hundred meters before he and Michl Dacher made a lightweight dash to the summit, bivouacking once along the way. Although they climbed without supplemental oxygen, the team employed two Balti porters to help ferry loads low on the route. So long as any would-be K2 summiteers accepted responsibility for fixing their own route and carrying their own loads, Messner felt that this hybrid strategy, which lay somewhere in between traditional siege tactics and pure alpine style, was a prudent approach to climbing the mountain.

"Whoever has humped up his own camps, installed his own camps, achieves a far more intimate feel for the mountain," Messner wrote of his climb. "He does not need to be told what increased risks he is taking. The difficulty of the mountain, the height, our own personal limitations do not permit us to go up into areas beyond our capabilities without outside help." In 1986, the Tyrolean summited Lhotse, at 8,501 meters the fourth-highest mountain in the world, becoming the first climber in history to climb all fourteen of the eight-thousanders.

Messner's groundbreaking stylistic advances might have changed the rules of the game of high-altitude climbing for everyone, were it not for another breakthrough that occurred on Everest the year before he finished his quest. In 1985, American Dick Bass, a fifty-five-year-old Texas oil tycoon–cum–ski resort entrepreneur, reached the world's highest summit and completed his own project: to climb the highest mountains on every continent. His achievement set the high-altitude community reeling, not so much because of the fact that someone had climbed the "seven summits," but because of how he had done it: Bass, a self-confessed amateur with a modest résumé of big-mountain experience, invested a small fortune to hire professional guides to organize each expedition and help him get to the top.

Separately, Messner's and Bass's achievements offered divergent visions of the future of the sport. Messner proved that the highest mountains could be climbed in a lightweight, minimal style, while Bass demonstrated that, using heavy-siege tactics, those same summits were attainable by ordinary, fit individuals with the requisite financial means and mental toughness. Paradoxically, the two milestones both highlighted the practice of collecting summits. Even Messner seemed to forsake challenge for its own sake in the last years of his eight-thousand-meter career. His final two summits, Makalu and Lhotse, were both ascended via their normal routes; a helicopter was used to transport him from base camp to base camp to maintain acclimatization and avoid wasting extra time on the low-altitude approaches. A harbinger of things to come, it would take another ten years, until the 1996 Everest season, for the disastrous consequences of the commoditization of eight-thousand-meter peaks to come home to roost.

Around the same time, the mid-1980s, the governments of the Himalayan states began to dispense with the old one-expedition-per-mountain regulations and issue permits for the same mountains at the same time to as many different teams as could pay. Pakistan was one of the first to initiate this trend, when in 1986 it issued nine permits for K2. An international convention of many of the world's leading alpinists (sans Messner) amassed on "the Strip" that summer, as K2's southern base camp on the Godwin Austen Glacier was dubbed. A cadre of Polish, French, British, Spanish, Austrian, Italian, and South Korean climbers eventually summited in a six-week period, most adopting the same hybrid strategy Messner had used on the peak. But, in the same time period, thirteen people died in a handful of separate accidents.

The 1986 season, which was ably chronicled by Englishman Jim Curran in his book *K2: Triumph and Tragedy*, was hard to categorize. Most fatalities occurred in ones and twos, until a catastrophic storm swept through late in the season, pinning seven climbers on the Shoulder. When the weather finally cleared, only two had the strength to survive the descent. Searching for a common thread among the complex causes for the loss of life, Curran himself could only offer this: "If anything was common to most of the deaths, it was that a lot of people were very ambitious and had a lot to gain by climbing K2—and a lot to lose as well . . . the word that comes to mind is overambitious."

By the last decade of the twentieth century, the governments of China, Pakistan, and Nepal had all embraced the policy of issuing unlimited permits for the same routes at the same time on their most popular peaks. As more and more people flocked to the world's tallest mountains, sharing the mountain with unknown climbers and different teams became an unavoidable demographic reality. Bureaucratic policy guaranteed that the so-called "normal routes" would be overrun with human traffic; the eight-thousand-meter base camps became great melting pots for expeditions from every conceivable corner of the globe. It also sounded the death knell for the minimal, self-sufficient ethos advocated by Messner and a return to more traditional siege tactics. Simply put, once a route is fixed with ropes and established camps, the nature of the climb changes for everyone, regardless of whether they would prefer to make use of that infrastructure or not.

It would be an exaggeration to say that all modern high-altitude climbers aspire to duplicate Messner's feat, but there is no mistaking the fact that the same individuals show up on the eight-thousand-meter peaks, year after year. None of the climbers vying for the top of K2 on the first of August, 2008, had designs to significantly alter the same proven strategy established a half century before. Indeed, much of the work of fixing rope and breaking trail on an eight-thousand-meter peak is the same in modern times as it was fifty years ago, regardless of whether there is one expedition or ten to share the burden. What had significantly changed was the organizational structure of the climbers on the mountain. Whereas the expeditions of the golden age fielded large teams of men within a single unified team, if anything one finds an even greater pool of available labor on modern eight-thousanders—but the manpower is dispersed, scattered among numerous expeditions. Interteam politics are another indelible part of modern high-altitude mountaineering.

In early June, the Internet site Explorersweb.com, a leading source for information about eight-thousand-meter climbing, reported that ten expeditions had received permits for K2, making for a total of fifty expeditions and more than three hundred people flocking to Pakistan's five eight-thousand-meter peaks. "Remember only a few years ago when K2 expeditions were rare, with several years leaving the mountain empty?" the Web site asked. "Ten years back only the most hardcore mountaineers went to Pakistan at all. Not anymore: With the recent events in China and Nepal; all of a sudden Pakistan seems the hub of safety and order while Himalaya climbing in general is taking off like never before."

The two largest groups on the mountain, the South Korean "Flying Jump" Expedition led by Kim Jae-su, and Wilco van Rooijen's Dutch Norit team, were both large and well-funded efforts. The Korean leader— "Mr. Kim," as he was known among base camp denizens—was forty-seven years old, and enjoyed lucrative sponsorship from Kolon Sports, a division of a large Korean corporation involved in everything from textile manufacture to water treatment to waste management, not to mention outdoor recreation. Kim registered eleven climbers on his permit, including four Nepali climbing-Sherpas. They would be attempting the Abruzzi Ridge. The Dutch Norit expedition had eight members, and opted to climb the SSE Spur, considered to be slightly steeper than the Abruzzi, though less exposed to rockfall. Like Kim, Wilco van Rooijen, the Dutch leader, was a professional adventurer, marketing himself as a corporate speaker with the slogan, "Business is your adventure, adventure is my business." He was forty years old, and back for his third attempt on the mountain. Wilco was a painstakingly thorough leader, not only assembling a strong team of climbers, but also recruiting a support staff that included a meteorologist, doctor, media spokesman, and webmaster, all of whom remained in the Netherlands.

Both men had designed their expeditions in the classic siege-style mold. In a series of forays, they would fix ropes up their respective routes, slowly carrying equipment and building a supply chain higher and higher. The two teams had been the first to arrive at base camp in early June, and each was single-handedly responsible for fixing the ropes as far as Camp III on their respective routes. As the season continued, teams of Serbs, Norwegians, Italians, and Singaporeans arrived. They all chose to follow the Koreans on the Abruzzi Route. It would have been difficult for any one of these groups, which were smaller in number, with five climbers or less, to independently perform the same job that the Koreans and Norit assumed on the Abruzzi and the SSE Spur.

But once fixed ropes are in place, anyone can use them, and there lies the problem. This tension between large expeditions that perform the lion's share of the work preparing the route, and smaller teams that appear to be taking advantage of their labors, is a recurring issue in the high mountains. Sometimes smaller teams and independent climbers share in the effort; more often they voluntarily make a donation of gear or money to the team that has orchestrated the prepping of the route instead. Occasionally, they are charged a fee.

Two more large groups occupied base camp. It is not accurate to call them singular teams, however, as they each contained internal factions and functioned more or less independently on the mountain. The phenomenon of climbers pooling together resources to pay for the logistical support is nothing new. It is historically rooted in a series of groundbreaking expeditions organized in the early 1980s between elite British and Polish alpinists. Today, they are especially popular in Pakistan, owing to its "one mountain—one price" permitting structure. There are several international agencies that specialize in putting these ventures together; others are privately organized among climbers and local tour operators. Most groups shared a permit fee, ground transportation, and base camp logistics, but were under no pretext of being a unified team.

The upshot of these arrangements was the most experienced alpinists on the mountain in 2008—the French trio of Christian Trommsdorff, Yannick Graziani, and Patrick Wagnon, who plotted an alpine-style ascent of the west face—were under the same permit as one of the least experienced, a twenty-three-year-old Californian named Nick Rice. A self-described "extreme high-altitude athlete," Rice brought a generator to base camp to power his laptop computer, iPod, and communications gear, and was somewhat of a tech guru around base camp. Though he stated on his Web site that his goal was to solo K2, Rice ended up partnering with another Frenchman, sixty-one-year-old Hugues D'Aubarède, who had hired two Pakistanis to help him reach the summit.

The second group was originally organized by a British commercial tour operator out of the United Kingdom named the Mountain Company. The expedition's leader, Roland Hunter, recruited a handful of climbers, most of whom were veterans of similar commercial trips up Everest, to try K2, without the bottled oxygen or professional climbing

Sherpa support used on Everest. But early on, Hunter dropped out from the trip. He passed organizational responsibilities off to one of his clients, an American with previous Karakoram experience named Mike Farris. The other team members—three more Americans, an Australian, a Swede, and one Nepali—joined independently or in pairs. The first time all of the individual team members of these two permitted groups, loosely called the French International expedition and the American International expedition, respectively, met was in Islamabad at the beginning of their trip to K2. Once on the mountain, they effectively split into smaller independent groups of climbers. The members of the American International expedition focused on the Abruzzi Ridge, while Hugues D'Aubarède and Nick Rice followed the Norit team up the SSE Spur.

Though traditional siege-style ascents of the golden age used a lot of fixed ropes, summit day itself was a different affair. Normally it came down to a single rope team, the expedition's two or three strongest climbers, to push from the high camp the final distance to the top. Once a single person succeeded, the entire expedition was deemed a success; there was little reason to equip the final climb to the top for mass numbers of people. Climbers simply soloed, climbing alone with no ropes to maximize their speed, as Hermann Buhl did on the first ascent of Nanga Parbat in 1953, or moved as independent teams with a line connecting them, as Hillary and Norgay did on the first ascent of Everest the same year. But as more expeditions and more climbers found themselves attempting the summit at the same time, the equation changed.

Until the mid-1980s, nobody bothered to take the precaution of fixing rope on summit day on K2. The first recorded fixed line above Camp IV arrived in 1986, when a South Korean team added a single length of rope to protect the traverse connecting the Diagonal with the top of the Bottleneck couloir. As the years went by, it started to make more sense, at least among the ever-growing and diversifying diaspora of climbers attempting K2, to add more sections of rope to the steepest sections of the route on summit day. Leaving a trail of line on the way up means you have something to follow on your way down. Fixed ropes also safeguard against a slip, and can be easily followed at night or in a whiteout. The trade-off is that fixing ropes requires more manpower and time. By 2004, the fifti-eth anniversary of the first ascent of K2, the entire portion of technical climbing had been draped with permanent rope. That summer, fifty peo-ple summited, in a record-setting season.

Of the teams vying for the summit four years later, the Serbs, Kore-ans, Norwegians, and Hugues D'Aubarède planned to use bottled oxy-gen. And roughly half of the expeditions, including the Koreans, Serbs, Italians, and D'Aubarède, had supplemented their manpower by hiring Pakistani or Nepali mountain staff. Variously called "guides," "climbing-Sherpas," "high-altitude porters," or simply "HAPs," each man's skill level and his particular responsibilities were ill defined and varied con-siderably from team to team.

But regardless of their differing choices concerning tactics, the expe-ditions leaving Camp IV for the top of K2 on August 1, 2008, seemed to be in general agreement on the overall strategy for the summit day. All teams had agreed to band together to help break trail and fix rope on summit day. In base camp, a series of meetings was initiated to hammer out a precise plan. It was a daunting task just to carry rope and hardware up the mountain to Camp IV. The expedition leaders haggled over what supplies and manpower each team should contribute; it was eventually decided that an advance team of eight to ten climbers would leave Camp IV at midnight to equip the route. The main body of climbers would depart two hours later. Six hundred meters of rope, it was decided, was enough to do the job.

It was three a.m. in the Netherlands and seven a.m. on K2 when Maarten updated the Norit blog again. On the mountain, the sun had just lofted above the Tibetan plateau to the east; ribbons of light cut down across the jagged peaks of the Baltoro toward the still-darkened glacier far below.

> Norit K2 members are complaining about cold feet, but it's a fact they are moving much faster than expected. In fact they are ahead of sched-ule by two hours.

A great rush of summit successes seemed to be in the offing. The weather, Maarten noted, was near perfect, with only a slight layer of clouds visible to the north, over China. With the genial air of a sports broadcaster, Maarten updated the blog again an hour later, at eight a.m. local time.

Wilco is almost at the top of the Bottleneck. Cas is right behind him. A bit farther down are Gerard and Jelle. In their view are the two Norwegian climbers, a couple of Serbs, one American with the first name Paul and our two Italian friends.

With characteristic punctuality, Maarten also posted the schedule for summit day.

> C4 start—03:00 a.m.
> Bottleneck—08:00 a.m.
> Top Bottleneck—09:00 a.m.
> Traverse—10:00 a.m.
> Start Last Climb—12:00 p.m.
> Summit—14:00 p.m.
> Back C4—20:00 p.m.

Maarten's phone rang again at seven forty-five in the morning in Holland. He recognized the number on the caller ID and answered immediately. "Wilco?"

A shrill voice rang through the earpiece of his receiver, each syllable half shouted in the strong diction of Dutch. "I am in the Bottleneck. A climber just fell. . . ." The torrent of words rushed into Maarten's ear, delayed half a second by the satellite connection. It took a heartbeat longer for their meaning to register. He knew better than to interrupt. "We don't know what happened. One second he was there, in the line— he must have unclipped. One of the Serbs. Dren is his name."

Wilco paused, gasping for air. Through the large bay windows of Maarten's kitchen, water shimmered in the morning sun. It was smooth and impenetrable, the color of tilled earth. Beyond, the lush lowland greenery of central Holland was slowly warming into a bright summer's day. It was the first of August, a Friday.

Wilco sounded annoyed. He explained that they were moving slowly. There had been problems with the fixed ropes, and now they were waiting while the final steep section of the climb was fixed with rope. In the background, beyond the static and the momentary delay, Maarten might have heard other voices yelling.

"He is stopped near the bottom of the Bottleneck. We can see him moving, I think. He is still alive."

There was very little more for Wilco to say. The Serbian's teammates had immediately begun to descend toward their stricken comrade. Other climbers from Camp IV were rushing to help the rescue. Maarten knew without asking that Wilco and the others would continue their push toward the summit.

Outside, a slender crew shell pulled by a team of rowers knifed down the canal, sending ripples that gently splashed against Maarten's houseboat. He wished van Rooijen a terse good luck, and they ended the conversation. They planned to speak again when Wilco reached the top of the Bottleneck.

Maarten van Eck smokes Marlboro Lights.

A methodical, middle-aged businessman who ran a profitable Internet company, Maarten was himself only an armchair climber. As a young man, he had done a few climbs in the Alps—but nothing extreme, nothing higher than the summit of western Europe's Mont Blanc. His passion for high-altitude mountaineering was completely satiated by remote involvement, but it was a passion nonetheless.

The Norit expedition was named for their chief sponsor, a Dutch water-purification company. The company had paid Wilco van Rooijen, the expedition leader, a hefty sponsorship fee in excess of ninety thousand euros. In exchange, Wilco and his team supplied a near-constant stream of live media coverage of the expedition: almost daily Internet dispatches, frequent photos, and even the occasional YouTube video. All the information was posted on the expedition's Web site, managed by Maarten in the Netherlands, or "K2BCNL," as he identified himself in his own updates.

Serving as the Norit team's chief administrator and webmaster in the Netherlands suited his organizational skills. "I like the idea of setting up a Web site so everyone can follow it, to show the management and organizational aspects of an expedition," Maarten says. "You have to arrange everything in advance; you have to think of a plan before you go. That's close to my usual work. . . . It's not too far from running a company, but in a small setting."

It was a role he had first performed during Wilco van Rooijen's first expedition to Everest in 2002 and had subsequently done with relish for a handful of his more recent expeditions. "Many years ago, on the first Everest expedition, we decided to build a Web site, and tell the story on a daily basis about what happens, acclimatization, how it works . . . make it as close as possible to normal people."

But K2 was something different. On Wilco's second attempt on the mountain, in 2006, Maarten had helplessly watched as the expedition unraveled into a string of accidents. Wilco's climbing partner, Irishman Gerard McDonnell, and several other climbers were hit by rockfall low on the Abruzzi Ridge, and then, soon after Wilco had given up his own bid for the summit, a team of four Russians was avalanched just below the top. All were killed. Maarten felt uneasy when his friend returned from Pakistan, sunburned and emaciated with stories of falling rocks that sounded like Formula One race cars, and said, "I will try one more time. . . ."

"Although I already read a lot about all kinds of mountains, I didn't like K2," Maarten confesses. "But K2 was one of the goals Wilco was really anxious to climb. I know the statistics on K2."

Everyone likes to reference the survival stats on K2. Among the climbers themselves, it was a topic that frequently came up, most often mentioned with a tone of macabre bravado. As one member of the Norit team said later: "Honestly, we did joke around about it. We knew the statistics: 25 percent who reach the summit die. . . . There was one Yugoslavian climber. We joked that it would probably be him."

Mount Everest will always hold center stage in the eyes of the unknowing public, but there is little argument within the eight-thousand-meter community as to what mountain presents the greatest challenge. Statistical evidence supports the conclusion that K2 is the more difficult and infinitely more dangerous summit to reach.

First, there is the historical record. After Everest was first climbed in 1953, the mountain was climbed three years later by the Swiss, again in 1960 by the Chinese, and again in 1963 by an American expedition: four successful expeditions in a decade. K2 was first climbed in 1954—and waited twenty-three years for a second ascent. More recently, Mount Everest had been summited every year from 1986 onward. K2, meanwhile, had gone without a single successful ascent five out of the last ten years since 1997: in 1998, 1999, 2002, 2003, and 2005.

As of the beginning of 2008, one expert calculated that Everest had been summited more than 3,689 times, while 210 climbers have been killed on the mountain. That makes a fatality-to-summit ratio of roughly 5.5 percent. Fifty-three summiteers were killed on the descent, meaning that if you are standing on the summit of Mount Everest, you have a one-in-fifty-six chance of not making it down alive. In comparison, K2 had been summited only 284 times before the 2008 season. Sixty-six had been slain on the mountain, resulting in a fatality-to-summit ratio of 23 percent. More than twenty-four of those fatalities occurred to successful summiteers on their way down, meaning that, should you find yourself on the summit of K2, you have almost a one-in-ten chance of not making it down alive.*

The only other eight-thousand-meter peaks that rival these figures are Nanga Parbat and Annapurna, the ninth- and tenth-highest mountains in the world, respectively. Annapurna in particular—a frightening fortress of a mountain in western Nepal—has edged past K2 in the numbers game. Since its first ascent, only 142 climbers have reached the top, but 58 climbers have died trying. That makes for a fatality rate of 40.8 percent. Adventure statisticians point out, however, that both Nanga Parbat and Annapurna's fatality count are skewed due to the high number of deaths

---

* These figures are accurate as of January 1, 2008.

during the mountains' early exploration. Their fatality rates are slowly dropping each season, while K2's have remained relatively constant.

But perhaps the most telling statistic is this: Over a hundred climbers have reached the top of Everest more than once, particularly the climbing-Sherpas who routinely summit each season. To date, only four climbers have been drawn to return to the summit of K2.

A half hour later, Maarten received a second phone call from Wilco. "We are at the top of the Bottleneck. Dren is dead," he said simply. The rescue party had reached the stricken climber at the bottom of the couloir as he took his last breaths, and the news was immediately radioed around the mountain.

Wilco hung up. They were late and he would call again when they had reached the end of the traverse. Maarten turned to his computer screen, his fingers tentatively pecking out a new dispatch.

Much to my regret I have to inform you that early this morning an accident occurred in the Bottleneck. . . .

The fact that a death had occurred did not surprise Maarten. "They were very confident that the weather was perfect; somebody fell; that's the price you have to pay. . . . And they are all very experienced climbers. This is not the first time that Wilco experiences [*sic*] dying mountaineers. He has seen a lot of these dead bodies on Everest and K2. So the news was upsetting, but not that upsetting that they would decide not to go. Because the rest of what you think would be any negative influence for the summit push—it was not there. It was perfect."

Maarten did not question the team's decision to continue, but Dren Mandic's death posed a sensitive question concerning protocol. "There is one golden rule," he says. "You owe it to the climbers' family members and the ghosts of the climbers themselves, that they are informed first before you shout out names. And you have to be very damn sure that you are talking about the right person." The meticulous Norit team had in fact collected documents stipulating the last wishes and contact information of next of kin from each member of the expedition, which Maarten had carefully filed away.

But Dren Mandic was from a different team.

As the teams of climbers attempting K2 had gotten to know one another, so too had the various "home teams" following their friends and loved ones on the mountain. The Norit team was not the only K2 expedition with an Internet site. In fact, almost every expedition had created some kind of Web site or blog to chronicle their adventures. Most were frugal affairs, like having a friend or family member post news on a free Internet site after each call home via satellite phone. They weren't typically updated until after the team returned to base camp. The Dutch Norit team, along with the Nick Rice, were the mountain's most reliable bloggers, almost always providing a daily report. The Dutch typically kept their posts punctual and happy, while Nick wrote with the gusto of a society gossip columnist. His writing documented not only his climb but also the political dynamics of base camp and the general inanities of high-altitude expeditioning. It made for excellent reading.

As manager of the mountain's most up-to-date Web site, Maarten had corresponded with many of the other home teams managing the blogs and other affairs of teams on the mountain. He had e-mailed with Hugues D'Aubarède's family in Lyons, for instance, and also Marco Confortola's brother Luigi in Italy. But he knew very little about the Serbian expedition, and had no way of contacting their home base.

Maarten's first update was vague. But by withholding Mandic's identity and publishing a report stating that an anonymous climber had fallen, Maarten knew he would be terrorizing the hundreds of friends and family who were monitoring his Web site. "That is very difficult because you know at the same instant there are a lot of people saying, 'Okay, it could my husband, son, whatever.'" If he published nothing at all, there was a good chance the story would get out anyway. Soon after, however, he realized that with a major summit push under way, all members of the Serbian expedition were most likely on the mountain, leaving nobody at base camp to help with their communications. He decided to revise his post.

Much to my regret I have to inform you that early this morning an accident occurred in the Bottleneck . . . Maarten announced. *The messages are erratic and chaotic but as far as I know now a (supposing) Serbian Climber fell several hundred meters down the Bottleneck.*

A mixture of conflicting emotions washed over Maarten as he composed the update. "Somebody died—that's not good, of course," Maarten explained later, pausing to exhale a terse stream of smoke. "But then again, statistics tell us that this could happen, it did happen . . . so then your mind says, Okay, if something bad already has happened, the rest will go flawlessly.

"That," he added ruefully, "was a stupid thought."

Five minutes after the message was posted on the Internet, a new e-mail pinged up on his e-mail. It was a strange address and the message was typed in poorly conjugated English. It was from the Serbian home team, asking for more information about the accident in the Bottleneck.

"I have a name," Maarten tapped out a response, "and I am 100 percent sure it is him."

It was four p.m. in Utrecht when Maarten's phone rang again.

"I'm on the summit of K22222222!" Wilco whooped in Dutch.

"Who is there with you?" van Eck immediately asked, the volume of his own voice noticeably increasing as well.

"Cas and Pemba and Gerard," van Rooijen answered.

Immediately after hanging up, van Eck composed a new entry to post on the expedition's blog. NORIT K2 SUMMIT! TOP! was the bulletin's headline. "Wilco, Cas, Gerard, and Pemba are at the summit of K2! All the way back to the source!" "In search of the source of clean drinking water," was the official slogan of the expedition.

Van Eck finished the report with a note of caution:

It is very late at K2 [*sic*]. We said it before and repeat it again. Now the most difficult part will start. The summit is only halfway! Light a fresh candle. We at K2BC Netherlands will start celebrations only if they are back safe in C4.

The message posted on the Internet at four p.m., Netherlands time. In under an hour, eighty-nine comments were posted, congratulating the team on its success. By then it was already nine p.m. in Pakistan. On the mountain, it was completely dark.

It was five a.m. in Anchorage, Alaska, when Annie Starkey's phone rang. "I was dozing on the couch," Annie remembers, "and half hoping that Ger would call and say they were back in Camp IV." Anchorage is fourteen hours behind Pakistan, and Annie instinctively calculated the time difference as she reached for the phone, knowing it was late for them to be on the summit. In Ireland, it was two p.m. in the afternoon, and some of Ger's family had gathered at his sister Martha's house to hear word of his imminent success—Gerard McDonnell was poised to become the first Irishman to summit K2. Like Annie, his family had spent the last twelve hours riveted to the Norit Web site as Gerard and his teammates made their final bid for the top.

Throughout the summer, Gerard had been unceasingly careful to keep Annie and his family updated on the progress of his expedition with his recently purchased satellite phone. He routinely text messaged with his siblings, spoke with Annie frequently, and most importantly, he saved his phone minutes for a weekly scheduled call to his mother. "One of the most important things to Ger was that nobody worried about him," Annie says. "One week he ran out of minutes and was in a panic that his mother would be concerned. He e-mailed and asked me to phone over immediately and let her know he was fine."

Annie picked up the phone and Gerard's voice came ringing through the receiver. They were on the summit. Annie's heart momentarily leapt. Gerard was elated, and he reported that his teammates—Wilco, Cas, and Pemba—were doing great. But it was far too soon to celebrate. Annie knew the most dangerous part of any mountain climb, in particular K2, was the descent.

JJ McDonnell, Gerard's older brother, would remember a similar feeling of foreboding. JJ's birthday was in late July, and he was away on holiday in Spain that week. In the midst of the summit push, his brother even remembered to send a text: *Happy birthday bro*. At nearly the same time Annie spoke to Gerard on the summit, the phone also rang at Martha's house, where the rest of the family was anxiously waiting for news. The phone rang. Certainly it was Ger, but when they answered—there was only static.

It must have been a bad connection.

Loud cracking noises could be occasionally heard around base camp as the Godwin Austen Glacier settled in the subzero darkness. A young Dutch climber, Roeland van Oss, paced around outside a cluster of tents. The light from a kerosene lantern shone dimly from the kitchen tent.

Roeland was twenty-nine years old. This was his first expedition to the Himalayas—indeed, base camp itself was higher than anywhere he had been before. Six months ago, Roeland had noticed an advertisement in a Dutch climbing magazine. It announced that an expedition was being organized to K2 that summer, and that Wilco van Rooijen, the team leader, was looking for motivated young climbers to round out his team. Wilco's invitation was prompted by the fact that he himself first visited K2 in 1995, as a rookie Himalayan climber invited by two experienced mountaineers, Ronald Naar and Hans van de Meulen, who became the first Dutchmen to climb the mountain.

Thirteen years later, Wilco carefully selected a team of eight climbers, built around the nucleus of him and Gerard McDonnell, whom he had met on K2 in 2006. Wilco also recruited his longtime partner Cas van de Gevel, and McDonnell invited a Sherpa acquaintance from Nepal, Pemba Gyalje. But Wilco saved two spots on the permit for a pair of younger climbers to join them. It was an admirable display of an old-fashioned mountaineering ethic, and continued the tradition started by Wilco's own mentors.

At Camp II, during an acclimatization climb, Roeland was stricken by carbon-monoxide poisoning from cooking with an isopropane stove.

Cooking in a tent, of course, is never recommended for precisely this reason, but the conditional realities of high-altitude mountaineering dictate that most of the time the only place to comfortably melt snow for water and prepare meals is inside. Carbon-monoxide poisoning is particularly dangerous if one is not careful to keep the shelter well vented, or if blowing snowdrifts around the tent, blocking vent flaps. Every couple of seasons, someone dies from it.

Roeland was lucky, but after the incident he decided to call off any more attempts on the mountain, and instead monitor the final summit push from base camp and look after communications. Besides the Pakistani cook staffs, base camp was largely deserted—after weeks of idle time, of friendly joking and stormbound rest days, the place had emptied with at long last a decent forecast and a chance at the top.

Roeland looked at the vast mountain above him. He could see the snowy sweep of the SSE Spur, peppered with protruding rocks, and farther up valley, profiled against the darkening skyline, was the flank of the Abruzzi Ridge. Both lines converged on the flat shoulder where Camp IV was located. Higher still, more than three thousand meters above where he stood, Roeland could almost see the summit of K2.

But most of the final portion of the climb, the route between Camp IV and the summit, was obscured by intervening terrain. Roeland could barely see the contour of the top of the great serac and make out the final section of snow immediately below the top, but a rock buttress hid the Bottleneck and the Diagonal, the most critical portions of the climb.

As Roeland gazed up into the gathering darkness, the first few stars winked on one by one in the deepening Karakoram sky. The hulking silhouette of Broad Peak could be made out across the Godwin Austen Glacier, opposite K2. Then he noticed something different. A light, just below the summit. It seemed to blink on and off, and Roeland realized it must be a headlamp, or several headlamps flashing back and forth in the twilight. He turned on his own light, trying to signal them by blinking the light on and off at regular intervals.

Those lights were his teammates, his friends. They were just beginning the descent.

2
STATUS: UNKNOWN

It's often said that above eight thousand meters the air has less than half the oxygen it has at sea level, but that is misleading. The proportional makeup of air on the summit of Mount Everest is the same as it is anywhere else: oxygen accounts for 20.9 percent of the matter in the gaseous atmosphere. But the pressure is less than half of what it is at sea level, meaning that the volume is more than doubled—and for each breath that is inhaled into human lungs at that elevation, less than half the number of O_2 molecules reaches the bloodstream.

The human body enters an inevitable state of physiological decay above fifty-five hundred meters. Above seven thousand meters, that decay accelerates, until above eight thousand meters, survival is measured in days. Above eighty-five hundred meters, it can be counted in hours.

Hypoxia, commonly known as oxygen deprivation, has many symptoms, including headaches, muscle fatigue, and shortness of breath. But strangely it manifests itself most noticeably through a series of psychological and judgmental distinctions. Poor coordination. Lethargy and lassitude. Visual impairment. Executing poor judgment. Euphoria.

Not surprisingly, a scientific study released in December of 2008 by the University of Ottawa and Massachusetts General Hospital concluded that "cognitive problems at altitude," rather than adverse weather or fluid flooding the lungs (pulmonary edema), were the most common factors in the 207 deaths on Mount Everest that had been recorded at that time. "We also were surprised at how few people died due to avalanches and icefalls in recent years," wrote Dr. Paul Firth, who led the study, purportedly the first detailed analysis of deaths on Everest.

But whereas on Everest climbers frequently slip into a beguiling state of exhaustion, eventually succumbing to the elements, the causes of death on K2 tell a different story. More than half of the fatalities that have occurred on the mountain are the result of traumatic events: twenty-two dead in falls and twenty in avalanches. Only fifteen deaths, meanwhile, are attributed to altitude sickness, exhaustion, or cerebral edema. Eleven more souls simply disappeared, their last living moments unwitnessed, their final fate lost forever.

The differing causes of death between the two mountains are partly explained by the topography of each mountain. Though six hundred feet lower than Everest, K2 is far steeper, its ridges and faces dropping precipitously on all sides to the glaciers far below. Some thousand miles north and west of Everest, the mountain is also colder, and subject to particularly strong and sudden windstorms. But it is the unrelenting steepness of the mountain that is most manifested in the two highest causes of death, falls and avalanches. Everest is a gentle giant, a place where the statistical evidence suggests that man's greatest enemy is himself. This is not true on K2. The extreme altitude may lull climbers into a state of hypoxic stupor, but the mountain rarely waits for its victims to expire from the natural causes of breathing air at eighty-five hundred meters, as happens on Everest. It lulls them into a state of hypoxic stupor, and then violently kills them.

In all of the satellite phone calls made from the summit of K2 on the evening of August 1, 2008, there was nothing blatant to suggest that the summiteers were in trouble. They were simply tired, happy adventurers calling home to share the thrilling news of their success. Even the death of one of their own, Dren Mandic, seemed temporarily brushed aside.

But their friends and loved ones were acutely aware of the risks they now faced. They knew that every second mattered.

In Breckinridge, Colorado, the silence told Tina Sjogren that something was wrong.

The Colorado Rockies are twelve time zones behind the Karakoram, and so, as her husband, Tom, slumbered peacefully, Tina spent the entire night of July thirty-first following the push to the summit. A freckled, forty-nine-year-old woman with a mop of coiled, untamed hair, she made a pot of coffee, hunkered down, and passed the early morning hours firing off dozens of e-mails and surfing among the various expedition Web sites. Maarten van Eck provided almost live-feed coverage of the summit climb on the Norit site, information that the Sjogrens quickly syndicated—with permission—onto their own Web site. But by six o'clock the next morning, as the thick glades of Aspen began to turn pink outside their ski chalet, there was still no word that the team had reached the top.

"I'm like, Shit—this is way after cutoff time," Tina remembers. "Now, we are not talking ten a.m., twelve p.m., two p.m., which is the usual cutoff time, four p.m., which is the really late cutoff time. In the previous years that we have been covering K2 climbers who have summited after four to five p.m., often they didn't make it back." Tina woke Tom, and told him something might be wrong.

For many mountaineers, the concept of a turnaround time is the foundation of summit-day strategy. You pick the absolute latest time you have to be descending, and schedule the day backward, leaving a comfortable cushion so that, if all goes well, you will be summiting well before then. Turnaround times are not universal law, however. As American climber Ed Viesturs says: "Turnaround times aren't an ironclad rule on K2, but I believe in them myself." In fact, most turnaround times are predicated on the assumption that once it gets dark, you will have to stop for the night. There's no arguing that route finding becomes far more difficult in the dark, but many of the world's great alpine climbers have successfully navigated down from the summit of K2 by headlamp. Whether or not a climber can continue through the night depends on the weather, the conditions, and the terrain, but, most important, on the physical and mental reserves of the climber. And these intangible qualities vary drastically from individual to individual. Whereas a typical mountaineer might be able to sustain sixteen to twenty hours of effort on a summit day, generations of standout athletes have pulled off nonstop pushes of thirty to forty hours on eight-thousand-meter peaks. When best utilized, turnaround times are a device designed implicitly to keep a mountaineer within his or her own limits.

A little after dawn, Tina rousted Tom. "You need to get up," she told him. "Something might be happening on K2."

"Maybe they just don't feel like calling home," Tom groaned, rolling over and brushing the sleep from his eyes. But his interest was piqued. He sat up and reached for a pair of jeans. A graying Swedish entrepreneur, Tom was remarkably trim for his forty-eight years. He counted as friends a good many of the climbers on the summit push.

As Tina fell fast asleep, word of success finally arrived at eight a.m. At eight forty-one, Tom wrote a quick e-mail to Annie Starkey. "Congrats to Gerard!" the message read. "We have been following his ascent closely. As requested, new minutes were added to his phone. We will continue to monitor his climb and hope for a safe descent."

Gerard McDonnell, along with a half dozen other climbers on K2, were the Sjogrens' clients: he had recently purchased a Thuraya satellite phone from one of the Sjogrens' businesses, Human Edge Technology. The company rents and sells remote communications equipment—satellite phones, small portable laptop computers, and solar panel chargers. It is run in close concert with the Sjogrens' other communications venture, the Internet site Explorersweb.com. The Web site is broken into various submenus such as "Everest," "Oceans," "Polar," "Space," and "K2," providing the latest news and gossip within the small, incestuous communities of each discipline. It would not be an exaggeration to say that the Sjogrens' living room was one of the single most important hubs for information in the world of extreme adventure.

And perhaps nobody embodied the realities and contradictions of that world better than Explorersweb's founders. Tom and Tina Sjogren had walked the walk, summiting Mount Everest in 1998 and skiing to both the North and South Poles in 2002. By the standards of the first decade of the twenty-first century, these achievements were relatively modest—as they would be the first to admit, the Sjogrens' were far from elite mountaineers. (Everest, after all, was first climbed more than fifty years ago, and man first reached the poles nearly a century before.) But neither, as it is often alleged in the media and assumed by the general public, were they wealthy clients with hired guides. They were indeed well-to-do, but on each of their adventures, the Sjogrens had run relatively bare-bones operations, with a minimum of team members, expenses, or fuss. And even if their accomplishments left them a step behind the leading edge of the discipline, each adventure still demanded plenty of grit and wilderness savvy. One might best describe the couple as a pair of passionate amateurs, individuals inspired more to simply repeat the historic achievements of the twentieth century than to exceed them. The same might have been said about most of the people who were on K2 during the summer of 2008.

The first global satellite phone company was founded in 1979. Inmarsat began as an intergovernmental nonprofit organization to provide communications for the maritime community. Heavy systems with large antennae were designed to be installed on ships, and later in the 1980s and early 1990s, smaller briefcase-size units became available. They were theoretically portable, but not practical. The purchase price ranged between five thousand and ten thousand dollars, and it cost as much as ten dollars per minute to make a call. The early units weighed twenty-five pounds, and had a bit transfer rate of only 2.4 kilobytes per second. Laptop computers, meanwhile, were still bulky and consumed lots of electricity. Solar technology that could quickly and efficiently charge all the necessary batteries in the field was lacking.

Up until the turn of the twenty-first century, only the most lavishly funded Everest expeditions could afford satellite coms. Still, it was an amazing thing: Mountaineers could conceivably call home from any base camp in the world. Once on the mountain, climbers still communicated almost entirely by radio, but it was possible to patch a call through, so that you could theoretically have global communication capability from anywhere on the mountain. During the infamous *Into Thin Air* disaster on Everest in 1996, when New Zealand guide Rob Hall lay stricken with cerebral edema on the South Summit after staying with a client, he was connected with his wife, Jan Arnold, for a heartbreaking good-bye, a link that was dependent on a dispatcher at base camp and powered by a vast array of communications gear.*

Iridium, the first widely available handheld sat phone, debuted two years after the Everest disaster, in 1998. The company promptly went bankrupt, and then was sold and relaunched in 2001. These were genuinely portable devices, manufactured by Motorola, and only a little bigger than a standard cordless house phone. Cheaper and more reliable, Iridium was a significant step beyond the old Inmarsat system. Two more rival companies, Thuraya and Globalstar, launched soon after Iridium.

Sat phones rely on a network, or a constellation, in industry lingo, of satellites in low-level orbit over the earth. Each company has its own network, which means that the phones are incompatible. The Iridium grid originally had seventy-seven satellites (iridium the element has an atomic number of seventy-seven). The Thuraya grid, in comparison, is much smaller, with only three operational satellites. They are more modern and powerful, however, and though they don't provide coverage in the western hemisphere, they are effective in Eurasia, Africa, and Australia.

Headquartered in Dubai in the United Arab Emirates, Thuraya is the most popular choice for Himalayan climbers, providing the best coverage and reception at the cheapest value. The phones, which are manufactured by Boeing, are lightweight, modern, and functional. The basic

---

* Interestingly, one thirty-pound sat phone belonging to the New York socialite Sandy Hill Pittman was hauled all the way to the high camp at the South Col on Everest in 1996. The effort of carrying the load exhausted American guide Scott Fischer's sirdar, Lobsang Jangbu—one of many small factors that contributed to the disastrous outcome of the climb.

model costs around seven hundred dollars, and prepaid phone calls can be purchased for fifty cents per minute.

The drastically reduced cost from the first generation of satellite phones meant that many of the summit party on K2 in 2008 had the potential to call home. Radios, however, were still widely used on the mountain, in part because they allowed many different parties to listen and talk on the same frequency. Most teams used handheld five-watt VHF-FM radios, similar to what are used in small civilian aircraft. Interference was rarely an issue—because of the sustained steepness of K2, climbers on both the SSE Spur and the Abruzzi Ridge are frequently in direct line of sight with base camp.

Most of the climbers on the summit push carried only one communication device—either a radio or a sat phone. A common strategy among the summit teams was for each mountaineer to pair up with a partner they expected to be climbing closely with, and make sure that one was carrying a radio and the other a sat phone. On the Norit team, Wilco and Gerard had sat phones; Pemba and Cas carried radios. And yet, for nearly five hours after eighteen climbers departed the summit, there were no reports that they had returned to Camp IV, no updates from other climbers camped on the Shoulder, no word from the mountain at all. It was "deadly silence," as Maarten van Eck would recall.

The news of Dren Mandic's death earlier that day had been sad, but not that surprising to many monitoring the climb. The situation was, in one sense, normal for a summit day on K2. Then, across the radio waves and satellite constellations, more calls from the upper mountain began to trickle in. At first they were confusing, almost indecipherable. But one thing was certain: Sometime soon after midnight, local time, on the morning of August second, the world heard the first murmurings of impending trouble—things had gone desperately wrong on K2.

At base camp, a burst of radio static startled Roeland van Oss from slumber. He was in his tent, having fallen asleep, utterly exhausted after monitor-

ing the summit push for over twenty hours. It was late, nearly one a.m.
Before dozing off, Roeland had been sure to leave his radio on.

"Roeland, base camp! Roeland, base camp!"

Roeland rolled over, his hand darting for the radio handset.

It was Cas.

He was calling from just below the Bottleneck. Pemba was somewhere in front of him, Cas was sure. Cas spoke lucidly, but the fatigue
in his voice was palpable. He was at the top of the Shoulder, still with
another hour to go to reach Camp IV. Later, Roeland would not be able
to recall whether Cas mentioned an avalanche or not, in that first conversation after the summit. But he would remember that Cas spoke with
concern, that it was obvious that something had happened.

"Wilco and Gerard are behind me. . . . They must have stopped above
the Bottleneck. . . . With the ropes gone, they are trapped!"

A moment later, Roeland unzipped the vestibule of his tent and
hurried over to the Korean base camp tent.

Maarten's phone rang an hour later. It was Roeland. Maarten immediately knew something was wrong: Roeland sounded worried, the concern in his voice bordering on panic. Maarten would remember it was a
short conversation, and the news registered in bullet statements:

"Something has happened—something bad. A piece of ice fell down
the Bottleneck. One of the Norwegians is dead. The fixed lines are cut.
The others are stranded above!"

"How do you know?" Maarten asked, trying to calm the young man
down, trying to make sense of the situation himself.

"I just spoke to Cas in Camp Four," Roeland explained. "Cas talked
to the Norwegians, and he will be calling you in a minute. . . ."

Five minutes later, Maarten's phone rang again and it was Cas. The
strain in Cas's voice was again palpable. "He was very, very, very tired,"
Maarten would say. Still Cas seemed generally okay.

"Cecilie says that Rolf is gone in an avalanche," he said. "And the
ropes in the Bottleneck are gone. It is very dangerous—Pemba and I are
lucky to have climbed down safely. We do not know where Gerard and
Wilco are. . . . We must go back up to look for them."

But it was obvious to both men that first Cas needed to rest. It was still dark, sunrise being another two hours away.

At midnight, Netherlands time, Maarten posted a new report. MAJOR PROBLEMS ON K2! it announced, clinically explaining the situation:

A big chunk of ice fell down and took a lot of the fixed lines with it. A large portion (latest estimate is twelve) of climbers who were descending canNOT move any farther. They halted before the traverse or before the Bottleneck. Cas and Pemba climbed without fixed ropes and are safe in C4 and resting. Wilco and Gerard are in the group with Marco and at least a couple of Koreans waiting (we think, and hope).

The Koreans had the most powerful radio base station on the mountain, so it was natural that Roeland went there. A handful of climbers huddled in the tent waiting for word from the summit team, including several Koreans, the team's Pakistani liaison officer, and their cook, an aging Nepali named Nawang.

Chris Klinke, an American member of the international team led by Mike Farris, soon joined the group. A Michigan-born financial manager, Chris had discovered mountaineering relatively late in life. He devoted his twenties to his professional career, and steadily worked his way up through a large financial services company to eventually become a vice president in his firm. But by his mid-thirties Chris was burned-out, and somewhat chagrined to discover that monetary success left him less than satisfied. After fourteen years, he quit his job and began to seriously consider a faded boyhood dream—to climb Mount Everest. With the money he had saved, Chris devoted himself to mountaineering, first joining several commercial expeditions to hone his skills and gain the requisite experience. In three years, he collected six of Dick Bass's seven summits, including Aconcagua, Denali, Mount Elbrus (at 5,642 meters the highest mountain in Europe), Kilimanjaro, Kosciuszko, and Everest.

Chris had descended the mountain with ominous news. He, too, had gone for the summit that day. But by seven thirty a.m., a little after sunrise, he was standing in a line of a dozen climbers while they waited for the ropes to be fixed above. By midmorning, it was obvious to him that the pace was too slow for him to reach the summit within his turnaround time. Klinke turned around. Returning to Camp IV, he met up with Italian Roberto Manni, and they decided to continue down the mountain together.

Right before the pair left Camp IV, Chris trained his camera at the Bottleneck and the Traverse, zoomed in as far as the optical lens would allow, and squeezed off two quick shots. Later, when he had the chance to examine them in detail, Chris realized they were remarkable pictures. Taken at twelve-oh-eight p.m., local time, they showed the entire technical portion of the route. At the bottom, one can see a small group of climbers clustered around a prone body. These were Chris's teammates Eric Meyer and Fredrik Sträng, and two of Dren Mandic's teammates, as they attempted to lower the body of the hapless Serb. Higher up, a long line of climbers snakes across the Diagonal. The resolution is so fine that you can almost recognize the different climbers by the color of their down suits. Higher still, one can see a lone soloist resting in the lee of a small serac at the beginning of the final summit slopes.

As they were descending toward Camp III on the Abruzzi Ridge, Chris paused to look back toward the summit. It was the last place on the route where there would be a good view of the upper mountain, and Chris was shocked by what he saw.

"This isn't good," he said to Roberto. It was three p.m. Since they'd left Camp IV, the climbers had barely moved fifty meters. And yet—they were still going up.

Chris and Roberto then turned and raced down the Abruzzi as fast as they could safely descend. By ten p.m. they were on the glacier, and, sometime after midnight, the two men trudged into base camp. Only then did Chris learn that something had gone seriously wrong.

The news coming over the communal radio frequency was sporadic and not entirely coherent, but none of it was good. Chris Klinke got a brief radio call from one of his teammates, Chhiring Dorje Sherpa. Like

Cas, Chhiring called to say he was down through the Bottleneck. He was descending with the Korean team's Sherpa, Pasang Lama, and was headed to Camp IV. Chris immediately contacted Eric Meyer, who was in Camp IV on the Shoulder, and told him to start up the stoves and begin melting water.

Then, sometime around two a.m. another call came through, a burst of rapid-fire Korean. Roeland couldn't understand a word of the message, but the look on their teammates' faces—concern, bordering on hysteria—was obvious. In the kitchen tent at base camp, he saw all the Korean faces turn ashen. Nobody spoke.

One finally turned to Roeland. "Radio from Camp Four," he said, pointing up the mountain. "Ms. Go . . . fell down." One of the Koreans began to sob quietly.

Maarten's first thought was to try to locate each member of his team. He knew Roeland was in base camp, while Mark Sheen, another team member who was hoping to make his own summit attempt on August second, was in Camp IV, with Cas and Pemba. That left three members unaccounted for: Wilco, Gerard, and Jelle Staleman, who had evidently decided to descend from the Bottleneck that morning. As he tried come to grips with the situation, Maarten had the peculiar sense that time was speeding up, racing ahead of him. New e-mails were popping up on his laptop almost constantly. He fielded several phone calls from concerned family members. Then Jelle Staleman's father called to report that Jelle was safe in Camp III on the SSE Spur.

"Impossible," Maarten replied. "Jelle doesn't have a sat phone with him." Jelle's father read Maarten a strange Thuraya number off of his caller ID. When Maarten cross-checked it against a list of phones of other expeditions, he discovered that it matched the number of American Nick Rice. Jelle must have been descending the mountain with him.

Next, news came from Italy: it was Luigi, the brother of the Italian Marco Confortola. During the weeks of bad weather on the mountain, Marco had been a regular visitor at the Norit base camp. Though he was climbing on the Abruzzi Ridge, he had eagerly planned the summit push with Wilco and Gerard. His own partner, Roberto, had called off his bid and safely descended with Chris Klinke. Marco was carrying a Thuraya phone, though neither Maarten nor Roeland knew his number. Luigi reported that Marco had just called him. He was bivouacked, waiting for dawn near the top of the fixed ropes, at eighty-four hundred meters. And with him, Marco reported, was "one of the Dutch."

It must be Wilco, Maarten thought. *Only he and Gerard are missing. But Wilco also has a sat phone. Why isn't he calling? What's going on up there?*

Yet another e-mail for Maarten came from Lyons, France. It was from the fiancée of Hugues D'Aubarède, asking if Maarten had any more information about what was happening. Over the past weeks, Maarten realized, the Norit team's punctual, up-to-date blog had become the go-to news source not only for those following his team, but for everyone who was watching the summit push—including the friends and loved ones of climbers on other expeditions. Maarten had no news to give them. In fact, he didn't even have all of the phone numbers of everyone on the mountain. He e-mailed Tom Sjogren and asked him to send the numbers of all the phones on K2.

Tom was one step ahead of him.

"Hi, Maarten," he wrote. "For your information I have requested five latest positions of Wilco's and Gerard's phones. It might take a while to get it and you might not even need it. . . ."

Sometime near dawn on the morning of August 2, another message came over the radio in base camp. Go Mi-yeong, the Korean woman, was alive. Evidently she and Kim Jae-su had descended the Bottleneck and arrived back in Camp IV. There was no more news from the upper mountain.

Chris Klinke and Roeland van Oss made a quick tally of the summit group. Nine climbers were confirmed as having arrived back in Camp IV: Lars Nessa, Oystein Stangeland, and Cecilie Skog from the Norwegian team, Cas and Pemba from Norit, Chhiring Dorje from the American team, plus Go Mi-yeong and Kim Jae-su and the climbing-Sherpa from the Korean expedition, Pasang Lama. Nine were still missing: Wilco and Gerard; Hugues D'Aubarède and his Pakistani guide, Karim; the Italian, Marco; and Kim Hyo-gyeong, Hwang Dong-jin, Park Kyeong-hyo, and their sirdar, Jumik Bhote.

Roeland and Chris began to discuss coordinating a rescue. By now, they knew from the sporadic radio calls from Camp IV that some kind of an avalanche had occurred and taken out a significant portion of the fixed ropes in the Bottleneck. In the relatively thick air of base camp, the thought—a natural reaction, almost—of sending a rescue seemed simple. They quickly realized they had scant resources available.

Their teammates in Camp IV—Cas and Pemba from Norit, Eric Meyer, Fred Sträng, and Chhiring Dorje from the American international expedition—were already on their second night at seventy-eight hundred meters, after having participated in a summit push the night before. The Norwegians were reeling from the apparent loss of Rolf. The Serbs, after losing Dren Mandic, were already on their way down. A team of Singaporeans were holding down Camp III on the Abruzzi Ridge, and Mike Farris was in Camp II on the same route—but they were still a day's climb from the Bottleneck. And no one was planning on going any higher for the time being. Regardless of manpower issues, mounting a viable rescue attempt through the Bottleneck faced another logistical problem: Where was the rope? According to radio reports, and confirmed by Chris, there had been no additional rope left in Camp IV that very morning, at the start of the push. Wasn't that the problem in the first place?

With no rope, there was no sense in asking additional climbers to return under the serac. How could they help climbers down without rope? The only positive sign was garbled at best. "We have two Sherpa," one of the Koreans said, bobbing his head optimistically. "Going up."

In Utrecht, Heleen van Rooijen had barely slept in two days. At least her parents were there to keep her company, and eight-month-old Teun, her and Wilco's baby boy, was a welcome distraction to all. A few sprigs of blond hair already shot from his soft scalp, and when he giggled he had the same warm cheeks, the vaguely cherubic face of his father.

Then, at six-thirty in the morning on August 2, the phone rang. It was Wilco.

"I'm alive," he said. "I'm okay."

He sounded remarkably composed, but both of them knew that wasn't the case. There was a pause; then Wilco went on: "I'm below the Bottleneck, somewhere on a south-facing wall. My altimeter says I am at seventy-eight hundred meters. I must be near Camp IV. My eyes are bad." Wilco spoke to his wife without emotion, consciously trying to convey as much pertinent information to her as quickly as possible to conserve battery power. After he hung up, Heleen called across town, brushing her deep auburn hair to one side in anxiety as she spoke to Maarten and relayed the news.

Why the hell is he calling his wife? Maarten wondered. Nevertheless, it was good news. The more phone calls Wilco made, the greater the chance they would be able to track his signal.

After hanging up, Maarten called Roeland in base camp, and Roeland radioed the news to Pemba and Cas in Camp IV. An hour and a half later, at eight ten a.m., Maarten crisply summarized what was happening on the mountain in a second emergency post on the Norit blog:

STATUS AS FAR AS WE KNOW
K2BC can see six people standing still in the Bottleneck. Two
HAPs are on their way up.
ROELAND in K2BC
CAS and PEMBA in C4
WILCO left bivouac, whereabouts unknown
MARCO left bivouac, whereabouts unknown
MARK in C4 and will move up with CAS to Bottleneck!
JELLE on his way down to K2BC
GERARD unknown
HUGUES unknown

By then it was noon on the mountain, and the reports coming down from Camp IV were not encouraging.

Soon after daybreak, Eric Meyer and Cas radioed down that they could see a cluster of dots high on the traverse, above the Bottleneck. None were moving. Cas and Pemba had evidently already searched the area around the Shoulder looking for Wilco and Gerard, but Roeland had a hard time understanding their vague reports. They were trying, though it was obvious that both men were exhausted. Then the weather began to deteriorate. A thick band of clouds wrapped over the Shoulder, cloaking the upper mountain.

By eleven a.m., Eric Meyer radioed to say that the remaining members of his team in Camp IV were going to begin their descent of the Abruzzi. Deciding that there was safety in numbers, Mark Sheen, the Australian on the Norit team, joined forces with the Abruzzi group, rather than descend the SSE Spur alone. The Norwegians had already left camp.

Around noon, a member of the Serbian expedition stomped into the Norit base camp tent and accused Roeland of not doing anything to organize a helicopter rescue. Roeland was confused: All of the missing climbers were last seen above eight thousand meters, high on the mountain. Because of the reduced air pressure, helicopters struggle to fly above six thousand meters. In 2005, Slovenian alpinist Tomaz Humar was stranded by stormy conditions at sixty-three hundred meters on the Rupal Face of Nanga Parbat. Initially, the Pakistani army refused to initiate a helicopter rescue above six thousand meters; his "official" altitude was thus amended to fifty-nine hundred meters so that the mission would proceed. Humar was successfully short-hauled from the mountain, but the Pakistani pilots were forced to push their machine to the absolute limit.

With an unknown number of missing climbers well above seventy-five hundred meters, Roeland knew that helicopters would not help the situation on K2. They could certainly be used to transport injured climbers from the base of the mountain to the closest medical care in Skardu, but that would be an evacuation, not a rescue. Still, he contacted both

Maarten and the Norit team's trekking agents in Islamabad and asked them to request that a helicopter be available, just in case. Roberto Manni, meanwhile, pressed the Italian embassy. But still—for some weird reason, the tall Serbian guy with a ponytail would not stop talking about a helicopter.

Among others in base camp, there was an imperceptible shift in focus on the afternoon of August 2. The thick cloud cap forming over the Shoulder was visible to all, and conversation began to center around making sure the teams from Camp IV got down the mountain safely. Both Camp III and Camp II on the Abruzzi were occupied. Radio calls went out for them to fire up the stoves and have water ready for the descending climbers. Meanwhile, there was no encouraging news from the upper mountain. The word "rescue" was still on everyone's lips, but in implicitly different terms. The goal was to rescue the climbers who were about to leave Camp IV, with eight thousand vertical feet to descend before they reached the glacier.

The prospect of using the signal from a satellite phone to locate a missing climber was an idea Tom had been kicking around for some time. He had seriously considered requesting coordinates in several instances before, like when two Mexican alpinists had gone missing on a peak in India, or when the Spanish climber Iñaki Ochoa de Olza was stricken with cerebral edema high on Annapurna. The circumstances had never worked out. The satellite network tracked the position only when the phone was actually in use. But every time a call was connected, the position was recorded on the computer database at the company's headquarters in Dubai. Tom needed access to the Thuraya database, and he needed more phone calls from Wilco and Gerard. Tom knew it was futile to try calling them—their phones would be turned off to save battery power. *How come they haven't called? What's happened?*

As a Thuraya dealer, Tom first contacted the regional distributor he knew, who passed the request on to the national office. But by then it was midnight on the East Coast, and the middle of the morning on a Saturday in the United Arab Emirates. Tom wrote several strongly worded e-mails, stressing the urgency of the situation. Thuraya responded promptly to explain their policy: They released coordinates of a phone only if the owner formally declared an emergency, or they had a court order. Satellite phones are frequently involved in kidnappings in Afghanistan and Pakistan, and Thuraya was taking no chances in giving out sensitive information. They kindly stated that they would release the coordinates from Wilco's phone when he himself called in and gave them permission. Tom felt his blood begin to rise. *Arabs*, he thought to himself. *Impossible to deal with.* His fingers hammered out another e-mail, adding a link to the Norit blog to highlight the exigency.

At one twenty a.m. in Colorado, Thuraya finally bowed to Tom's persistence and released the coordinates of the last five calls from Wilco's phones.

35.815908	76.39118
35.877704	76.52544
35.878393	76.52675
35.897963	76.50139
35.920259	76.59613

Tom immediately forwarded the raw data to Maarten, and began plotting the position on a software program. The data was not consistent. "I have tried to place the positions on Google Earth and three are irrelevant and clearly wrong. Two positions seems to be confirming that he was at that time at around 7,500 meters and pretty much straight up from the Pyramid," Tom hastily explained in another e-mail to Maarten.

The Black Pyramid was a series of steep rock cliffs between the Abruzzi Ridge and the SSE Spur routes. If the altitude was correct, it would mean that Wilco had somehow bypassed Camp IV and was now three hundred meters *below* the Shoulder. Maarten phoned the information to Roeland. By then it was already two fifteen in the afternoon on K2.

Wilco made a second call to Heleen. Heleen called Maarten. "He says he sees two climbers, that he is in Camp IV, but he can't find Cas," she told him. Maarten could feel the tension in her voice.

What? Maarten wondered. *How could Wilco be in Camp IV and not find other people? It must be the altitude. His eyesight is bad; he is beginning to hallucinate. . . . Why isn't he calling anyone else?* Then it occurred to Maarten: *If he is having problems seeing . . . he can't use the address book in his phone! He is dialing the only number he can remember!*

Maarten suppressed his own frustration and collected himself. "If he calls again," Maarten told Heleen, "tell him to leave his phone on, and then call me immediately." In the background, he could hear the baby begin to cry.

JJ McDonnell was due to return to Ireland from his vacation on Sunday, but as the news from Pakistan went from bad to worse Saturday morning, he and his partner impulsively decided to pack their bags and go to the airport in hopes of catching an earlier flight home. In Alaska it was still Friday evening, and Annie was waiting alone for more news from the mountain. She finally called a close friend, Evie Whitten, and asked if she would come over and keep her company.

"We are going to *will* him off that mountain," Evie said when she burst in the front door of Annie's home, her abdomen bulging with the third trimester of pregnancy. She found Annie glued to the computer—it struck Evie as a little strange how much information was available on the Internet. A half dozen Web sites covered different expeditions on K2; Annie compulsively clicked from one to the next, hoping for new information.

The evening only became more surreal. Fevered reports were popping up on the Web, written in rough English and several other languages.

A group of climbers can be seen standing still above the Traverse. Two HAPs are on their way up.

Evie and Annie wondered: What did that mean? They scrutinized every piece of information—every sentence of every damn post. Each single word made a heartbeat of difference: were they *standing still*, or *still standing*? Just changing the *order* of words conveyed two very different realities. The only thing that was obvious was that a lot of people were in serious trouble, and trying to relay useful information to the best of their capabilities while under tremendous stress.

Evie realized that she was going to be at Annie's for the long haul. She called her neighbors, and asked them to go over to her place, feed the dogs, and then let them back inside. Sometime, late in the night, the Norit site updated again.

We have not heard or seen anything of Gerard.

"What does this person know that we don't know? What aren't they saying?" The words came fast and impulsively to Annie. The tears swiftly followed.

"It's a strange thing about Holland," Maarten later observed. "The Netherlands is a very flat country, but we love our mountains very much." Indeed, the ninety-thousand-euro sponsorship check from Norit was good evidence of mountaineering's popularity, and generating publicity through the expedition's Web site was an implicit part of Maarten's job. But by the morning of August 2, his goals had narrowed to two simple objectives: keep the channels of communication open for the network of friends and family, and provide Roeland with whatever logistical help he needed to organize an efficient rescue. He had no time for the mainstream media.

Around nine a.m. on Saturday, August 2, Maarten's neighbors heard a commotion on the leafy side street that paralleled the canal. They peeked out from behind their window blinds to see several TV trucks pulled off of the road. A crew was setting up on the lawn in front of the canal. It had been the same when Wilco summited Everest back in 2004. It was possible that some of them came without knowledge of the impending disaster, just looking for a good human-interest story about a hometown mountain climber. They found a tragedy unfolding.

The Dutch had prepared two press releases for the culminating summit push. One enthusiastically claimed the summit; the other regretfully announced that they had been defeated. The team also had a public spokesman—a friend, Michel Schuurman, who had volunteered to deal with the media. But after weeks of delays, Michel had finally left Utrecht for a holiday in Austria with his family. Maarten contacted him, but first he had to drop off his wife and kids at the hotel. While Michel downed a quick espresso and raced the twelve hours back to Holland, Maarten was left on his own to deal with the media.

It wasn't just the TV crews outside; Maarten's phone was constantly ringing. Somehow they even knew his cell number. The BBC, CNN, Al Jazeera—suddenly everyone wanted to talk to him. He abruptly became *the* source to find out what was happening on K2.

Maarten began to worry that he wouldn't be free to take the important calls. If Wilco did try to reach him, the line could be busy. Maarten asked his wife, Henrietta, to go borrow a phone from one of the neighbors.

Maarten had anticipated that the Web page would experience a sharp wave of hits during the summit push. Two to five thousand unique visits per day might have been average during the beginning of the expedition, but he expected that to increase to ten thousand or more in the days leading up to the final climb. Maarten thought there was a chance it might climax in the fifty-to-one-hundred-thousand-hits range. But by Saturday afternoon, the traffic was going . . . off the charts.

Late that afternoon Roeland received another radio call from Cas at Camp IV. They had found Marco Confortola. He was alive, though suffering from advanced frostbite. He and Pemba were almost hit by an avalanche below the Bottleneck that afternoon. Cas had no more information to offer regarding Gerard McDonnell, Hugues D'Aubarède, or Karim.

It was a quarter to six in the evening at base camp when Chris Klinke trained a telescope on the SSE Spur. The cloud layer that had obscured the route above Camp III was beginning to lift. Suddenly, he saw something: a tiny fleck of color against the monochrome mountain hues of ice and rock.

A tiny orange dot.

Fifteen minutes later, Maarten called Roeland with a position for Wilco based on his sat phone calls: seventy-five hundred meters, somewhere by the Black Pyramid. The elevations were the same, but the linear locations were off: The Black Pyramid was to the right of the SSE Spur, between it and the Abruzzi Ridge, while the orange dot was way to the left.

Evie dozed off a few times Friday night. She'd feel the weight of her head pulling down toward her stomach; then the baby might have kicked once or twice; but then she'd close her eyes, just for a minute. And each time she opened them, Annie was there, staring at the computer screen, exactly the same as she had been before Evie went to sleep.

Sometime before dawn, Annie decided to light a candle. It was silly, but wasn't that what the summit report on the blog had said? *Light a candle.* She had a big red one sitting on her coffee table—it was eighteen inches tall, six inches in diameter, of the variety one finds at fairs and craft shops. The thing flamed and spit dripping wax, making a mess of the table around it. But it was comforting, cheerful even.

A little after morning broke, Annie pressed the reload button on her Web browser. There was a pause, and the screen blinked: USER ERROR. She pressed the reload button again, slapping down on the mouse pad. The computer blinked, but . . . *nothing happened.*

3

SIGNALS INTERFERENCE

*L*ater on, in the aftermath of the disaster, there would be hard feelings
among some of the K2 expeditions. The central points of contention
would be who contacted the media first, and what information they released, and when they released it. But there was little animosity in base
camp as the tragedy was still unfolding. Everyone personally knew the people who were dead, or still missing, and a somber cloak of brotherhood and
mutual aid settled thickly over the Godwin Austen Glacier. All parties involved would claim they acted in that spirit, trying to help in the communal
effort to set the rumors straight and provide accurate information—with
special concern for the families riveted to their computers, waiting for the
next blog posting, e-mail, or telephone call.

For the first thirty hours of the summit push, the Norit team was
the primary news source coming from K2. A few other blogs posted
sketchy reports, or copied from the Norit blog, but Maarten van Eck's
Web site was the predominant center of information from the mountain. In addition to his own team, he quickly assumed the responsibility
for monitoring the last-known whereabouts of Nick Rice, Hugues
D'Aubarède, Marco Confortola, and the Norwegians. Maarten's reporto-

rial style was conservative. He withheld many details from the press, instead issuing bullet-point statements that were vaguely reminiscent of a quarterly financial report. Climbers were either accounted for, confirmed dead, or "status unknown"—and he had pointedly chosen to suppress information that did not conclusively change any of those categories.

But on the afternoon of August 2, Norit's monopoly on the flow of information from the mountain began to change. Other individuals— some recently arrived in base camp, some still on the mountain—began to offer their own reports, their stories. With the Norit team's spokesperson, Michel, racing back from Austria, Maarten van Eck had neither the time nor the inclination to give detailed statements to the press. All of his energy was focused on the mountain. He tried to ignore the media. But suddenly, the media had other sources calling *them*, offering pitch-perfect sound bites and vivid descriptions of the tragedy.

Both Tom Sjogren and Maarten van Eck later blamed the crash of the Norit Web site on these new independent sources, which tipped the mainstream media off that something major was happening on K2. Of course, the international press was bound to get wind of the story sooner or later, but in Tom's and Maarten's estimation the process was unnecessarily accelerated by a crucial twenty-four to forty-eight hours, so that the families and loved ones anxiously waiting for news began to hear unattributed, anonymous body counts at the same time that the Norit site crashed, severing the most reliable informational link with the mountain. It wasn't long before Maarten himself was being bombarded with queries from the media asking if he could confirm the rising death toll. "Before Pemba and Cas got down, there was no way anyone could have known for sure," he insists. "No way."

At approximately the same time Chris Klinke looked through the telescope in base camp and noticed a faint flash of color, a short article began to appear in various European online news sites. Produced by the Swedish syndicated news service TT, the piece ran under the headline, Swedish Climber in K2 Death Drama. "Swedish mountaineer Fredrik Sträng was forced to break off his expedition to help another team to safety as four people were killed in avalanches on the notoriously challenging Mount Godwin Austen," the article began, incorrectly calling K2 by an antiquated, colonial name.

The article identified the source as Joachim von Stedingk, the spokesperson for Fredrik Sträng, who was a member of the American international expedition led by Mike Farris. It did not identify anyone other than Sträng by name, but offered this tantalizing report: "Sträng's team broke off its ascent and went to help another group to safety after one of its members had been killed. As they climbed down, another climber lost his life and Sträng almost went down with him." The article then summarized the situation with the following quote, also attributed to von Stedingk: "This avalanche caused a further two deaths and at least eight people are completely cut off now. How they will come down now nobody knows."

Those informed readers who had been following the Norit blog might have been able to deduce that Sträng's report referred to the aborted rescue of Dren Mandic—but the majority of readers perceived only a chaotic, desperate inferno of avalanches and falling climbers. If factually vague, the article was notable for the profound sense of futility it conveyed. It made no mention of any organizational plan or ongoing rescue efforts—the tragedy was a fait accompli.

The article was posted at one forty-five p.m. Central European Time, which meant it was five forty-five in the evening at K2 base camp—almost exactly the same time that Marco Confortola had been affirmatively located alive in Camp IV, and Chris Klinke noticed the orange dot high on K2. Sträng did not know that two of the eight missing climbers had been found because he was not yet in base camp—he was still descending the Abruzzi with the large group of climbers who had left Camp IV late that morning. "Right now, his team is climbing down to a lower level with injured and shocked climbers," the article explained. "The teams are presently at 7,500 meters, which significantly worsens rescue services' chances of helping them."

Meanwhile, the young pair of Nick Rice and Jelle Staleman reached the bottom of the SSE Spur around six p.m. Both were still in their twenties, new to the altitude game, and had made conservative decisions on summit day. Separately, they had turned back early in the morning on August 1, then shared a tent in Camp III and decided to descend the rest of the route together the next day. Nick learned of the situation on the upper mountain when he checked messages on his satellite phone in the morning.

"I received a disturbing SMS from my mom," Nick wrote, "saying that a big chunk of ice had fallen off the serac above the bottleneck, and cut the fixed lines, stranding the climbers above the Bottleneck." It was a bizarre twenty-first-century information loop: Nick's mom in Hermosa Beach, California, was quoting the news almost verbatim from the Norit blog, and reporting it back to her son on the mountain. And, as one of the mountain's most reliable bloggers, Nick wasted no time posting his own dispatch that evening. "Hoselito (Serbian) was at the base to meet us," he wrote, "and told us of the tragedy that was unfolding high on K2. He set the death toll at nine. . . ."

> The climbers were still stranded above the Bottleneck, aside from Pemba and Cas (Norit team), who had managed to down climb the Bottleneck without fixed lines. The Italian, Marco, and Irish, Gerard, had apparently made a bivouac, and then in the morning had headed the opposite direction from each other. Marco made it back down to Camp IV with severe frostbite on his hands and feet. Gerard had been sighted heading toward the Chinese side of the summit.

Nick did not specify his sources for these statements. It might have all come from the Serbian, Hoselito Bite, or it simply could have been the buzz around base camp. The news of Marco's survival most likely came from a radio call between Cas and Roeland, and the news of Gerard must have come, however indirectly, from Marco. The Norit site, meanwhile, was updated simultaneously. It confirmed that Marco had been found—but made no mention of Gerard or his whereabouts. So far as Maarten van Eck was concerned, the vague report that he had been seen "heading toward the Chinese side of the summit" was a rumor not worthy of public mention, and his real status remained unknown.

In subsequent statements, both Nick Rice and Fredrik Sträng would claim that they were motivated by a desire to clear up base camp rumors. This may be true, though neither Maarten van Eck nor Roeland van Oss, who were in direct contact with Pemba and Cas and thus had access to the most accurate two sources of information on the upper mountain, recall any agreement where it was decided that Nick or Fredrik would act as spokesman. Ultimately, their personal stories became some of the dominant accounts of the tragedy for two simple reasons: They had the technological resources—sat phones, portable computers, Web sites, even a media publicist—and they had the willingness to step into the public limelight.

But, for better or worse, they would become two of the most quoted sources in the mainstream media in the days to come—both gave numerous follow-up interviews from base camp over the next few days. Again and again, the media would return to the sense of confusion and hopelessness they expressed. It would be expounded on with vivid imagery and eyewitness accounts, news specials and op-ed pieces, until the spin itself threatened to taint the survivors' recollections and the factual evidence at hand.

Maarten van Eck wrote Tom Sjogren asking for help at five seventeen on the afternoon of August 2. The subject line of the e-mail read in bold letters:

> Norit K2 Web site is crashing under the pressure of way too many page visits. We try to update but it is difficult. If we send information by e-mail to you will you please publish?

Tom called Maarten on the phone. "Give me an hour," he said. "I think I can come up with something better."

Tom hung up and turned to his office computer. An hour later he had

designed a rough approximation of the Norit team's site and posted it on
the ExplorersWeb server. Then he linked the new site to the original Web
page. The traffic load was now balanced between the two servers, the
stress on the Norit server dropped, and the Web site was again operational. After Tom finished designing the mirror site, he called Annie.

"Have you seen Nick Rice's blog?" Tom asked. "I think you really
should contact him. He might have information about Gerard."

Annie and Evie typed in the address of Nick's Web site. They quickly scanned
his latest report. Gerard had been last seen . . . heading toward *China*?
Annie found Nick's contact e-mail address and wrote a hasty query: Whom
did he hear about Ger from? Did he have any more information?

At the same time, JJ McDonnell started making phone calls. He
quickly learned that the Pakistani military had a plane on standby, but it
was forbidden from entering Chinese airspace. *This is crazy,* JJ thought.
*This is a life-and-death emergency, and there's no procedure, no way to get
permission?* He began trying to get in touch with the Irish embassy in
China to organize an aerial search on that side of the mountain.

A little while later, Annie got a reply. It was from Nick's mom. Nick's
mom e-mailed Nick at base camp, and when Nick replied to her, she
wrote again to Annie: Nick didn't know anything more about Gerard. He
had heard that bit about China from someone in base camp. It was just
a rumor.

Another of Annie and Gerard's close friends, Jo Fortier, arrived by
midday Saturday. The three spent the rest of the day pinned to the Internet. Annie started scribbling notes, making lists of where people were
on the mountain, trying to make sense of it all.

A couple of hours later, the hard drive inside Ger's computer began to
heat up and make funny whirring noises, the screen washed an ominous
shade of blue, and the computer went entirely unresponsive. "Oh, shit,"
Evie said. The exact same thing had happened to her own computer once
before and the thing had been completely fried. Evie jokingly called it the
"blue screen of death."

"What does that mean?" Annie asked.

"It's not good, Annie." They called up another friend who lived nearby and asked if she could drive over her computer.

In Ireland, they were having computer troubles too. Damien O'Brien, who was married to Gerard's youngest sister, had been up for two days with the rest of the family. They were still gathered together at Martha's, with several laptops between them, surfing the Web for more news. But the router was somewhat antiquated and the connection excrutiately slow. By now, the Irish media had begun trying to contact them. Pat Falvey, one of Ireland's most experienced mountaineers, who had climbed Everest with Gerard in 2003, offered to act as the spokesperson for the McDonnell family. Late Saturday afternoon he called Kilcornan.

"They can see an orange dot near Camp III on the South-southeast Spur," he told Damien. "It might be Gerard." It was the third different rumor Damien had heard about Gerard. First, he had been told that his brother-in-law might have been killed in the initial avalanche that took Rolf Bae. Then it was reported that Ger was last seen heading to China. And now this. The family knew that Gerard's high-altitude suit was red and black, not orange, but the news was still somehow comforting. In Spain, JJ decided to return to his hotel to spend the night before flying home the next morning, and Damien went home for a few hours of much needed rest.

"But, Pat, he doesn't have an orange suit. That must be Wilco, not Gerard," Annie said when Falvey rang her with the same information.

"But it could be him," Pat urged. "It's something positive to say to the family. . . ."

Annie could never be sure if Pat really believed that it was Gerard, or if he was just saying it to keep everyone's spirits up. Ultimately, Falvey—an experienced mountaineer himself—must have known that he was clutching at straws, trying to keep some candle of hope burning as the bad news came crashing in. But despite his best intentions, it would only make the events that were soon to follow more devastating.

———

Just after midnight, a halting procession of headlamps bopped across the moraine of the Godwin Austen Glacier. As the lights approached the lit tents of base camp, Roeland and Chris could see the vague forms of their friends and teammates, shoulders sagged and foot-worn from the tortuous descent from Camp IV. The Serbians had arrived earlier that day, and the Norwegians only a few hours before. Now, with the arrival of the American international expedition, many of the climbers who had participated in the summit push were off the mountain. The Abruzzi Ridge was largely vacated, except for Marco Confortola and his two hired Pakistanis at Camp IV, and the Koreans and Singaporeans in Camp III.

For Eric Meyer, the descent started out well enough. The Singaporeans had plenty of water and hot tea waiting in Camp III, and Mike Farris joined them in Camp II. Each step downward brought them more oxygen and warmer temperatures. They were making good time, and Eric hoped they could reach advance base camp on the glacier before dark.

Getting down the Abruzzi Ridge is largely an exercise in descending fixed ropes. Several miles of line stretched in a continuous path from just below Camp III, at the top of the Black Pyramid, to the bergschrund on the Godwin Austen Glacier at the very bottom of the mountain. Most expeditions try to attach new lines at the beginning of every season. Rarely, however, does anybody bother to remove the old ropes, and so often climbers are confronted with tangled nests of weakened, sun-bleached cord. Anchors of pitons, ice screws, or slung blocks are generally placed every one hundred to two hundred feet. Depending on the steepness of each pitch, a climber might decide to rappel down the rope using a friction device, or, if the terrain is more moderate, clip into the rope as a tether and descend by walking, with one hand wrapped around the rope for extra support. Once the climber reaches the bottom anchor point, they can clip into the next rope and continue the descent. Technically, the process of going down fixed ropes is as simple as clipping a locking carabiner from one section of rope to the next, but it demands unwavering attention to detail.

Eric was below Camp II, rappelling a section of sixty-degree mixed ice and rock. At the top anchor, he saw that there were two ropes fixed on the next pitch. He chose the newer-looking line—eight-millimeter polypropylene—and threaded it through his ATC friction device, and clipped his tether to the other rope, as a backup. Two-thirds of the way to the next anchor, the line suddenly exploded, the crinkled, weather-worn fibers tearing inside Eric's belay device as he watched. A moment later, before he had any time to react, Eric was somersaulting backward. He saw a clear image of Broad Peak against the blue sky behind him, and tried to throw his arm up to catch the other rope. He felt his tether come tight just as his forearm hooked the second rope.

Australian Mark Sheen had been just in front of Eric and watched the fall, powerless to help. Now Meyer was ten feet below the anchor, his weight resting on the one remaining rope. "I thought you were a goner, mate," Mark deadpanned to the incredulous Meyer.

As if I needed another sign that we had to get off this mountain, Eric thought to himself. The team continued down, following the lower ridge as it weaved around gendarmes and gargoyles of rotten rock. Finally, a little after dusk, they set foot on the glacier and trudged toward the advance base camp. The American international expedition's cook, Deedar, had hiked up to meet them with food and water for the exhausted climbers. The solemn group continued the last several hours to base camp in silence.

Roeland and Chris were monitoring the situation on the SSE Spur. Pemba and Cas had departed from Camp IV a little after dark, and were descending toward Camp III on the SSE Spur, where the vague orange dot had been seen late that afternoon. By midnight, Pemba radioed to report that he had reached Camp III. He had become separated from Cas, however, who was missing somewhere on the fixed lines between Camp IV and Camp III. Nor had Pemba located the mysterious missing person. Roeland and the Sherpa agreed that there was little more that could be done until morning.

Pemba signed off on the radio, and evidently crashed into deep sleep. Roeland and Chris greeted the climbers returning from the Abruzzi Ridge, and slowly they tried to piece together what had happened up there.

Rolf Bae was confirmed dead. No one had seen Cecilie since the Norwegians arrived in base camp early that evening, but their teammate Lars Nessa solemnly confirmed the news. To Chris Klinke and Roeland van Oss, it was almost unbelievable. Fun-loving and approachable, Rolf was one of the most popular guys in base camp, and acknowledged as one of the best climbers on the mountain to boot. Nobody thought it would happen to him.

Lars and Cecilie had summited together, just ahead of the Koreans. Rolf, who had evidently not been feeling his best that day, held back above the fixed lines and did not continue to the top. Instead he waited for his wife and teammate to return, approximately halfway between the fixed lines and the summit. The Norwegians had set a strict rule for themselves of arriving at the top anchor before sunset. "We knew we could follow the fixed ropes down to the Shoulder in the darkness and be okay," Lars later recalled. The three reached the top anchor with fifteen minutes to spare.

One by one, they rappelled down the first rope, which protected a steep section of water-ice on the side of the serac. At the next anchor Lars turned to Rolf and asked who should go first. The two had already agreed to keep Cecilie between them. "He wanted himself to go first, and me to wait for Cecilie," Lars remembered. "He asked me to watch Cecilie, to make sure our Italian hitches were tied correctly." It was now completely dark. As the three traversed the fixed lines down the Diagonal, Lars heard the sound of ice collapsing. The sudden noise was disorienting: It was impossible for him to tell whether it was right in front of him, or twenty kilometers away. Then he heard another noise: Cecilie, calling out for Rolf in the night. But Rolf was gone.

So was the Serbian, Dren, who had fallen late in the morning of summit day. Chris Klinke's teammates, Eric Meyer and Fredrik Sträng, who turned around early on August first, rushed up the Shoulder to help as soon as they heard a climber had fallen. By the time Fredrik reached Dren's teammates—Iso Planic, Predrag Zagorac, and Pakistani Muhammad Hussain—at the base of the Bottleneck, it was too late. They placed

Dren's body in a sleeping bag, shrouded with a Serbian flag—the same flag they had planned to unfurl on K2's summit that day.

The sad episode might have ended there. But one of the Serbians—and afterward no one was sure who—decided they should lower the body back to Camp IV for a burial in a crevasse. Body recoveries at high altitude are rarely performed; it was later asserted that the unusual decision was made by the Serbians' expedition leader, Milivoj Erdeljan, who was monitoring from base camp. Erdeljan denied this charge in his own expedition report, and the confusion is difficult to resolve. But as they began to lower the body, Jehan Baig, another Pakistani who was descending from the Bottleneck after carrying a load of oxygen for Hugues D'Aubarède, arrived on the scene. Jehan apparently wanted to help, but he seemed unstable in crampons, and then became tangled in the line they were using to lower the body, and fell. He crashed into Fredrik Sträng, wrenching him off his stance. One of the Serbians lost his footing as well.

Startled, Sträng cried at him to get off of him, that he would kill them all. "He neither used his ice ax, his crampons, nor made any effort to ease the strain on the rope," Sträng wrote. "We continued to shout at him. Nothing happened. Then he lost his grip on the rope and began to slide down the mountainside, at first on his backside; then he flipped over so that he was sliding headfirst." Jehan held an ice ax in one hand, but Meyer would remember that he made no effort to self-arrest, a basic mountaineering technique to stop a fall. They watched helplessly as gravity took hold of the man and swept him out of sight. The others abandoned their efforts to bury Dren Mandic and returned to Camp IV.

As the early morning hours of August 3 waned toward sunrise and the details of these grim events were passed around base camp, most people dropped into their tents to try to get a few hours' rest. Still, Chris and Roeland could directly account for the deaths of only three people: Jehan Baig, Dren Mandic, and Rolf Bae. There were rumors of a much greater loss of life, to be sure, but the only source for substantive reports was via radio or satellite phone. The language barriers, limited battery power, and incomplete transmissions made the communications so unreliable that Roeland resolved to wait. Until Cas and Pemba got down the SSE Spur, or the Koreans or Marco descended the Abruzzi, nobody in base camp could personally confirm anything at all from the upper mountain.

Chris Klinke was up at dawn.

The thickly built financial manager pressed his bearded face up to a telescope and scanned the SSE Spur for life. The little orange dot was still there, about three hundred meters west of Camp III and a hundred meters above it. Then Hoselito, the Serbian soloist, spotted a second dot descending the fixed ropes below Camp IV. *That must be Cas*, Chris thought to himself. There was no luck on the radio raising Pemba, who evidently was still asleep, and so all of base camp held its collective breath, watched through telescopes, and waited for the inevitable rendezvous.

Finally, a few minutes after Cas reached Pemba's tent, radio communication resumed with base camp. "Start calling Wilco's name—he's to your west, to the left," Roeland urged his teammates. A subtle terrain feature between the missing climber and Camp III prevented the two parties from seeing each other. Chris and Roeland radioed directions to Pemba and Cas, and watched as the final drama played out in telescopic detail.

As soon as Pemba and Cas started yelling, Chris saw the missing climber abruptly stand up and begin traversing toward the camp. He could see the climber punching his fists into the slope of the mountain, overdriving each step with fatigued determination. Now Cas was leaving camp in the direction of the missing climber, and Pemba exited the tent to follow. Now Cas was slowly rounding the broad pillow of snow that blocked their view. Now it looked like he was waving. In base camp the last agonizing minute slipped by in the still early morning air, and then— the radio squelched to life.

They had found Wilco.

———

Late on Saturday night, Tom spoke again to Annie: "There's still a little time left," he said. "We need to get them to organize a new rescue effort. I think you should be more aggressive. It's not too late, Annie."

Okay, fine, Annie thought. *Just tell me how I do that.* Then she heard another phone ringing in the background. "Oh, that's Maarten," Tom said. "I need to call him back."

Ten minutes later, Annie's phone rang again. It was Tom.

"Annie," he said, "Maarten is going to be calling you, but I told him I'd talk to you first, because we have been in touch. I'm afraid Ger's been killed."

Silence. Annie would remember the rest of the conversation quite clearly.

"Is there no hope at all?" she asked.

"I'm afraid not," Tom said. "We've heard from base camp that Marco says he saw Ger's yellow boots in an avalanche."

Annie's living room seemed to list at an odd angle. She knew that pair of bright yellow boots well. They were modern, double-insulated with integrated gators, cost nearly a thousand dollars retail, made by the Italian company La Sportiva specifically for the intense cold of eight-thousand-meter climbing. Ger had bought his first pair of La Sportivas for his K2/Broad Peak expedition in 2006. Over the course of a single summer in the Karakoram, the soles had completely worn off their tread. Afterward, Ger sent the boots away to have the soles replaced. When they returned from the cobbler, the boots had a new tread, but they were heavier than the factory-made originals—just a few ounces more, but Gerard, ever the methodical engineer, wanted them lighter. So La Sportiva had eventually sent him a pair of their state-of-the-art, 2008 Olympus Mons model before he left for Islamabad that spring. A shiny new pair of bright, fluorescent yellow boots.

"Well," Annie asked, "could they be someone else's boots?"

"Annie, I don't think so. I'm afraid not. Ger's boots were the latest model; they only started making them in yellow this year," Tom stammered on.

"No, Tom." Annie was insistent. "They were yellow in 2006—other people have to be wearing the same boots up there. . . ."

Tom didn't know what else to say.

"Annie, I'm so sorry. . . ."

Damien O'Brien's phone rang at five a.m. on Sunday morning. He listened for a few moments, and then got dressed and drove over to tell the family to prepare for the worst.

Tom stormed into the loft bedroom of their rented chalet, waking Tina. "That's it! Time to wake up." He was half talking to Tina, and half talking to himself. "Now we are going to get them and we are going to get them good!"

Tom was, in Tina's own expression, "mad as a hatter." After two days of unceasing effort supporting Maarten any way he could—tracking the Thuraya signal, the sleepless night of furious programming to get the Norit site back up and running, and then the excruciating phone call to Annie—as he had been doing all that, climbers in base camp were— *giving interviews*?! To Tom and Tina, it was appallingly insensitive and completely tactless.

ExplorersWeb's e-mail in-box was inundated with requests for information and material from journalists around the world; Tom had just deflected requests for interviews from CNN and the BBC. August is historically considered a slow news month for the mainstream media. Although 2008 was an election year in the United States, by midsummer the candidates were retreating from the spotlight, preparing for their party conventions scheduled later in the month. The vague reports and thirdhand accounts that had began trickling out of base camp late Saturday evening had coalesced into a media firestorm. K2 became *the* news story of the weekend. And everyone was asking the same question: How many are dead?

Modern adventure seekers such as the Sjogrens have a penchant for counting and records. After all, there are few singular "firsts" remaining to be achieved by which to distinguish one's accomplishments. A substantial part of Explorersweb.com (dubbed Adventurestats.com) is dedicated to keeping track of who did what when—one can read, for instance, the names, vessels, and dates of the 259 people who have sailed solo around the world, or the 71 people who have made solo, unsupported, and unassisted journeys to the South Pole (both figures are current as of January 1, 2009). A detailed glossary of definitions is provided as well, to ensure that all achievements are measured using (more or less) the same rules. This tendency toward quantification applies to tragedies as much as it does to triumphs. And so far as Tom saw it, the problem was that all too often the mainstream media willingly accepted the unsubstantiated claims of modern adventurers without bothering to do their homework.

The "official" death toll, as reported in the media, seemed to rise with each wave of news updates. Early on Sunday morning, Reuters reported that five climbers were missing after an avalanche on K2. Then the AFP (Agence France-Presse) released a new story confirming seven dead. Then, at two thirty-five Central European Time on August 3, or approximately five p.m. local time in Pakistan—as base camp prepared for the imminent arrival of Pemba, Cas, and Wilco, who were still on the mountain, nearing the bottom of the SSE Spur—came this headline from TT: *K2 Mountain Drama Over: 11 Deaths.*

"I carried both the living and the dead down from the mountain," the story quoted Fredrik Sträng, now in base camp, as saying. "At one point I was terrified as a Pakistani Sherpa fell on my back with all his weight. I was in a panic that he would drag all of us down with him, and screamed for him to use his ice pick, but he lost hold of it and flew off a three-hundred-meter precipice. . . . The accidents could have been prevented. These mountains attract more and more inexperienced and naive people who completely rely on the resources that are there, Sherpas, oxygen gas and weather reports."

Most of the other news stories cited statements from Pakistani officials or domestic tour companies in Islamabad who were providing base camp logistics to each K2 expedition. Everestnews.com published a report from Mike Farris, the leader of the American international team.

"Up to eleven climbers are confirmed dead, or missing and presumed dead," he wrote. But still, the Norit site publicly confirmed only a single fatality—the Serbian Dren Mandic, who had fallen from the Bottleneck early in the summit push.

Moreover, no names were released in any of the revised death counts, making the different reports maddeningly hard to reconcile. Tina, a journalist herself, understood the well-rehearsed, unverifiable lexicon that was sometimes employed by the media. "Missing and presumed dead" was a great catchall phrase that was impossible to clarify or confirm.

Presumed dead by whom? Tina wondered. *Anytime the shit hits the fan on some peak and it starts making headlines,* Tina thought to herself, *there's always some profiteer waiting in the wings, some self-styled hero standing by to profit from the drama.*

Feisty and outspoken, neither Tom nor Tina was inclined to shy away from public debate. On the contrary, the Sjogrens felt it was their duty not only as a journalistic assignment, but a moral obligation to defend the core values of the sport. In a feature-length profile on the pair in 2007, *Outside* magazine summed up their often divisive style: "Day after day, it is ExplorersWeb that practically tape-measures the claimed feats of dozens of adventurers, often causing anger, outrage, and embarrassment." Bryant Urstadt, the author of the story, which ran under the title "The Grudge Report," went on to say:

> Their reportorial style often skips the norms of American journalism: Personal invective is seen as fair play, and source attributions can be maddeningly vague. . . . But, during my own research, I didn't come across any substantive fact-based rebuttals to their stories, and so far no one has sued them for libel.

Tina sat down that morning and began to hammer out a new screed. "'Confirmed dead' must be done by a coroner or judge in most countries in the world," she wrote. "In the mountains we need an eyewitness or sufficient time to pass. . . . It's only 12 hours since Wilco was found and even though hope is very slim, we should not declare people dead that are still missing." Tina singled out Fred Sträng's comments, and those of his teammate Mike Farris. ExplorersWeb had specifically e-mailed Farris asking if he could confirm Gerard McDonnell's death, to which Farris had responded: "Tell the family that we presume Gerard is dead, but won't know for the next twenty-four hours."

Circling in for the kill, Tina brought her piece to its conclusion: "While his statement on EverestNews clearly says 'up to 11 climbers lost their lives,' fact is that Farris has no idea." With a special flourish, she pecked out a title: "K2's Double Tragedy—Blowing out Candles for Scoops and Fame." The editorial was classic ExplorersWeb: timely and thought provoking, morally charged—and way over the top. Tom and Tina didn't stop there. Five days later, they ran an in-depth piece investigating Fredrik Sträng's claims on previous mountaineering expeditions; in several instances ExplorersWeb found him guilty of making minor embellishments on his résumé.

A month after the tragedy, Sträng would vehemently deny those charges and defend his integrity and that of his teammates on his own blog. "Early on 2nd August news of the drama on K2 was leaked to the world," he wrote. "We in the International K2 Expedition and many others on the mountain know . . . who reported the news, but our position was not to say a word until we had the situation on the mountain under control. We prioritized attempts to save life." According to Sträng, "Nobody wanted to shoulder the task of speaking to CNN, BBC, etc. . . . The responsibility fell to me. . . . When I informed the media that 11 people had died it was an established figure and communications central were in possession of the official list of names of the deceased." He also suggested that ExplorersWeb was attacking him out of jealousy because his team had been providing exclusive reports to Tom and Tina's rival, EverestNews.com.

Nick Rice, for his part, is more introspective about the role his blog played in covering the unfolding disaster. "That's the power of keeping a daily blog," he says. "You can't change the dates. You can't change the times. . . . There's not the hindsight of a couple of months. It's a real record of what people believed was happening."

4

WILCO AND MARCO

*R*oeland van Oss spent Sunday, August 3, nervously watching the three *specks of life descend the SSE Spur. The sunny weather of the past several days changed conditions on the lower mountain, significantly melting snow and making the bottom sections of the Abruzzi Ridge and SSE Spur dangerously exposed to rockfall. In radio communications, Cas, Wilco, and Pemba spoke coherently and reported that they expected to reach base camp under their own power. But all were without question physically and mentally spent; the two Dutchmen, Roeland knew, suffered from advanced frostbite. Yet Pemba, who was saddled with the responsibility of escorting the two injured climbers down two thousand meters of terrain, was uncharacteristically forceful. They didn't need a rescue.*

Over the radio that morning, Pemba had expressly forbidden Roeland from sending any parties to help them down. Crowding the route with more people, he said, would only make the situation more dangerous for all involved. Instead, Roeland, with Jelle Staleman, Chris Warner, and the Serbian Hoselito, decided to climb the bottom four hundred meters of the SSE Spur, adding more fixed lines to help their teammates over the final sections of wet, shattered rock and sloughing snow. Then they turned around and waited on the glacier, watching the three minuscule dots inch their way down the mountain.

Roeland stayed in hourly contact with Maarten van Eck in Holland. Maarten was already coordinating a helicopter evacuation from base camp for the following morning, in addition to keeping up a running dialogue with several embassies and the Alpine Club of Pakistan, and sharing what news he could with the families and loved ones of those still on K2. Each time they spoke, Maarten asked Roeland the same questions: "What do you know about Gerard? Hugues D'Aubarède? Rolf Bae?" Maarten would patiently check the status of each missing person.

All day Sunday, rumors and unsubstantiated reports crackled around base camp, but Roeland found the details devilishly hard to confirm. Someone had seen Hugues fall. The Koreans lost three team members and a Sherpa. Gerard was last seen heading toward China. It was all secondhand information, mostly people repeating news from someone else who said they heard it had been radioed down from Camp IV. In fact, everyone in base camp had left Camp IV by noon on August 2; the only people who might personally have witnessed the final disastrous hours of the summit push were still fighting their way down the mountain. Despite the rampant gossip, there was nothing Roeland could publicly confirm.

Now, the young climber sat perched atop a boulder tucked into the rocky folds of the Godwin Austen Glacier. In a sinking arch, the sun had curved behind the flying buttresses of the South-southwest Pillar, a route Messner himself had nicknamed "the Magic Line." To the right, his eyes followed his teammates as they skirted the edge of the broad snow gully that formed the start of the SSE Spur, turned their backs on the mountain, and plunge-stepped toward him through the thick, slushy snow. The summit of K2 was in shadows, and behind them, the sun's last rays played on Broad Peak's western flank. It occurred to Roeland that eight weeks ago, when the expedition first convened in Islamabad, he had been thrilled to join a team that included Wilco, Cas, Pemba, and Gerard. They were all strong, confident climbers with decades of experience, mentors and friends who welcomed him on the expedition and coached him through his first high-altitude experiences.

They were not the same three men Roeland met in the cooling, dusky twilight.

Pemba arrived first. Roeland watched the Sherpa's compact form scramble around a few rocks resting on the glacier and hop a small crevasse. He expected Pemba to be exhausted, but he looked startlingly fresh. Pemba dropped his pack and took a long swig from the bottle of Coca-Cola Roeland offered him. Then he ate a bit of chocolate.

"There were too many people. Too many people not experienced enough to climb K2," Pemba said. He was animated. Agitated. Angry, even. His face was darkened from days of exposure to intense solar radiation, save for two lighter circles of skin where his goggles had been. They accentuated his eyes, making them bigger than they were. Cas and Wilco lagged behind in the deep, isothermic snow. After a few minutes' rest, Pemba stood up, put his pack back on, and began walking the last hour to base camp alone.

Pemba's surprising energy only underscored Wilco's and Cas's condition. They were entirely depleted, at the end of their bodies' physical reserves. Both Dutchmen cut tall, strapping figures, standing well over six feet high. Now their height seemed a disadvantage, as they wobbled like drunken sailors, pitching in and out of balance with each step across the pocked surface of the glacier. They dropped to the ground when they met Roeland.

Cas and Wilco were old friends—friends from adolescence, when they had first dreamed of traveling the world and seeking adventure. As young men, they drove a jeep across Africa, learned to climb in the Alps, and went on their first expeditions to the Greater Ranges. But as they matured as mountaineers, their climbing careers each developed a distinct flair. Cas was drawn to technical alpine climbing, quietly climbing impressive routes in Peru and attempting steep test pieces on six-thousand-meter peaks in the Himalayas. In 2003, he established a new route on the ice-wreathed, near-vertical Northeast Face of India's Thalay Sagar. Wilco evolved into an adventurer in the more classical mold. He climbed Everest without oxygen, skied to both poles, and frequently participated in grueling long-distance mountain runs around the Alps. If he didn't have the same technical background as Cas, Wilco was generally acknowledged to be an extremely tough and physically fit guy.

The two men lived only a few miles away from each other in Utrecht, and often teamed up for short trips to the Alps, when work allowed. Wilco had studied to be an electrical engineer, while Cas carved out a living taking on small carpentry jobs, to ensure he had plenty of time to climb. Wilco, who had always been talkative to a point bordering on compulsion, began to give more and more lectures about his adventures, and slowly it dawned on him that he could perhaps make a career as a professional adventurer—especially if he could break into the realm of lucrative corporate-speaking engagements. One of his first clients was Norit, and the presentation was such a success that he quickly negotiated a deal to become a sort of adventure spokesperson for the company. The deal was a major windfall for Wilco's family: that spring, only a few weeks before leaving for Pakistan, Wilco and Heleen purchased a wonderful old barn out in the country, a ninety-minute train ride east of Utrecht. In the fall, they would move there and begin renovating the old agrarian structure, and get down to the business of raising their family in the countryside. All Wilco had to do first was climb K2.

Now Cas and Wilco, the last members of the Norit team to make it off the mountain alive, shakily stood. They could still walk, but it was necessary to stop every two hundred meters to rest. By headlamp, the tiny party slowly escorted the survivors of K2 toward the lit village of tents below.

On the surface, Eric Meyer well fits the Westernized ideal of the twenty-first-century mountain adventurer. A slightly built, athletic man of forty-four, he had earned his medical degree from the University of Washington and gone into anesthesia, eventually settling in Steamboat Springs, Colorado. Soft-spoken and handsome, he frequently sported a shock of neatly cut platinum blond hair. His interests spanned from yoga, skiing, biking, and trail running to flying small aircraft, climbing eight-thousand-meter peaks, and volunteering for medical-aid programs in the developing world. Though his primary goal in Pakistan was to climb K2, the expedition proved to be one of the hardest missions of his career.

It was a job that started on day one of the approach. Porters and villagers would seek out the American doctor each evening with a litany of health problems—intestinal pain, fevers, infections, malnourishment. Eric took satisfaction at being able to help the local population on the trek to the mountain. But after arriving at base camp, he was somewhat dismayed to realize that he was the only doctor among the sixty-odd climbers attempting K2. He was routinely sought out by people for help—amoung other things, he prescribed medicine to a Korean climber with gastric reflux, diagnosed a French climber with appendicitis, and answered countless questions concerning altitude-related illnesses. "Around base camp, I was a busy guy," he says laconically of the weeks leading up to the summit push. "But it helped our expedition form strong bonds with the Koreans, and other teams too."

While Roeland hiked over to meet Wilco, Cas, and Pemba at the base of the SSE Spur and accompany them back to camp, Eric set about improvising a triage center. He cleared out the Norit team's mess tent and made a bed out of foam pads and blankets. The Norwegian expedition donated an inflatable couch. Eric unpacked his medical kit on a table and readied two IVs, and then he asked the cook to boil a large pot of water.

At nine p.m., his first patient, Wilco, arrived, followed shortly by Cas.

As a mountaineer, Eric Meyer knew the debilitating effects of high altitude firsthand. The average adult male is made up of 60 percent water (women have a slightly lower water content, about 55 percent). Human life is predicated on several basic requirements to sustain our predominantly liquid bodies: warm temperatures, an abundance of water, and oxygenated air. The environment on the world's eight-thousand-meter peaks is cold, dry, and depleted of O_2. Confronted with extreme conditions, the body will undergo a series of involuntary changes to preserve its basic functions. In periods of prolonged cold exposure, signals

are sent to the blood vessels in the arms and legs, causing them to constrict, reducing flow to the extremities. This increases more blood flow
to the vital organs, while at the same time minimizing heat loss by exposing less blood to the cold temperatures at the skin. If this process
continues, a compensatory action known as the hunter's response is trig-
gered. Blood vessels in the extremities will periodically dilate, allowing
blood flow to increase and preserving some measure of functionality,
before they constrict again. If the body senses a serious threat of hypothermia—that is, its core temperature dropping below 98.6 degrees—it
will begin to permanently restrict flow to the extremities. That is when
serious frostbite begins.

The fluid inside of human tissue cells doesn't actually freeze. That
kind of injury might rarely occur when the skin is exposed to rapidly freezing conditions, like coming into direct contact with supercooled metals.
But more often than not, frostbite injuries are the result of damage in the
intracellular spaces and vascular tissue. Two different processes happen
in succession. The first occurs during the initial freezing, when water in
the intracellular spaces begins to freeze into ice crystals. This sucks more
water away from the cells, and the resulting cellular dehydration destroys
the tissue. The second and more insidious destruction happens when the
damaged body parts are rewarmed. As blood flow returns, the initial damage already done to vascular tissue causes further blood leakage, clots, and
obstructed circulation. Inflammation frequently occurs next, compound-
ing these problems. The final amount of tissue damage is largely deter-
mined by the extent of these processes.

Wilco and Cas slumped side by side onto the makeshift gurney in the
Norit tent. Because deep frostbite wounds also inflict significant damage
on the nervous system, there is little pain associated with the initial
freezing. But once the body parts are rewarmed, returning blood and
oxygen to the region, the pain can be extreme. Eric's first concern was to
minimize their discomfort. A small crowd of base camp denizens peeked
in the doorway, waving hello, or stood outside with arms somberly
crossed. Eric applied IVs to both Wilco and Cas, then administered a
moderate dose of morphine and valium. Rehydration was also vitally

important. Thermoses of warm tea, bottles of electrolyte sports drink, and the ubiquitous bottles of Coke were all on hand. Then someone brought them their first real meal in days—steaming plates of hot rice and chapatis.

Wilco's feet were the most pressing concern. The leader of the Norit expedition had spent two nights lost on the mountain, and gone for nearly seventy-two hours without shelter, water, or having the luxury of removing his boots. Now, as they unzipped his gators, untied the boot laces, and removed his sweat-stained socks, was the moment of reckoning. All of his toes, on both feet, were an inanimate, waxen shade of white.

Cas's worst damage was to his fingers. As he and Pemba had hastened to descend to Camp III in an effort to find the mysterious orange dot, the batteries in Cas's headlamp had unexpectedly died. Realizing that he carried more AA batteries in his radio, Cas had tried to switch them into his light. At sea level, this might seem a basic, even mindless task, but such are the effects of prolonged exposure to high altitude that it was challenging. Cas couldn't seem to open the small plastic door to the battery case in his radio. He removed his gloves for greater dexterity. A carpenter by trade, the lanky Dutchman gripped his ice ax and gave a few sharp swings at his radio. The door exploded open, sending batteries jumping down the mountain, into the night. With no light, and no means to continue his descent until dawn, Cas removed his sodden sleeping bag from his pack and draped it over his head as he sat at an anchor. Somewhere in the episode, one of his gloves disappeared.

Frostbite treatment has changed little over the last twenty-five years. Eric knew it was critical to thaw the injured extremities slowly. If he were to rewarm the frostbite too quickly—for instance, by immersing one's fingers in a pot of boiling water—it would only exacerbate the damage by shocking the vascular system back to circulation. The accepted protocol is to apply soaks of lukewarm water, between 100 and 102 degrees, until the injuries are entirely thawed. The process takes hours. There is little that can be done to reverse the effects of deep frostbite. As with burn victims, it is largely an exercise in minimizing what damage has already been done, controlling post-injury infections and inflammation, and waiting to see how much tissue revives—and how much is permanently dead.

Several large pots of water were brought in from the kitchen. Eric poured in a few cups of boiling water from a thermos, stirring the fluid and carefully checking the temperature with a thermometer. As the climbers' unfeeling feet and hands dipped beneath the warm, rehabilitating water, steam rose from the surface and quickly evaporated in the cold glacial air.

There are few proven strategies for more aggressive treatment. Eric was familiar with one experimental study conducted by the Burn Center at the University of Utah Hospital. There, doctors had given victims of severe frostbite a high-powered drug called alteplase, generically known in medical parlance as a tissue plasminogen activator, or tPA. Alteplase stimulates enzyme production in the cellular tissue lining the blood vessels. Because it artificially raises the levels of plasmin, the enzyme responsible for breaking down blood clots, alteplase is commonly used as a drug of last resort for treating victims of severe heart attacks, strokes, and pulmonary embolisms.

But what about using it against the debilitating effects of thawing? The few studies that had been done on the subject were promising, but it was far from proven. Eric had two vials of alteplase, and three potential patients: Cas, Wilco, and Marco Confortola, who was still descending the Abruzzi Ridge. For heart attacks and strokes, alteplase has to be administered as quickly as possible, preferably within an hour of the onset of symptoms. For frostbite injuries, that window widens—the University of Utah study recommended treatment within twenty-four hours.

Cas's injuries fell wholly within that time frame.

Wilco's did not . . . but it might be worth a try.

Marco, still at least twenty-four hours from base camp, was beyond help.

Cas and Wilco each got one dose of alteplase.

Their hands and feet, meanwhile, slowly thawed. Small flecks of skin pealed from the ashen-hued digits floating in the tepid bath. Both survivors had arrived in base camp in relatively stable mental shape. They were exhausted, yes, but alert and oriented to their present time and circumstances and in good spirits, all things considered. They talked sporadically of the last few desperate days, but their memories were disjointed, nonchronological. One or two visitors murmured a word of congratulations, and a few halfhearted jokes were cracked. But most present didn't have much to say. Certainly no one felt the need to ask any questions in detail. After a while, once Wilco and Cas had eaten as much as their stomachs would allow, they each wrapped themselves in a sleeping bag. Conversation drifted off. Eric, Chris, and Roeland had to admit to themselves that they were nearly as tired as their patients. By then, the two Dutchmen had passed into heavy sleep, snoring next to each other, their hands and feet still submerged in pans of 102-degree water.

Eric Meyer kept the soaks going until five a.m., when he judged the injuries to be well thawed. One at a time, he removed each appendage and carefully wrapped it in thick gauze dressings. Roeland was already busy readying for the helicopter evac, which he hoped was only a few hours away.

Pemba, Meyer recalls, had barely said a word all night. He stood around for the first hour or two, looking after his teammates in silence, then retreated to the cluttered confines of the kitchen tent. There, he sat in deep conversation with several climbing-Sherpas from the Korean team. Eric noticed that they crowded over one another, passing a digital camera back and forth so that they all could look at the glowing display screen.

Looking back on it now, Evie Whitten can't remember a definitive moment or single point in time when the awful truth hit them. Her memories of the long weekend are more those of a protracted siege of emotional trench warfare, in which they were forced to retreat, inch by inch, foxhole by foxhole, trying to hold out hope and resist the mounting evidence of a terribly different reality that was now regularly being cited in the news. It was all about flow. With the inevitable pull of gravity, she felt their optimism slowly drain until everyone must have been thinking the same thing, though no one was ready yet to say it out loud.

Ger McDonnell was dead.

After the conversation with Tom, the rest of the weekend passed in a strange blur for Annie. Jo kept urging her to try to sleep, to rest, to at least eat something. Annie was still glued to the computer. Meanwhile, her friends worked on arranging a bereavement ticket to Ireland—they eventually found a ticket on a red-eye flight that evening, leaving Anchorage at one a.m. There was so much to do: A call to Annie's office to explain that she would be taking an immediate leave of absence. Bills to pay. A bag to pack. Annie had no interest in going through the rack of outfits in her closet.

The candle still sputtered and spit as they prepared to take Annie to the airport Sunday evening. Jo would accompany her on the first leg of the flight, to New York. Annie was still at the computer, surfing the Web for more news. Evie warned her that she could miss the flight. Annie finally stood up, vacantly looking around her apartment one more time.

"Is it crazy to still have hope?" she asked.

"No, it isn't," Evie told her.

She had one more thought: *I don't want to see the candle go out.*

And so Annie left for the airport, and Evie Whitten stayed, waiting until they had pulled out of the driveway and around the corner from her residential street. Then she blew out the candle, turned off the lights, and locked the door to her friend's empty apartment.

At ten a.m. on Monday, August 4, the low-frequency, mechanized beat of rotors echoed off the lower flanks of Broad Peak. The sound slowly built, throbbing across the Godwin Austen Glacier until an olive green Pakistani army helicopter lumbered into view. It orbited K2 base camp several times, the pilot checking the wind and eyeballing the rough landing area that had been hastily cobbled together the evening before. The ship gently touched down and a small procession trudged toward it, their heads down to protect from the gravel and silt thrown in the sixty-mile-an-hour backwash of the rotors. Two men were loaded on board. Their feet and hands were bound in thick swaths of gauze. Seconds later, the French-made turbine helicopter from the Askari Aviation unit rose back into the air, turned, and clomped back down the glacier.

Wilco and Cas were transported straight to the Combined Military Hospital in Skardu. The local authorities, perhaps motivated by a desire to turn the rescue into some positive publicity, allowed a photographer and video crew to document their arrival and initial treatment. The world was about to get its first pixilated glimpses of the survivors of K2. They would be haunting images.

Among Western mountaineers, the military hospital in Skardu has a mixed reputation for patient care. Though the Pakistani army is known for its institutional professionalism, many injured climbers who have been admitted to the facility report unnerving experiences that are less than confidence inspiring. Gerard McDonnell had one such story. After he was hit by rockfall in 2006, he was evacuated by helicopter to have his head wounds treated. The facility had no local anesthetics in stock, and he was asked to sign a waiver so they could put him under general anesthesia to clean and dress the deep gashes in his scalp. Gerard signed the paper, the drug was administered, and then they wheeled him into the operating room. It "looked like a slaughterhouse," he would recall, with antiquated surgical equipment and filthy walls. He was lifted onto a cracked leather operating table, and they firmly strapped his arms and legs in place with thick buckles. Then, as the injured Irishman lay waiting for the anesthesia to take hold, one of the doctors began to taunt him. "Where are your friends now?" he asked the helpless climber. The drug he had been given, Gerard would later learn, was most commonly used in veterinary medicine.

Now, two years later, Gerard's teammate Wilco found himself in a similar situation. The doctors wanted to operate immediately on Wilco, an idea the Dutchman flatly refused. But his satellite phone, which he still carried with him, had finally run out of batteries and he couldn't get hold of Maarten or his expedition doctor in Utrecht. The rest of the

Norit team would be marching out from base camp; it would likely be a week or more until they were reunited. For the time being, Wilco and Cas were on their own. The hospital staff wouldn't provide him with a phone call, but willingly allowed the photographer and cameraman to keep filming their star patient as he lay on a cot being evaluated. Wilco's atrophied form was wrecked from his escape off the mountain, and a strong dose of pharmaceutical-grade painkillers coursed through his bloodstream.

Nevertheless, Wilco talked to the media. That evening, Reuters and the Associated Press published the first eyewitness accounts of the disaster online. Here, at last, was a survivor who had witnessed the accident firsthand—someone who had conquered the mountain and survived. Wilco's initial statements presented only a piecemeal account of the disaster. He himself still seemed to be searching for the answers. But it made great copy, and Wilco van Rooijen's remarkable story of survival made headlines around the world.

Marco Confortola, whom the media had already coined the "last survivor" of K2, was still struggling down off the mountain.

Marco was thirty-seven years old, tall with an athletic build, a closely shaved head, and a gold hoop earring in his left ear. He was an accomplished eight-thousand-meter climber, with the summits of Cho Oyu, Shishapangma, Annapurna, Broad Peak, and Everest to his credit, putting him well on his way to completing all fourteen of the eight-thousanders. A professional mountain rescuer, he worked in the Italian Alps on a helicopter team, but enjoyed considerable corporate sponsorship as well, including the Credito Valtellinese bank. Outgoing and social around base camp, Marco radiated a peculiar brand of backslapping, cheerful Italian machismo. During the stormy July days, he had become especially good friends with Wilco van Rooijen and Gerard McDonnell, and been a fixture in the Norit mess tent.

K2, Marco liked to say, was "Italy's mountain." Moreover, Achille Compagnoni, who had first summited K2 in 1954 with Lino Lacedelli, was from Valfurva, Marco's birthplace. Marco had attempted K2 in 2004, on a large, well-organized expedition to mark the fiftieth anniversary of the first ascent. But an unexpected windstorm had demolished the team's tents at Camp III on the Abruzzi Ridge, and he was forced to descend to base camp empty-handed, tears of disappointment streaking down his face. "I had opened an account with K2," he said, "and as such, I returned in 2008 and asked K2 if I could try to summit."

If K2 had granted the Italian permission to climb it, the mountain now exacted a cruel price for the success. He left Camp IV on Sunday morning alone, though his two hired Pakistanis had waited for him and would be descending behind. By then, the third day after the start of the summit push, the frostbite in his feet was extreme. His feet had partially thawed in the sleeping bag the night before, and now the piercing pain made each step down the Abruzzi Spur an excruciating trial.

In the course of the descent, Marco was in frequent contact with friends and family in Italy via his Thuraya satellite phone. His brother Luigi, who helped manage his sibling's Web site, stepped into the role of media spokesperson. On Monday, Marco spoke to Agostino Da Polenza, his old leader from his first K2 attempt, in 2004. "My hands are fine, while my feet are black from frostbite. Anyway, I can walk and I want to descend to the base camp," he was quoted on Da Polenza's Web site as saying. "I never gave up in my life; I am surely not going to give up now."

In base camp, Marco's partner, Roberto Manni, was doing everything he could to organize help, but found few resources to mount a rescue. Most everyone who had participated in the summit push was out of commission, too tired or too distraught to climb up the Abruzzi Ridge to meet the descending climber. There also was talk of getting a helicopter to try to evacuate him from the mountain. At sixty-seven hundred meters, a Lama helicopter might just barely be able to fly high enough to pick him via a cable winch. On Monday, as Wilco and Cas were flown to Skardu, a Pakistani pilot had picked Roberto up and made a brief sortie to see if it was possible. Ultimately, with the weather questionable and Marco evidently still capable of descending by foot, the military decided against attempting the risky maneuver. Meanwhile, Roberto found a small team that was willing to ascend the lower Abruzzi and help Marco down the final descent. George Dijmarescu, a Romanian national living in the United States, agreed to climb to Camp II with two climbing-Sherpas and shepherd Marco through the final stage of the descent.

The once-proud *alpinista extremo* limped into base camp late on Tuesday afternoon. The weather had turned squally and gray, and wet snowflakes fell as Marco made the final, agonizing steps across the glacial talus. Despite the relatively warm temperatures, he still wore his fluorescent green down suit and climbing harness, a sign of how depleted his body must have been. At the edge of camp, Marco dropped in front of a small stone chorten. He sobbed for a moment, pressing forward against the glacier's cold mass. Then he sat up and closed his eyes, his lips moving softly in silent prayer.

When Marco was finished, he stood back up and was ushered into the Norit mess tent. Eric Meyer had managed to get a few hours of fitful rest that day, and now he quaffed down a cup of strong black tea and turned to greet his next patient. Like Wilco, Marco spoke in disjointed ramblings as Eric gradually warmed his congealed, lifeless appendages through the night. The Italian's condition was notably worse than that of the two Dutchmen he had treated two evenings before. While he'd endured an extra day and night on the mountain, the frostbite advanced past the first knuckles; now a malignant line of pallid skin stretched beyond his toes to the balls of his feet. Eric put him on an IV as soon as possible, and Marco received a strong dose of morphine for the pain. There was no alteplase left, but, considering that the onset of Marco's considerable injuries were more than seventy-two hours previous, it wouldn't have made the slightest difference.

As Tuesday, August 5, drew to a close, the collective spirit in base camp ebbed into empty, bottomless exhaustion. The weather high on the mountain had completely broken down, and gale-force winds lashed the summit. Neither Eric Meyer nor Roeland van Oss recalls Marco giving a decisive explanation of what happened to the others, but it was painfully obvious that all missing persons—the distant black dots seen high above Camp IV, the names that Maarten van Eck still assiduously maintained were "status unknown"—were dead.

"There was a time," Roeland recalls, "when we just stopped talking about it." Teams began making arrangements for the return trek to Skardu. Requests for porters were sent down the glacier. The expended adventurers began to pack up their belongings, the thoughts of those who survived turning to the long journey separating them from home. The names of the dead were checked with each expedition one more time, and then captains Azimullah Beg and Sabir Ali Changazi, two Pakistani liaison officers attached to the Korean and Serbian teams, respectively, phoned their superiors in Islamabad. Scrawled in rough penmanship the final list read:

1. Mr. Kim Hyo-Gyeong—Korean
2. Mr. Park Kyeong-Hyo—Korean
3. Mr. Hwang Dong-Jin—Korean
4. Mr. Jumik Bhote—Nepali
5. Mr. Pasang Bhote—Nepali
6. Mr. Jehan Baig—Pakistani HP
7. Mr. Meherban Karim—Pakistani HP
8. Mr. Hugues D'Aubarède Jean-Louis Marie—French
9. Mr. Gerard McDonnell—Irish
10. Mr. Dren Mandic—Serbian
11. Mr. Rolf Bae—Norwegian

5

DEATH IN THE INFORMATION AGE

*S*atellite communications and the Internet notwithstanding, the unseemly race to report news of the tragedy and the sensationalized coverage that quickly followed had lengthy historic precedent. Pundits would
soon lament the phenomenon of turning life-and-death adventure into public spectacle as an example of modern commercialism intruding into a once
sacred endeavor, but for many of the K2 survivors, the blogs and online news
sources reporting their struggles, even accusations of muckraking between
Everestnews.com and Explorersweb.com, all of it was merely part of a game
that explorers have played for centuries. The contemporary rules of the
tradition had its roots in the great polar achievements of the early twentieth
century—a true heyday of modern exploration.

By 1900, the scientific advances, new technology, and accumulated
wealth produced in the wake of the Industrial Revolution provided humankind with the resources to explore the farthest limits of its world. Of
course, humankind has always been exploring and having adventures,
searching for food, or new grazing land, or other people to trade with,
but it was quite a different thing to set off in search of a precisely defined
yet entirely abstract destination: ninety degrees north latitude.

Another modern phenomenon stirred the pot, making each achievement a watershed moment in human history. The rise of mass-production daily print media meant that events in the most geographically remote places on the planet could be quickly and cheaply communicated to large populations. Amundsen and Scott, the Wright brothers, Lindbergh and Earhart, Peary and Cook, Hillary and Norgay: their achievements were exceptional, but the newspapers made them legends.

In 1896, a young, energetic publisher named Adolph Ochs purchased a small daily with a circulation of nine thousand called the *New York Times*. Ochs had an instinctive feel for human-interest stories, and recognized the power of adventure stories to boost circulation. In 1908, he spent four thousand dollars for the exclusive rights to report on Robert E. Peary's attempt to reach the North Pole on his eighth trip to the Arctic. Before Peary returned from his expedition, however, a onetime companion turned rival, the media-savvy Dr. Frederick Cook, returned from the Arctic to announce that he had beaten Peary and reached ninety degrees north latitude. Ochs's rival, the *New York Herald*, immediately offered Cook twenty-five thousand dollars for the scoop. Two days after the story broke, the *Times* received a telegram with urgent news from Peary. He had just reached port in Labrador, and he also claimed to have succeeded in gaining the Pole, a year after Cook's alleged success. Ochs swung his newsroom into full spin, churning out five pages of triumphant coverage of the event. Controversy quickly ignited, and for weeks the *Times* and the *Herald* featured dueling editorials and splashy new revelations as each publication supported its man.

One might be justified to conclude from the conflict that the media was more interested in tales of adventure and adversity because they sold papers, rather than accurately recording the facts and offering clear-eyed analysis. The *New York Times* almost conceded as much in an editorial on September 9, 1909. It generally supported Peary's claims while questioning Cook's motives, then went on to summarize the debate with an attitude of laissez-faire indifference. "The one thing certain is that the North Pole has been discovered by an American explorer," the piece finished, tacitly acknowledging that there was a chance its own vigorous defense of Peary was misplaced. *Who really cares*, the paper seemed to be asking, *so long as an American gets the credit?* Among exploratory historians, however, the controversy refused to die and—an incredible seventy-nine years later—on Tuesday, August 23, 1988, the *Times* ran a correction acknowledging Peary's own inconsistencies and the paper's bias:

> Peary's expedition was sponsored by the National Geographic Society. The *Times* had exclusive global rights to the story. Thus both may have failed to scrutinize adequately what they yearned to believe. The error was doubtless committed in good faith, but most authorities today agree that no one has an untainted claim to be first—neither Cook, nor Peary, nor the two Eskimos and the American black, Matthew Henson, who accompanied Peary.

The belated addendum to the historic record is respectable, but one is left very much in doubt whether the *Times* or the *Herald* regretted the controversy. After all, controversy boosts sales, and both papers profited enormously from the incident.

Peary and Cook's competing claims helped spark a second polar race. Englishman Robert Falcon Scott had been preparing a highly publicized attempt to reach the South Pole for some time. He was docked in Australia, already en route to the continent, when he received a telegraphed message announcing that Norwegian Roald Amundsen had just set sail with the same goal. Amundsen, who had discovered the Northwest Passage, was allegedly preparing a North Pole expedition of his own, but after learning of Cook's and Peary's claims, he turned his focus to the South Pole instead.

On March 7, 1912, Amundsen's ship *Fram* docked in Hobart, Tasmania, with news of his success. Amundsen had shrewdly sold the rights for an exclusive account of his expedition to the *London Daily Chronicle*, which in turn sold the U.S. rights to the *New York Times*. Amundsen cabled his story in secret, but several competing papers promptly plagiarized the article. Such was the intense media interest in Amundsen's expedition that, on March twelfth, the explorer agreed to sign an affidavit before the American consul in Hobart certifying that he had reported only to the *Daily Chronicle* and the *New York Times*. Back in New York, Adolph Ochs swiftly brought lawsuits against any publications that threatened his exclusive rights on the story.

The *London Times* owned exclusive rights to the 1953 British Everest expedition. When Edmund Hillary and Tenzing Norgay set foot on the summit on May twenty-ninth of that year, a twenty-seven-year-old reporter named James Morris was waiting in Camp IV in the Western Cwm. A day after they reached the summit, Morris met the descending climbers, improvising a hasty interview with Hillary at twenty-two thousand feet. Reflecting on the story of a lifetime, Morris would later say: "In a moment of wild optimism, the *Times* could conceivably print the news on the very day of Queen Elizabeth's coronation."

He immediately raced down to base camp, where he dispatched a runner with a brief announcement of the success. Morris had served in the British SS during World War II, and took care to encrypt the news, as he knew the rival *Daily Telegraph* and *Daily Mail* had both dispatched reporters to Kathmandu to scoop the news. The messenger ran down twenty miles of rugged Himalayan country to reach a government outpost in the village of Namche, where the news could be radioed to Kathmandu and then relayed by telegraph wire to London. On the morning of June 2, 1953, as Londoners took to the streets for the crowning of a new monarch, a special edition of the *London Times* announced both the coronation and that Mount Everest had at last been conquered. Five hours later, the *New York Times* ran its own banner headline:

2 OF BRITISH TEAM CONQUER EVEREST; QUEEN GETS NEWS AS CORONATION GIFT; THRONGS LINE HER PROCESSION ROUTE

Separately, the conquests of the North Pole, South Pole, and Mount Everest were each a major news event in its time. It is no accident that each undertaking was couched in the rhetoric of a competitive race; in those days exploration *was* a race to be first. But the lasting lesson of each episode, something that was implicitly understood not only by media barons like Adolph Ochs, but also by the explorers themselves, was that the finish line was not crossed until the news had been published—even if less than the full story made it to print.

Monday, August 4, 2008, was a quiet news day. The ongoing energy crisis dominated the headlines—the price of crude oil had dropped to a hundred and twenty dollars a barrel, and two presidential candidates skirmished in dueling press conferences over whether it would be necessary to tap the strategic petroleum reserve or permit offshore drilling. Two American soldiers died in a roadside bomb while patrolling a neighborhood in eastern Baghdad; a general with close ties to the president was assassinated in Syria; sixteen Chinese border police were killed in the town of Kashgar, the victims of an attack by Islamic militants. And the first two survivors of the K2 catastrophe, Wilco van Rooijen and Cas van de Gevel, were evacuated by Askari Aviation to Skardu. Marco Confortola would join them two days later. The international media, alerted to the unfolding drama since late Saturday afternoon, at last had direct access to the tragedy's main celebrities.

"Everything was going well to Camp Four," Wilco told the Associated Press, speaking directly by phone from the military hospital in Skardu, "and on [the] summit attempt everything went wrong." "The biggest mistake we made was that we tried to make agreements," he said in another interview to Reuters. "Everybody had his own responsibility and then some people did not do what they promised."

The problems began with several time-consuming delays early in the summit push. Both Wilco and Marco singled out the advance rope-fixing team for improperly preparing the route. Evidently, they began fixing rope too early and ran out of line at the top of the Bottleneck, the most critical place in the entire climb. Most climbers were forced to stop while several ropes were cut and leapfrogged up from below. "We were astonished. We had to move it," Wilco said to the *Guardian*. "That took, of course, many, many hours. Some turned back because they did not trust it anymore."

"I think we arrived late on the summit of K2 because the technical equipment was low quality," Marco said to the Italian news agency ANSA, noting that some of the rope "wasn't fit to tie bales of hay." "Nobody was willing to go up first," Marco said to the *Independent*. "We didn't have the right ropes for that part of the climb. But I started shouting. I told them that the first person to reach the summit of K2 [in 1954] did it at six p.m., so let's move!"

Wilco van Rooijen and Marco Confortola had been among the last to leave the summit. They recalled little of their initial descent from the summit, only that it was dark and they were tired and they feared they would become lost, still high above the top of the fixed lines. "We were very tired; we said then that we would bivouac for the night," Wilco said to Andrew Buncombe, a reporter for the *Independent*.

Marco reported that he and Gerard McDonnell decided to stop together. To journalist Omar Waraich, he described the scene as they scratched meager seats into the snowy skin of the mountain, and kept vigil until dawn. "Since Gerard was having a difficult time, I made his hole bigger to help him lie down for a little bit. Gerard was very cold. I was also cold and began to shiver on purpose to create heat. I was wasting energy, but I needed to get warm." Later in the night, they were joined by van Rooijen.

The next morning, as they made their way down the mountain, they came upon a harrowing scene: "There was a Korean guy hanging upside down. There was a second Korean guy who held him with a rope but he was also in shock and then a third guy was there also, and they were trying to survive but I had also to survive," Wilco told Stephen Graham of the Associated Press. By then, the Dutchman was beginning to go snow-blind. The distressed Koreans, who must have been Hwang Dong-jin, Kim Hyo-gyeong, and Park Kyeong–hyo, indicated that a rescue party was on its way up. "He offered help but they declined, believing help was already on the way," the Associated Press article read. Van

Rooijen gave one of them a pair of gloves, and then explained that he had to continue down because of his failing eyesight.

Marco and Gerard, who were descending behind Wilco, came upon the Koreans soon after Wilco had left them. The *Independent* reported that they worked together to try to free the tangled team. "For three hours, McDonnell and Confortola tried to right them, but it was in vain. All three died. It was at that moment, 'for some strange reason,' that McDonnell began to walk away. It was the last time Confortola would see his friend alive." Separately, both Confortola and van Rooijen managed to down-climb the Bottleneck and became lost in a cloud that enveloped the upper mountain.

By now they had been out for more than thirty hours and were suffering from overwhelming exhaustion and experiencing vivid hallucinations. According to the same interview given to the *Independent*, Marco passed out in the snow, only to be awoken by the sounds of an avalanche. "All of a sudden I saw an avalanche coming down. It was only 20 metres to my right. I saw the body of Gerard sweep past me," Marco tearfully recounted. The Italian was apparently located and revived by rescuers, only to be struck by another avalanche: "It hit two Sherpas who were helping us. And an oxygen bottle came cascading down and hit me in the back of the head," he said to the *Independent*. Wilco, meanwhile, was nowhere to be found. It would be nearly another twenty-four hours before he was located, stumbling toward Camp III, more than a thousand meters below the Bottleneck.

In their interviews, the two European characters seemed almost archetypal. Cool and calculating, Wilco played the role of a dispassionate Dutchman, perhaps not universally liked around base camp but respected for his organizational skills, and willing to speak frankly about the decisions he made. Confortola came across as an emotional, chest-thumping Italian, one moment denying that it was a bad idea to summit so late in the evening, and the next breaking down and sobbing uncontrollably about the loss of his companion Gerard McDonnell.

From his hospital bed in Skardu, Wilco gave a chilling sense of the desperation that swept the doomed summit party that night. "They were thinking of using my gas, my rope," he said of the others, "so actually everybody was fighting for himself and I still do not understand why everybody was leaving each other." Wilco never explained precisely what he meant by these comments, and given his fragile mental state, it's really impossible to know.

The 1996 Everest disaster marked a turning point in how the sport of high-altitude mountaineering was perceived by the general public. The annals of Himalayan climbing are rife with large-scale disasters from every era, like when sixteen climbers were snuffed out in a single avalanche on Nanga Parbat in 1937. In 1972, another slide took fifteen lives on Manaslu, the eighth-highest mountain the world, and in separate events, K2 killed thirteen climbers during the season of 1986. But Everest in '96 was different. At the center of the tragedy were two commercial expeditions. The realization that the world's highest summit was available to any reasonably fit, wealthy individual cast mountaineering in a new light. The conflicts and contradictions of the burgeoning guiding industry on the world's highest peaks were left starkly exposed to the public eye. Since the polar feuds of the early twentieth century, media controversy was an intrinsic part of exploration—but back then, few seriously questioned whether climbing mountains or traversing continents was worth it. The value to greater society seemed self-evident. But after Everest in 1996, public sentiment began to change. The postmodern era of mountaineering had begun.

In the decade after the *Into Thin Air* debacle, little happened to change that attitude. A dozen more climbers joined Messner's exclusive eight-thousand-meter club, but most had reached their summits via the traditional, normal routes, with plenty of logistical support. More climbers flocked to Everest than ever before, and few were surprised when twelve climbers perished on the mountain in 2006. Among the dead was David Sharp, an Englishman who fell at eighty-five hundred meters on the North Ridge. More than thirty climbers passed the comatose but still breathing man on their way to the summit. Most rationalized that he was beyond saving. That same autumn, as tens of climbers sat in base camp beneath Cho Oyu, the sixth-highest mountain in the world, a group of Tibetan refugees attempted to cross the Nangpa La pass into Nepal. In plain sight of base camp, Chinese soldiers opened fire on the fleeing pilgrims, killing two people, including a seventeen-year-old nun. Most startling about the incident was the fact that despite the dozens of international climbers who witnessed the shootings, it was not reported until days later. Evidently, Chinese soldiers had menaced many of the climbers in base camp to stay silent, and large numbers of climbers decided that reporting the incident was a lesser obligation than climbing the mountain.

The news of this new tragedy on K2 was largely placed in the same context as these sordid episodes, and the outrage began almost immediately. "We cannot sit as a spectator to this," said Shahzad Qaiser, a top official at the Ministry of Tourism, the governmental organization responsible for issuing mountaineering permits and overseeing the commercial tour operators that provide logistical support for expeditions. "This accident is a very sad and disastrous event in our mountaineering history." Yet Qaiser stopped short of explaining what, if anything, could be done. His statement only hinted at the impotent rage that was slowly seeping into the public consciousness as the media storm continued. To most casual observers, the precise circumstances of the tragedy mattered little. Everyone was looking for someone to blame.

On Monday, August 4, the guru of eight-thousand-meter climbing weighed in himself. "People today are booking these K2 package deals," Reinhold Messner told Germany's N24 news station, "almost as if they were buying some all-inclusive trip to Bangkok. Something like that is just pure stupidity; that is not professional."

The uproar climaxed on Wednesday, with a front-page article in the *New York Times*. Adolph Simon Ochs's great-grandson, Arthur Sulzberger Jr., the current chairman and publisher of the *Times*, is known to be an enthusiastic amateur climber himself, often seen frequenting the steep quartz-conglomerate crags of the Shawangunks, two hours' drive north of New York City. How much Sulzberger's personal passion informs his paper's predilection for articles on outdoor adventure is anyone's guess, but the contemporary *New York Times* undeniably holds to the same strategy recognized by Adolph Ochs: stories of life-and-death survival sell papers. A three-column, thirteen-hundred-word article, complete with two color photographs, graced page A1 under the banner headline: CHAOS ON THE "MOUNTAIN THAT INVITES DEATH."

Cowritten by Graham Bowley and Andrea Kannapell, the piece was a succinct summary of what was known at the time. Like many of the stories that ran in the mainstream media about K2 that week, it contained little original reporting, and instead borrowed liberally from the expedition blogs and previously published statements from Wilco and Marco. What was notable was the reaction the article produced. The "comments" section attached to the online version buzzed with hundreds of anonymous messages. Few were sympathetic to the victims of the tragedy.

"Climbers are herd followers, aimlessly searching for a thrill and self-esteem outside of themselves," one reader opined. "It is a supremely selfish act. At minimum, should someone who needs to justify their own folly, they MUST do so with the understanding that THERE BE NO RESCUE." "Utterly pointless. What a waste of time and lives. Who cares about this stupid mountain? Visit by helicopter. Ridiculous, though sad for those killed," another wrote. "These climbers are always some white guy trying to see if he could conquer another mystery of natural beauty of this world. . . . Sorry, I feel no sympathy for this outcome," a third stated bluntly. And finally: "Heroes, my ass. No one should feel an inch of sympathy for these eggheads."

The fact that nowhere in any of the *Times*'s coverage of the tragedy were the survivors declared heroes and that helicopters can't fly anywhere near the summit of K2—none of it made any difference in the midst of an anonymous online discussion forum. In fact, many of the commenters seemed to direct their anger partly at the *Times* for covering the event in the first place. As one reader wrote: "I have no objection to mountain climbing or mountain climbers—just don't report on the subject any longer. Let them risk their lives in anonymity."

The vitriol of the debate is explained only by taking into account the morally charged ground on which the K2 tragedy became implacably stuck. Comment after comment circled around one simple question, a question that seemed to drive to the heart of the issue. As one *Times* reader asked: "What these men and women do is impressive, but are they heroes? They go out of their way to experience something very dangerous that has zero utility except to themselves. Some of them die in the process. For me, it's too solipsistic to qualify as heroism." Or as another put it: "'Heroic'? 'Legendary'? How can these words apply to people who choose to get out of their easy chairs and walk to the very edge of the drop into oblivion, and then to climb off that edge?"

In answering these questions, some pointed out that K2 had been climbed many times before. Modern mountaineering was not about exploration, they asserted, but ego. "'Spirit of exploration,' please," one commenter wrote. "K2 has been climbed before. Many times. It was 'discovered' a long time ago. . . . Climbers today climb 8,000-meter mountains for only one reason: themselves." Or, as another succinctly put it: "This was not a voyage of discovery; it was an ego trip, as most mountain ascents are today."

Lost in the reckless words of the Internet chat room, a single voice spoke up with surprising eloquence: "This is such a sad story, and as Ger's cousin I write this with such a heavy heart. He had passion in life and followed his dreams. He was a hero to me and many others in my community even before he conquered K2. And yes, in my opinion he died a hero. . . . He wouldn't leave an old lady alone to cross the road; therefore he wouldn't leave anybody struggling behind."

Meanwhile, in the op-ed section, pundits weighed in to put a more nuanced spin on the story. Maurice Isserman, an academic historian who has authored books on the history of mountaineering, wrote that "mountaineering has become more dangerous in recent decades as the traditional expeditionary culture of the early- and mid-20th century, which had emphasized mutual responsibility and common endeavor, gave way to an ethos stressing individualism and self-preservation." Isserman went on to contrast the current tragedy with a much-revered saga from the golden age, the 1953 American attempt on K2. In the midst of that expedition, a team of eight climbers, led by Bob Bates and Dr. Charlie Houston, were forced to make an epic descent of the Abruzzi Ridge in an effort to save the life of a teammate stricken with a pulmonary embolism, Art Gilkey. After summarizing the teamwork and camaraderie of the now mythical expedition, Isserman reached the inevitable conclusion that while twentieth-century mountaineers enjoyed a sacred brotherhood, "Today in contrast, as was evident last week on K2, climbers enter the mountains as strangers and tend to leave the same way."

Graham Bowley touched on this same theme in a separate editorial piece that ran on the same day: "Fifty years ago, when mountaineers were conquering the world's last great unclimbed peaks, they set out to make names for themselves and their countries and to make history for all of us," he wrote. "It was heroic stuff. . . . But the world's tallest peaks have long been conquered; the byways of Everest are well trod. So when 11 people died last weekend on K-2, a 28,000-plus-foot peak that is the world's second-tallest mountain, in one of the worst disasters in mountaineering history, among the questions being asked were: Was it worth it? And, should we still care about their exploits?"

Everyone—survivors at base camp, commentators in the media, friends and family scattered around the globe—agreed on one thing: There needed to be a thoughtful, thorough discussion of what precisely had happened on K2, and why. "When all this calms down I would like to do a real debrief with you guys and find out the real facts," Tom Sjogren wrote to Maarten van Eck. It is an accepted tenet of any police investigation to interview witnesses as soon as possible, knowing that an individual's memory of an event is most accurate and detailed when it is still fresh in his mind. Even before Wilco arrived in base camp, Maarten had reminded him in a sat phone call directly to Camp III to conduct a thorough debrief with Roeland and Chris before he was evacuated. Online, the Norit site publicly promised a detailed report. Meanwhile, in Islamabad, the Ministry of Tourism announced an official press conference and investigation to look into what had gone wrong.

But nothing happened. Chris Klinke, Roeland van Oss, and Eric Meyer remember hearing plenty of anecdotal stories in base camp, but no attempt was made to comprehensively record their memories. As Chris remembers: "Wilco talked a lot, but it was mostly disjointed. Cas, on the other hand, was nearly silent, and there were serious language problems with Marco, when he got down." The Italian's English, marginal under the best of circumstances, was virtually unintelligible in his overwhelming fatigue. "He made a lot of hand gestures, but it was hard to know what he meant precisely," Chris says.

In Islamabad, the press conference turned into a grim recap of Marco's and Wilco's stories, but offered no new substantive information. Afterward, the two survivors returned to Europe and began long convalescences, finally claiming the private rest they so desperately needed. As the days passed by and the articles became less frequent, little more factual evidence was entered into the public record of the disaster. Having raised all the inevitable questions, and pointed out all the unavoidable criticisms, the mainstream media dropped the story without ever bothering to piece together the disparate narrative of what had really happened. "The events on K2 will no doubt be debated among climbers as more facts emerge but it seemed clear last week that many climbers had already moved on," Bowley observed in his editorial. Even among those climbers closest to the event—those who had been on the mountain or in base camp and watched as the chaos engulfed their friends and teammates—there was no final understanding as to what had happened.

Marco's and Wilco's accounts had some extraordinarily strong imagery: the tangled Korean climbers, hanging helplessly at eighty-three hundred meters; Marco seeing the body of Gerard McDonnell sweep past him in a fatal avalanche; Wilco's haunting descriptions of chaos in the night. But both Marco and Wilco also experienced vivid hallucinations and unpredictable swings in consciousness as they battled to survive the mountain. "There were so many moments when I thought I saw a climber and thought I heard voices, but I knew there couldn't be people there. It was a scary moment when I knew I was reaching my limits," Wilco told *National Geographic Adventure*. On his descent of the Bottleneck, Marco described involuntarily "falling asleep" on two separate occasions, and such was his condition when he was found by Pemba.

Wilco and Marco were under extraordinary stress, alone in a difficult foreign city, severely injured, and under heavy doses of pain medication, their bodies broken from days of intense struggle. But they still found the energy to speak to the press. In those first days, they gave not one, or two, or five interviews—but *dozens*. Rightly or wrongly, the spin undeniably began to orbit around the two surviving Europeans. As Ed Viesturs put it, "The media . . . focused on the survival stories of Marco Confortola and Wilco van Rooijen, reporters hanging on every word the Italian and the Dutchman uttered from their hospital beds in Islamabad." Later, sympathetic friends would argue that they had been besieged by the press, and had no option but to cooperate. This is at least partially true, but the third evacuee set a more humble example.

Cas van de Gevel never came into the media spotlight. In article after article, he appeared as Wilco's silent companion, perhaps lending a brief quote to the journalists, but never offering his full personal story. Few realized at first that Cas was the last person to see Hugues D'Aubarède alive. As Cas had descended from the summit, in the dark, moonless night of August first, he had caught up to the Frenchman in the middle of the Diagonal, still a little above the Bottleneck. Hugues let Cas pass, conceding that the Dutchman was moving faster. Farther down, after Cas had discovered the ropes in the couloir were missing and was in the midst of down-climbing the steep snow solo, he heard a muffled noise and looked to his left in time to see a dark form tumbling past. In a flash, he thought he recognized Hugues's backpack. Hugues's body was never positively identified, though Cas later felt certain he had perished in a fall that night. The reason no one knew about Hugues was that Cas did not even tell Roeland over the radio, and waited instead to personally carry the news to base camp.

In Islamabad, Cas was forthright in answering questions posed to him, but he didn't put himself out there the same way Marco and Wilco did, giving highly emotional and free-reining confessional-style interviews. It may have been due to his shy personality, or the fact that he made it down the Bottleneck that night, without having to stop to endure a harrowing bivouac so high on the mountain. Or perhaps it was because, unlike Wilco van Rooijen and Marco Confortola, he was an amateur. The critical dose of alteplase Eric Meyer administered in base camp ultimately spared Cas's hands from any significant damage, and Cas, the soft-spoken carpenter who liked to build doghouses and garden sheds, knew his professional prospects would not be altered one way or another by any media coverage.

In all, the first wave of media coverage could detail the circumstances of the deaths of only four men: Dren Mandic, Jehan Baig, Rolf Bae, and Hugues D'Aubarède. Seven more souls' last moments remained shrouded in mystery—Koreans Hwang Dong-jin, Kim Hyo-gyeong, and Park Kyeong-hyo, Nepali climbing-Sherpas Jumik Bhote and Pasang Bhote, Pakistani Karim Meherban, and Irishman Gerard McDonnell.

Cas van de Gevel had no recollection of seeing Karim Meherban, Hugues D'Aubarède's high-altitude Pakistani porter, when he passed Hugues in the middle of the Diagonal on the descent. The three Koreans, Hwang, Kim, and Park, were last seen tangled in rope near the top of the fixed lines at the upper end of the Diagonal snowfield, according to both Marco and Wilco. And the two climbing-Sherpas—well, nothing in the media really explained what had happened to them. Amid the waning news coverage, a single statement was issued concerning their deaths. The source was not identified, the information quietly buried among a list of the confirmed dead, and one might not have thought anything of it were it not for one unqualified word.

Jumich Bhote—Trapped in Bottleneck When Rope Cut by Serac Fall
Pasang Bhote—Died in Rescue of Jumich Bhote from Serac Fall

Rescue. Pasang Bhote was not included in any of the lists of those who had summited. The report suggested that he had been going *up* the Bottleneck on August second, at the same time Marco and Wilco were struggling down the same terrain. Neither Marco or Wilco had any memory of seeing him as they descended. But dancing on the shadowy limits of the Norit blog and the published accounts, the vague presence of other men was palpable.

"Two HAPs are on their way up . . ."

"In position for rescue efforts are a number of altitude staff . . ."

"Two Sherpas helped me down . . ."

Nothing more was said in the mainstream media about a rescue attempt reaching the Koreans, or the ghostly saviors who seemed to drift in and out of the narrative, silent as a snow squall. More than a dozen Westerners had been in high camp the morning after the summit team had disappeared. All were too tired, too shell-shocked, or deemed it too dangerous to reclimb the Bottleneck and look for survivors. For the most part, the climbing-Sherpas and high-altitude porters (a euphemism for Pakistani porters or guides) remained anonymous background characters.

Other contradictory statements swirled just below the surface. The European survivors had criticized the advance rope-fixing team for causing the early delays on summit day—but no one bothered to identify who they were, what the prearranged "plan" had been, or why it had gone wrong. In fact, not a single Western climber had been a member of the eight-man advanced group—it was four Sherpas, two Pakistanis, and two Koreans. Eight Asians. And none of them had explained what happened.

Another inconsistency concerned the eight climbers' decision to bivouac above the Bottleneck on the night of August first. Again and again, it was repeated in the media that the climbers were "stranded." As the *New York Times* re-created the scene: ". . . as night fell and the temperature plummeted, the climbers struggled with an awful choice: wait for rescue in the death zone, or descend without fixed ropes." However, from their own stories, it was clear neither Wilco nor Marco knew the ropes were gone in the Bottleneck at the time they decided to stop. Instead, the two men cited fatigue, and fear of getting lost and not being able to locate the top anchor of the fixed lines. According to interviews, they had separately stopped to bivy, Wilco alone, and Marco with Gerard McDonnell, and rendezvoused only sometime in the middle of the night, when Wilco, who was still searching for a way down in the darkness, noticed Marco and Gerard's headlamps and stumbled to meet them. In several interviews, Marco mentioned seeing a group of headlamps disappearing in front of him. Wilco would later estimate the location of their bivy as being *above* the serac, some three hundred linear meters from the site of the avalanche that had killed Rolf Bae and stripped the couloir of rope.

Marco and Wilco agreed that the Koreans were in bad shape: "They were still alive, but two of them were in very critical condition," Marco would tell Michael Kodas, writing for *Outside Online*. In several newspaper articles, Marco was quoted as saying that two of the three were unconscious; Wilco described them as being in a state of "shock." Wilco spent little time with the Koreans, but Marco reported he and Gerard stopped for over three hours, trying to help the stricken team. Debate over what happened next would linger for a long time to come.

The article in the *Independent* seemed to suggest that the three Koreans died in their presence, and then Gerard McDonnell disappeared: ". . . McDonnell and Confortola tried to right them, but it was in vain. All three died. It was at that moment, 'for some strange reason,' that McDonnell began to walk away." A lengthy article in *Men's Journal* written by Matthew Power (who also was in Islamabad interviewing the survivors) reported that: "By mid-morning, Marco and Gerard had left the Koreans and continued toward the traverse. . . . Suddenly, Marco said later, Gerard turned around and began to climb back up the slope, back toward the Koreans, offering no explanation." Finally, Michael Kodas wrote in *Outside Online*: "They spent three and a half hours trying to free the Koreans but gave up when the glacier let loose nearby and reminded them of their perilous location. McDonnell, perhaps confused by the lack of oxygen, climbed back up the slope toward the summit. Confortola shouted to his friend but couldn't get his attention. Then he heard an avalanche and recognized two yellow boots in the slide."

Days slipped past. The truth of what transpired on the upper slopes of K2 from the evening of August 1, when eight climbers failed to return to Camp IV, to the afternoon of August 2, when the last survivor, Marco Confortola, was found just below the Bottleneck, settled into shadows cast by the intense emotions and fragmented accounts of those tragic days. The general public, by and large, was content to overlook the subtle inconsistencies and understood the saga of the 2008 K2 season, one of the deadliest chapters in modern mountaineering history, to be that which they were conditioned to believe. It was a terrible story, a reflection of how far the values of the sport had fallen, a case study that proved self-preservation to be the final principle of the high-altitude mountaineer, a uniquely modern tragedy—a tragedy with no heroes.

But other histories do exist. Other stories are told and repeated in different tongues above the hissing din of kitchen tents. After the long return trek from base camp, and two days of grueling road travel down the roughly hewn Karakoram Highway, the remnants of each team reached Islamabad in dusty convoys of road-weary climbers. They showered and cleaned, gorging themselves on Western-style buffets, held their press conferences and meetings with the Ministry, and then departed to Benazir Bhutto International Airport and the final legs of their journeys home. They flew to Amsterdam and Denver, Oslo, Seoul and Sidney, back into their lives of men with busy careers and the responsibilities of fathers and husbands, and families to feed.

Four such men flew to Kathmandu, and their names were Chhiring Dorje, Pasang Lama, Tsering Bhote, and Pemba Gyalje.

PART TWO

*B*y the time I finished college, climbing was the overwhelming purpose in my life. I was hopelessly in love with the mountains, and hopelessly addicted to climbing them. I tried to do it all: short rock and ice routes around New England, big walls in Yosemite, and habitual alpine trips to hard-core peaks in Alaska, Patagonia, and Asia. But the one genre of climbing I did not sample was the eight-thousand-meter peaks. I always assumed that someday I would, but for a young climber without significant financial backing, the price tag was prohibitively expensive. That, and the reputation of eight-thousand-meter climbing was that the normal routes were crowded, nontechnical "walk-ups," choked with fixed lines and wealthy paying clients. Or as Bart, my main climbing partner during those formative years, succinctly put it: "Dude, for us, climbing an eight-thousand-meter peak would be like paying ten grand to go for a snow hike with a bag over our heads. Fuck that—let's do Cerro Torre instead."

So I stayed away from the world's highest summits, and instead concentrated on self-contained, lightweight dashes up obscure routes at moderate elevations. Everything else in life organized itself around my need to climb. I took seasonal employment as a guide in New Hampshire and Alaska and began contributing short pieces to climbing journals. The thought of miss-

ing a good weather window in Patagonia to spend Christmas with my family, or not being in the Alaska Range for May, when conditions were typically
best for high-end technical routes, was unthinkable. Still, the game I played
had very little to do with the modern world of high-altitude climbing.

In 2005, a friend and I started up the Diamond Arete on Mount Hunter
in Alaska, a hideously steep mixed route that demands a uniquely high level
of commitment. Because the base of the route was littered with crevasses,
threatened by exposure to serac fall, and guarded by an impassable icefall,
retreating or even getting rescued by airplane simply wasn't an option: Our
pilot could barely land, drop us off, and have room to take off with an empty
payload. Getting airborne with two extra bodies in the craft would be out of
the question. We began the route knowing we had to succeed by traversing over
the summit to the other side of the mountain to reach a glacier from which an
airplane could pick us up. We carried no sat phone, and saw only a single
plane during the three days it took us to race up and down the two-thousand-
meter route. It was a one-way ticket, and at the time, I loved that too.

Then suddenly one day in August 2008, mountaineering was on the
front page of the New York Times. And everyone was trashing it, lending
their considered opinions on how the true spirit of mountaineering was
dead. Of course, I shared many of the same critical feelings being expressed
about the modern culture of peak-bagging. But there was something about
the tone of the story, how it was being told. . . . It pissed me off.

I don't have a subscription to the New York Times; I read it for free
online. The Internet's a funny thing: With a few strokes of the fingers and
a tap of the mouse, it has the power to propel you to the farthest corners of
human experience. I spent a good deal of time that week absently surfing
the Web, searching for news from K2. What happened up there? None of
the interviews and articles gave a complete account of the tragedy. Many
were merely well-written syntheses of the expedition blogs—it was easy to
trace one rumor from story to story, rippling across the media establishment.
I found myself trapped in a labyrinth of circular references, like a research
librarian chasing his own tail. It was slowly apparent that most of the re-
portage on the accident was based on the accounts of the two Europeans
who survived the Bottleneck on August second.

If most stories did little to further a rational understanding of what had caused the disaster, they did produce a complex and contradictory emotional response. Reading each report was like walking into a darkened movie theater in the middle of an epic saga. The first photos of Wilco showed an emaciated figure lying on a Spartan hospital cot. His feet were covered in thick bandages, and a saline drip hung nearby, connected intravenously to the right forearm. In one shot, a Pakistani medic in army fatigues leaned over the bed, dabbing Wilco's burned nose with ointment. In another, a hand extended from out of the frame, thrusting a television microphone toward the patient.

Wilco's face was ringed by a matted gray beard and a head of tousled, unkempt hair. His lips were tender and swollen. The flesh around his visage seemed to have shrunk, drawing his cracked skin tight against the skull so that the rim of his occipital lobe was faintly visible. His face was the color of worn leather. But most arresting were his eyes: In each photo, Wilco gazed perfectly straight ahead. But his vision wasn't focused on any object or person close at hand. His eyes were wide open, evenly meeting the camera's gaze, as if they looked through the lens and out to the newspapers and magazine articles. A dim red light glowed beyond the irises.

Clicking from blog to blog and article to article elicited a fleeting, shamefaced melancholy. It was that same feeling you get when you turn your head despite yourself while passing the scene of a car accident. Was the news media about objectivity or voyeurism?

I wrote a short analysis of what was being said, trying to explain that fixed ropes aren't really necessary to climb K2, that the mountain was first climbed without oxygen in 1978, that Sherpas aren't actually from Pakistan. A few days later I received a query from Alison Osius at Rock and Ice, *one of the three niche magazines in America specifically aimed at the climbing community, asking me if I'd be willing to do a write-up on what happened. I had six weeks before I was due to fly to Kathmandu for my next expedition to Kangtega, an obscure sixty-eight-hundred-meter mountain just south of Everest. It seemed like the perfect project to fill in a few weeks before I could get back to the mountains.*

6

A CINDERED PLANET

In the fading twilight of another Karakoram sunset, a Sherpa gazed on the final, wind-hardened snow slopes leading to the summit of K2. A shiver knifed through him. The Sherpa was clad in knit wool sweaters, knickers, and nailed leather boots, and a bulging pack hung from his back. He stood on a steep, impossibly exposed ridge at eighty-three hundred meters—less than a thousand feet separated him and the Bara Sahib from the summit of the unclimbed mountain. To his right, he could look directly across at the profile of the great serac, jutting into the deepening cobalt sky like a ship's prow.

His name was Pasang Lama, and the year was 1939.

A braided hemp rope connected Pasang Lama to the Bara Sahib, the German-American Fritz Wiessner. No men had pressed so close to K2's summit; indeed, only a few Englishmen on Everest had ever stood higher on any mountain at that time. For a month their expedition had pushed up the Abruzzi Ridge, driven by Wiessner's climbing prowess and indomitable drive. After finally establishing Camp VIII just below the Shoulder, Wiessner and Lama left their faltering companion, Dudley Wolfe, and pushed on to make a final assault on the summit. Wiessner discounted the obvious snow couloir leading underneath the serac—it was too dangerous, he felt. Instead Wiessner, a brilliant rock climber, chose a canny zigzagging line up the rocky ridge just to the south. On July 19, 1939, they left their top camp for the summit.

For nine hours, the two men had struggled upward: Wiessner in the lead, weaving an improbable route over broken ground, Pasang belaying and following steadily behind with a large pack of equipment. And now, as shadows seeped slowly into the valleys around them, Wiessner called down to his partner. He could see the route to the summit. All that remained was a twenty-five-foot traverse to reach an easy snow ridge that would take them to the top. Wiessner estimated that the summit was only three or four hours away.

Pasang Lama hesitated. They would surely be benighted, and forced to undertake a long and taxing descent the next morning. Wiessner again extolled his companion to continue, and began to make his way across the final rock traverse. Pasang Lama looked around him. The weather was perfect, but he could feel the foreboding chill of the coming night.

"No, Bara Sahib," he said. Pasang Lama held fast to the rope, refusing to pay out slack so that Wiessner could continue across the traverse. Wiessner considered untying from the rope and pressing on alone, but ultimately consented to descend to their camp. The weather was perfect, he thought, and they would try again for the summit.

Pasang Lama's story—the story of how a Sherpa of Tibetan ancestry, born in the Khumbu Valley of Nepal and living in Darjeeling in British India, came to be so high on a mountain in Baltistan, more than two thousand miles away—is the story of relationships. It's not only the story of how the first generations of European climbers venturing into the Himalayas perceived their Sherpa employees, but also of how the Sherpas recognized the power of mountaineering work to advance their own socioeconomic position, and how mountaineering eventually changed even their own self-image. Their story truly originated sometime in the mid–sixteenth century, when two clans of Tibetan people made the dangerous trek over the Nangpa La pass to settle the Solu Khumbu Valley in what would become the Kingdom of Nepal. But its most dramatic chapter began in 1921 in Darjeeling, India: the year of the British Everest reconnaissance expedition.

In the first two decades of the twentieth century, a Scottish geologist named Alexander Kellas had quietly mounted a series of small exploratory trips into the Himalayas. Often traveling alone with only a few hired porters, Kellas formed close bonds with several Sherpas, whom he began to employ on technical mountaineering excursions and taught some rudimentary climbing skills. A picture taken on one such expedition shows Kellas's original cadre of Sherpa guides. They are wearing wool smocks, loose-fitting shawls, and beaded necklaces. One has a formidable knife visible, carried on his belt. All sport long braids of hair tucked underneath small caps and tightly bound turbans. Kellas is the only white man in the photo. The Scotsman became the first true champion of the Sherpas' natural skills in the mountains. It was thanks in part to his urging that among the legions of Tibetans hired from the local coolie labor force for the reconnaissance expedition, there were several Sherpas from the Solu Khumbu.

The next year, 1922, the British were back for a serious attempt on Everest, and the expedition was led by General Charles Bruce. Bruce was a dashing presence, often portrayed as the archetypal swashbuckling colonial adventurer—though his true character was more complicated than that. Over the course of his long career, he had participated in numerous military campaigns and expeditions to all regions of the Himalayas, learned to speak fluent Nepali, and was even known to engage in wrestling matches in the traditional Punjabi style. As a young man, Bruce had participated in the first serious attempt on an eight-thousand-meter peak, an expedition to Nanga Parbat with Albert Mummery in 1895. By 1922, he probably had amassed the greatest record of any Himalayan explorer of his day.

But Bruce was first and foremost a product of the army, and since the Great Mutiny of 1857, the recruitment policies in the Raj—the British dominion of India—had been a subject of much debate. Since large numbers of Hindus had revolted, the English naturally began to look to

other races to serve instead. The new strategy was codified in a prepos-
terous body of pseudoscientific anthropological study that became known
as the martial races theory. As General Sir O'Moore Creagh wrote: "In
the hot, flat regions, of which by far the greater party of India consists . . .
are found races timid both by religion and habit, servile to their superiors, but tyrannical to their inferiors, and quite unwarlike. . . . Where the
winter is cold, the warlike minority is to be found."

With thirty years' experience commanding the 5th Gurkha Rifles of
the Indian army, Bruce had a keen if still patriarchal view of Himalayan
peoples. (The famed Gurkha regiments were recruited from the ranks of
at least four different tribes in the midland hills of Nepal, who became
in effect mercenaries to fight for the Crown.) It was natural that when
he showed up in Darjeeling to attempt Everest, he looked around for the
strongest, most reliable tribe of people fit for the high mountains. When
Charles Bruce returned in 1924 to lead a second attempt, his nephew,
Geoffrey, handled the hiring of porters for the expedition. Bruce the
younger later described the interview process, laying the groundwork for
a new body of racial theory: "Our experience proves that the clean, well
proportioned, clean-bread man is the one to take. All carrying porters
should be either Sherpas or Bhotias."

Seven Sherpas died in an avalanche while approaching the North
Col of Everest in 1922. They were the mountain's first victims. Still, not
only did the Sherpas continue to work on expeditions, but they actively
sought to establish themselves as the best group for high-altitude work.
Why did they do it?

The simple answer is that life in the Solu Khumbu was hard. The
Sherpas were mostly farmers, but as the valley grew slowly more popu-
lated, there was less farmland to go around. It was Sherpa custom that
all inherited wealth was evenly divided among all the sons in a nuclear
family, thereby subdividing property into smaller and smaller pieces with
each successive generation. By the turn of the century, there were few
options open to a young man from a working family: His parents might
place him into indentured servitude to a wealthier family, or he might be

sent off to a monastery, or he might end up carrying loads around the valley to make ends meet.

There was a final option. He could run away, and seek his fortune in Darjeeling, a three-week walk away from the Solu Khumbu. And it was in Darjeeling that the first Sherpas—all of whom were essentially young, unlanded farmers—were hired for the first Everest expeditions.

They realized immediately that the job was lucrative. After one season of expedition work, a man could make enough money to return to the Khumbu and buy a few yaks or a small plot of land. Those Sherpas returned home relatively wealthy, their heads held high, and their neighbors quickly saw that the Englishman's strange predilection for climbing mountains might provide a means for rapid upward mobility in their otherwise static, agricultural-based society. More Sherpas journeyed to Darjeeling in search of work.

Their biggest competition was their ancestral cousins, Tibetans and Bhotes. Anthropologist Sherry Ortner writes that during the 1922 Everest expedition, "The Sherpas made a point of competing with the Tibetans, volunteering for all the difficult high-altitude jobs, and bringing themselves to the sahibs' attention as less 'superstitious,' more willing, and more disciplined than the Tibetans." The effort paid off in 1924, when the British formally divided their labor between low-altitude porters (the Tibetans) and high-altitude specialists (the Sherpas). In 1930, a group of Sherpas actually brought a lawsuit against the pay officer of an international expedition to Kangchenjunga because they felt Tibetan coolies had unfairly received better compensation than themselves, and threatened not to work again with the leader of the expedition if he hired any Tibetans on future climbs. Sherpas also began to resist load-carrying duties at lower elevations, on the approach to base camp—even staging a strike during the 1935 Everest expedition over the matter. They began to see themselves not as menial coolie laborers, but something akin to skilled tradesmen.

In the Karakoram, local porters from the Hunza and Balti tribes had been employed by a German expedition to Nanga Parbat in 1932. They were in many ways similar to Sherpas: two mountain tribes accustomed to hard, agrarian work, load carrying, and a cold climate. But politically, they were pressed into working for the German team because each man owed a corvée labor tax to the autocratic ruler of the region, the Mir of Hunza. They expected to receive little or no pay out of the deal. Sherpas, meanwhile, entered the coolie labor market in Darjeeling essentially as independent contractors, well aware that future employment and higher wages depended on their performance. The Hunza and Balti porters on Nanga Parbat in 1932 protested and continually had to be coaxed up the mountain by the German climbers. The expedition turned into a slow, grinding failure—there is little wonder that the Hunzas appeared, in the words of one of their employers, "capricious and temperamental." Word spread quickly through the Himalayan exploring community that, for future expeditions to the Karakoram, it would be far preferential to import Darjeeling Sherpas rather than hire local labor.

And so, on April 27, 1939, nine Sherpa men arrived in Srinagar. Their sirdar was Pasang Kikuli, who had also served as Sherpa leader on a highly successful reconnaissance expedition the year before. The Sherpas' appearance, as historian Jonathan Neale notes, had markedly changed in only a single generation of high-mountain work. In place of the traditional Tibetan coats and long braids of hair worn by Kellas's protégés, they were clad in modern European suits and neatly trimmed haircuts. Beneath these visible changes, one senses a deeper shift. The Sherpas had traveled more than two thousand miles by train and car to join the team; they bore with them the confidence of men who knew their skills were in demand. "They are proud," Neale writes.

The mountain was first seen by Western eyes three years after the "discovery" of Mount Everest. On September 10, 1856, Lieutenant Thomas Montgomerie of the Great Trigonometric Survey arrived at a recently constructed surveying station positioned on the flank of fifty-three-hundred-meter Mount Haramukh, overlooking the valley of Kashmir.

The weather was clear, and as Montgomerie caught his breath from the arduous four-day climb, he gazed to the northwest and sighted two large masses of land some hundred and forty miles distant:

> There was nothing remarkable in the first six or seven ridges . . . beyond came the snowy points of the Karakoram and behind them I saw two fine peaks standing very high above the general range.

Lieutenant Montgomerie took rough bearings on the two summits and sketched a quick drawing in the margin of his notebook. He designated the two mountains K1 and K2. The "K" stood for Karakoram.* In his notes on the two peaks he surveyed that day from the flanks of Mount Haramukh, Montgomerie wrote: "Every effort will be made to find a local name if it has one." K1, it was soon learned, was known to the Balti people as Masherbrum, but the locals only shrugged in a bemused manner when asked the name of Masherbrum's taller neighbor.

The mountain was not visible from any villages or permanent human settlement. As was imagined by the writer-photographer Galen Rowell, it is possible that an errant shepherd from Askole, the closest permanently inhabited village, wandered above the grassy summertime pastures of Paihu and followed the deep swath cut by the Baltoro Glacier to reach the glacial confluence now known as Concordia. From there, it might have been possible to catch a fleeting glimpse of the summit, still some fifteen miles distant. But most likely, even if this occurred, all the wayward pastor would have seen was a churning mass of cloud and storm.

---

* Though it is seldom noted today, the British made an admirable effort to ascertain the local names of the geographic features they surveyed and officially record them as such. By and large, the mountains and rivers and lakes of the Himalayas carry the names of the people who lived closest to them. The world's highest landmass is the one glaring exception to this rule: George Everest was the surveyor general of India from 1830 to 1843. He officially forbade his men from naming things after Westerners, but he couldn't quite stop it when his successor (and Montgomerie's superior) Andrew Waugh decided to name the world's tallest peak after him.

Pasang Lama and Wiessner limped into base camp on July 23, five days after they had crept so close to the summit of K2. They were weary and dehydrated; Wiessner was so parched that he had trouble speaking. In rasping tones he exploded at his teammates for having abandoned them.

On the midnight descent from their high point so close to the summit where Pasang Lama had refused to climb higher, both men's crampons, which were lashed to the pack he carried, became loose and dropped into the void. After a day of rest at their high camp, Wiessner resolved to try for the summit again, this time following the narrowing snow couloir under the massive serac. But, lacking crampons, they were forced to cut steps—an exhausting, time-consuming process—and both men quickly realized that their second attempt was also futile.

Pasang Lama and Wiessner descended to Camp VIII, where Dudley Wolfe was still waiting.* Wiessner optimistically hoped he could pick up more provisions, a spare pair of crampons, and a new Sherpa partner, as Pasang Lama was quite tired from their efforts—and then immediately return to make a third bid for K2's summit. But the men found no more provisions in Camp VIII and no more teammates, save for the weakening Dudley Wolfe.

Wolfe had by now spent eight nights at Camp VIII. A large, convivial man, who also happened to be quite wealthy, he possessed marginal experience—at best—to be so high on such a serious mountain. Wolfe had not been able even to properly light a stove, and after running out of matches he had survived the last several days by melting snow during the abnormally sunny weather. Pasang Lama, Wolfe, and Wiessner continued down to Camp VII, barely avoiding total disaster in a terrifying fall in the process. They found no one in Camp VII waiting for them, and no sleeping bags or mats either. What to do? The next morning, Wiessner made his decision: He and Pasang Lama, who were in far better shape, would continue descending to the lower camps to resupply.

---

* Located just below the Shoulder, close to the location of modern Camp IV

Wolfe would remain. But as Pasang Lama and Wiessner scurried lower and lower down the Abruzzi Ridge, they found no sleeping bags left behind in any of the six lower camps.

Now, in base camp, everyone realized that Dudley Wolfe was frightfully alone and in effect marooned high on the mountain. A rescue effort was immediately launched the next morning by American Jack Durrance and three of the Sherpas. But Durrance lapsed into altitude sickness and descended, leaving two of the Sherpas, Phinsoo and Kitar, at Camp IV, seven hundred meters below the stranded Wolfe. Wiessner was still wrecked from his summit attempt the week before, and his other teammates were incapable or unwilling to lead another effort. When it most mattered, the expedition was suddenly perilously short of rested, capable manpower.

Dudley Wolfe's best hope lay with Pasang Kikuli. In ten years of mountain work, the twenty-eight-year-old Pasang Kikuli had amassed a résumé that placed him in the highest echelon of Himalayan climbers. He had climbed on Kangchenjunga, Nanda Devi, and K2 the previous year, but his most formative experience was a German expedition to Nanga Parbat in 1934. On that climb, a large summit party was caught in a sustained storm high on the mountain. The fittest Germans, who carried skis, rushed down the mountain ahead of the others, and by the time it was all over, three sahibs and six Sherpas were dead. Pasang Kikuli was a professional, but that did not mean that his ensuing actions on K2 were motivated by money, or that Wiessner ordered him to do it, as his critics later claimed. As Jonathan Neale hypothesizes:

> His [Kikuli's] lesson learned on Nanga Parbat was that in extremity only Sherpas could be counted on to behave decently and look after each other and the other climbers. And it probably followed that if he was only person who could lead a rescue, it was his duty to do so.

Nanga Parbat had left Kikuli with lasting frostbite injuries to his toes, and as he left base camp to bring Dudley Wolfe down he must have known he risked seriously reinjuring them. Nevertheless, Kikuli, with another Sherpa, Tsering Norbu, left base camp on July 28 and climbed straight to Camp VI, where they rendezvoused with Phinsoo and Kitar. The next morning, Kikuli, Phinsoo, and Kitar ascended to Camp VII, where they met Wolfe. The American was in bad shape, having not eaten or drunk in days. He could barely walk, and begged the Sherpas off, asking for another day of rest before descending. Modern physiologists immediately recognize that Wolfe, having by now spent an incredible *thirty-eight* consecutive days above sixty thousand meters, must have been in a state of total physical exhaustion. But little was known about the effects of altitude in 1939, and there was nothing the three Sherpas could do. Kikuli agreed to descend to Camp VI, where they had left their overnight supplies, and return in the morning.

A short storm prevented the Sherpas from mounting another effort the next day, and so it was only on July 31 that Kikuli again led Phinsoo and Kitar to Camp VII to rescue Wolfe. They never returned. Tsering Norbu arrived alone at the foot of the Abruzzi Spur on August 2. He reported that Kikuli's final plan was either to rescue Wolfe, or make his employer sign a written document (a "chit," in the colonial lexicon) absolving him of responsibility.

The 1939 K2 expedition was a turning point in the Sherpa-Sahib relationship. Pasang Lama's partnership with Wiessner, and Pasang Kikuli's leadership during the attempted rescue, showed for the first time that Sherpas could perform in the mountains on an equal footing with their employers. Sadly, that realization was punctuated by tragedy, not success. If nothing else, the ill-fated 1939 expedition illustrated just how important an abundance of fresh manpower was in a crisis situation on K2. As would happen again, it was the Sherpas who proved to be by circumstance those strongest and best positioned to help.

In his diary of the climb, Wiessner described Pasang Lama's decision to descend on their summit push, a decision that in all likelihood cost him the summit. "He didn't have the heart for it," Wiessner wrote, a vague statement that could be attributed to Pasang Lama's physical condition, his mental commitment, or his psychological willingness to continue on and face a very real and increasing chance of death. But then he continued: "Since the day before [Pasang Lama] had no longer been his old self; he had been living in great fear of the evil spirits, constantly murmuring prayers, and had lost his appetite."

It's not surprising that a Tibetan Buddhist from the respected Lama caste would experience K2 in religious terms, but it's also hard to fault the Sherpa for preferring to retreat rather than be overcome by darkness without supplemental oxygen very near to the summit of K2. Ironically, sixty-nine years later, experienced climbers like American Ed Viesturs would criticize many of the summiteers for continuing to the summit in nearly the exact same situation that Wiessner and Pasang Lama faced. The 1939 expedition's tragic ending ultimately proved Pasang Lama's fears—regardless of how he expressed them—were only all too justified.

Nepal's borders finally opened to foreigners in 1950. That same year, a French expedition wildly succeeded on Annapurna, making the first ascent of an eight-thousand-meter peak. The golden age of Himalayan climbing had begun. One principal reason that the world's highest summits were conquered in such a short span of time is that, after a generation of apprenticeship, mountaineering Sherpas had acquired enough skills to be very effective in supporting a high-altitude climb. Pasang Kikuli's final act of bravery in 1939, as well as a hundred other acts by Sherpas embedded into twenty-nine years of mountaineering efforts, all coalesced into one pivotal realization: Sherpas had earned their employers' trust.

On Annapurna in 1950, Ang Tharkay, the expedition's sirdar, was invited to join Maurice Herzog and Louis Lachenal on the summit climb. Ang Tharkay declined. He was worried about getting frostbite and he had already done his job: getting the sahibs and enough equipment to a well-stocked high camp, so they could go on and reach the top. "How oddly their minds worked," Herzog reflected as Ang Tharkay and Sarki, the expedition's two stongest Sherpas, turned to descend. "Here were these two men, proverbial for their trustworthiness and devotion, who quite certainly enjoyed going high on the mountains, and yet, when on the point of reaping the fruits of their labors, they prudently held back. But I don't doubt that our mentality struck them as even odder."

The summit of a mountain was nothing special to Ang Tharkay; nor were summits important to the vast majority of Sherpas engaged in mountaineering work. But it was different for one man: Tenzing Norgay Sherpa. "Always as a child, a boy, a man, I have wanted to travel, to move, to go and see, to go and find," Norgay wrote in his autobiography. Others noticed it too. Tenzing Norgay served as sirdar for two successive Swiss expeditions to Everest in 1952. It was obvious to the Swiss that not only was he a capable leader and organizer, but that he desperately wanted a crack at the summit himself. Tenzing formed a special bond with a strapping guide named Raymond Lambert, and they were designated as the summit team. The pair got close to the top, almost all the way to the south summit, but ultimately they were forced to turn around.

Britain's turn at Everest came the next year. Like the Swiss, they offered the critical job of sirdar to Tenzing, but the Sherpa hesitated. The Swiss were already planning a return in 1954, and Tenzing had his heart set on reaching the summit together with Lambert. But the Swiss guide interjected and insisted that his friend try with the British. Compared to their close relationship, Hillary and Tenzing were more akin to amiable business partners.

When the well-timed news of their success rocketed around the world, Tenzing's fame was notched even higher by one small and often overlooked fact: There were no summit photos of Hillary. From New Delhi to New York and London, when people picked up the newspaper and saw documented proof that man had reached the top of the world, they were looking at a photo of a Sherpa.

A second and slower change began in the 1950s, which helped cement the Sherpas' public image. With Nepal opening its borders, Westerners could visit the Solu Khumbu. Returning from the first reconnaissance of Everest's southern approaches in 1950, Charlie Houston wrote: "I remember walking . . . through the autumn gold, reflecting on what we had seen, and what damage we and others like us might have set in train for this innocent, backward, beautiful country." A generation later, those words would seem prophetic, as thousands of international visitors flocked seasonally to the region. The burgeoning tourism business would undoubtedly have profound effects on Sherpa culture, and Houston's concerns were heartfelt, but there is also more than a hint of old colonial perceptions in his characterization of the Sherpa homeland.

In 1954, the year after Everest was climbed, a large team of Italians succeeded on K2. Ascending the Abruzzi Ridge, two men, Lino Lacedelli and Achille Compagnoni, cramponed up the same gully that Wiessner had first avoided, then skirted left around the serac to reach the top of the Karakoram. Since Pakistan had become an independent nation after Partition in 1947, a new law stipulated that all expeditions must use only local labor. Like the Germans in 1932, the Italians relied on Hunza porters.

Over the years, other names had been suggested for the mountain discovered by Montgomerie. Chogori, an amalgam of two Balti words meaning "big mountain," was one suggestion, as were Dapsang and Lamba Pahar, two Urdu words meaning roughly the same thing. A group of Englishmen proposed naming the mountain Mount Godwin Austen, in honor of the British explorer who was one of the first to reconnoiter the base of the mountain. The Chinese, meanwhile, officially labeled the peak Qogir, a rough translation of Chogori.

The subtle controversy had simmered for almost a century. But none of the names stuck. None seemed right to describe the mountain that for time immemorial stood so isolated from humankind. It was another Italian, Fosco Maraini, who put it best. "No country claims it," he wrote in 1959, "no latitudes and longitudes and geography, no dictionary words. . . ."

No, just the bare bones of a name, all rock and ice and storm and abyss. It is atoms and stars. It has the nakedness of the world before the first man—or of the cindered planet after the last.

As I dug into researching the tragedy for my *Rock and Ice* assignment, I noticed a backlash of sorts in the media. In reaction to the many articles that were quick to compare what happened on K2 to the 1996 Everest disaster, some began to mount a defense, stating that there were no guided parties on K2 and that everyone was qualified to be there. Sitting decidedly in this camp were Wilco van Rooijen and Marco Confortola. The *Independent* published the following paragraph in an article about Marco, which seemed to contradict his earlier criticisms of the advance rope-fixing team:

> The Italian climber shrugged off suggestions that the six teams—from Ireland, South Korea, the Netherlands, Serbia and Italy—had displayed poor judgement, insufficient preparation and had caught so-called "summit fever." "We were well prepared," he says. "We had made our plans—even the weather was good."

The *Men's Journal* article concluded with the following quote from Wilco: "I have nothing to hide. . . . With this tragedy, if you're really surprised about this, then you don't understand anything about it. If you don't want to face the risk, don't go to K2." The net result of these kinds of "shit happens" public statements was to partially neutralize any constructive debate about what went wrong. Even ExplorersWeb, embroiled in their own media feud with Fredrik Sträng, defended the experience of the other teams on the mountain while trying to quantitatively discredit Sträng's teammates: ". . . except for their expedition Sherpa summiteer, this expedition had a total score of 8000er summits barely equaling two of the Korean climbers."

Part of the problem was the vocabulary being used to describe the relationships on the mountain. In mountaineering circles, a *guided* expedition is commonly understood to provide professional mountain guides trained to Western standards to accompany their clientele up the mountain. The guides are responsible for fixing ropes, establishing camps, cooking meals, and dictating the strategy that will provide their clients with the best possible chance to reach the summit. More often than not, the guides supplement the expedition's manpower by hiring high-altitude support staff that are domestically available in any of the Himalayan states.

On K2, there were no Western guides. But other trappings of guided climbing—notably Sherpa and Pakistani support climbers, and the heavy-handed use of fixed ropes—were readily present. I began to notice a vague body of assumptions that were never directly mentioned but frequently implied in many of the newspaper stories and personal accounts of the disaster: Many, both on the mountain and in the press, took it for granted that responsibility for fixing the ropes would be assumed by someone else. The following blog, for instance, written by Nick Rice, gives a sense of how much even the independent climbers were relying on the Pakistanis and Sherpas on the mountain:

> The Serbians have three high altitude porters and have 24 bottles of oxygen in Base Camp. If they use oxygen, they will be able to work very efficiently when fixing the lines in the bottleneck, and this will help us all. . . . We also spoke of Pemba, Qudrat, and Karim working together on the Cesan Route to fix the final 250 meters of ropes to Camp IV (or the shoulder).

Nowhere in this dispatch did Nick mention any specific commitments of his own to help establish the route. Moreover, Nick's suggestion of having Hugues D'Aubarède's professional help, Qudrat and Karim, team up with Pemba was strange in light of a statement released by the Norit team ten days after the tragedy began.

On August 10, a new update appeared on their Web site, detailing the whereabouts and travel arrangements of the ill-fated team. At this time, the remaining members of the expedition, including Pemba Gyalje, had just arrived in Skardu after a weary trek from base camp, and now faced the specter of a grueling, two-day jeep ride down the Karakoram Highway to reach Islamabad. There, they would be reunited with their frostbitten teammates, Wilco van Rooijen and Cas van de Gevel, who had already arrived from Skardu via airplane. As Pemba and his teammates checked into a hotel for their first hot shower in months, and then placed phone calls home to tell family and friends they were finally safe from the mountains, Maarten van Eck issued the following statement about Pemba:

> Possibly superfluous for the faithful readers of this Internet site, but for all clarity we find it important to communicate the following once again. In many media expressions Sherpas and HAPs are depicted as bearers and aid troops of climbers. With emphasis I can tell you a different story about OUR PEMBA. Pemba is and was an entirely equivalent climbing partner in this expedition. We are exceptionally proud of his performance and his incredible commitment during the entire expedition and in particular during the dramatic events of the previous days.

The statement didn't bother to specify what those deeds were; nor were any details offered elsewhere on the Norit Web site. But by then, a week after the disaster, rough accounts of Pemba's tireless efforts to rescue survivors of the disaster had leaked into other media reports.

Another clue appeared the day before, when the *Independent* ran a story on Italian Marco Confortola's harrowing fight to descend K2 alive. Omar Waraich, the reporter who interviewed Confortola in Islamabad and authored the piece, wrote the following account of his rescue, in which Marco was found lying unconscious in the snow at eight thousand meters:

> Shortly afterwards, one of the Nepalese porters appeared and offered oxygen—which he gratefully accepted. . . . "When we were walking down another avalanche struck. It hit two Sherpas who were helping us. And an oxygen bottle came cascading down and hit me in the back of the head." Confortola bends forward to reveal a round black mark near the base of his skull.

It was at this point that Confortola was certain he would die. "I was falling," he says, gesturing animatedly. "The avalanche would have taken me away with it. But I was lucky. One of the Sherpas, his name was Pemba, grabbed me from behind. He was holding my neck. He saved my life."

In another account, Confortola went even a step further, telling of how Pemba jumped out to grab his neck as blocks of ice fell around them, "like a lioness protecting her young." None of the articles mentioned that Pemba had then immediately descended all the way to Camp III on the Cesen Route by headlamp, and spent much of the night searching for Wilco van Rooijen. He finally located his lost teammate early the next morning, and then safely shepherded him and Cas van de Gevel down to base camp.

If anyone was deserving of public recognition for bravery or selflessness during the disaster, I realized, it was the quiet man whose hometown was listed as the village of Kari Kola in Nepal's Solo Khumbu Valley. But in the initial media accounts he appeared only as a gauzy cutout of a person, at the periphery of the real story, which was van Rooijen's and Confortola's fight for survival. Other than a copy of his climbing résumé and a few low-quality, pixilated images posted on the Norit site, I could find little information or specifics about the man.

Next I spoke to Eric Meyer. Eric had just returned to the States; I caught him while he was actually visiting his parents in Montana. Three weeks after the disaster, the fatigue and confusion were still palpable in his voice. I asked him how Chhiring Dorje, the Sherpa member of their team, felt about working on K2. Eric quickly corrected me.

"Chhiring was on our team because he wanted to be there—he wanted to be the first Sherpa to climb K2 without supplemental oxygen," Eric told me. "And we wanted to be part of the movement to support Sherpas as real climbers." Then he added, almost conspiratorially: "Did you hear about how he down-climbed the Bottleneck with Pasang Lama hanging from his harness? *That one* hasn't made the newspapers yet."

The vague reports of the Sherpas' heroism, as well as the subtle yet meaningful subtext to the assertion that both Pemba and Chhiring climbed as "equivalent climbing members" of their respective teams, fascinated me. Why would someone who earned an annual income of less than fifteen thousand dollars humping loads and fixing ropes choose to climb a mountain for the fun of it? Did the fact that Pemba and Chhiring were not acting in a professional role somehow make their actions more noteworthy?

The positions and duties of the Pakistani and Nepalese climbers involved in the disaster were frequently misidentified and rarely explained in the mainstream media. Consider the excerpt from the *Independent* article quoted above: In the same breath, Pemba is referred to as a "Nepalese porter," and then simply a Sherpa. Elsewhere, the four Nepalese who took part in the summit push were repeatedly called "porters" or "HAPs" (high-altitude porters, a euphemism most frequently used for Pakistani mountain staff). Surprisingly, this trend continued even in well-informed stories that ran in *Men's Journal* and *Outside* magazine online months after the disaster. Yet the published death tolls listed their identity only by nationality; no mention was made of whether they were on the mountain as employed workers or pleasure climbers.

Most mainstream journalists covering the story seemed unfamiliar with the intricacies of Himalayan climbing, and willing to use the terms carelessly and interchangeably. But within the climbing community, there are marked differences between each title. A "porter" refers to an unskilled local laborer hired to transport equipment and supplies to base camp. Porters don't venture onto technical terrain and they had no role in what happened on K2. "Sherpa" is fundamentally an ethnic distinction, but their role in Himalayan mountaineering history was so critical that today, it has become standard practice in Nepal and Tibet to describe all native high-altitude support staff as "Sherpas," or perhaps "climbing-Sherpas." The appropriation of a tribal identity to describe a form of labor ignites charged debate in many quarters, but one reason the new definition stuck is that there was no existing word that quite fit what they did.

From the first Everest expeditions of 1921–1924 through the 1950s and 1960s, the prevailing ethic was that the Western climbers fixed the route, and the Sherpas followed with the loads. With few exceptions, both parties saw their relationship in a formal, almost colonial context. But sometime in the 1970s, a curious thing happened: The Sherpas stopped calling their employers "sahib," and started using their first names instead. In the 1970s and 1980s, they also began to assume more responsibilities on the mountain, tasks that increasingly resembled the skill set of a Western guide, like fixing rope, breaking trail, short-roping clients, and managing the group. And during the same time period, men from different tribal backgrounds than purebred Sherpas (in the ethnic sense) also began to compete for mountaineering work in Kathmandu. They summarily were included as being Sherpas (in the job description sense), further muddying the waters.*

Pakistan also had its own tradition of mountaineering labor, though the Hunzas and Baltis never benefited from the special relationships that allowed the Sherpas to make their remarkable advances. Today, it might be said that the Pakistanis are seeking to follow the same path as the Sherpas, but got a later start, and in general (with a few notable exceptions), their skills are not on par with that of Nepali climbing-Sherpas. Pakistani mountain professionals also face a marketing hurdle: Whereas Sherpas brilliantly branded their own ethnicity into an image of a sort of rough-hewn, indefatigable mountain guide, Pakistanis commonly are given a far less romantic title—high-altitude porter, or HAP.

Given the factual errors that were popping up daily in the media about the climbing-Sherpas on K2, Norit's statement about Pemba's status as an "equivalent climbing member" of the team made sense. It was meant to correct the record, and also to draw positive attention to Pemba's extraordinarily selfless deeds. But despite the annoucement's gracious intentions, its subtext was troubling. Addressing Pemba's status on

---

* On their own recommendation, I have chosen in this book to refer to modern Nepalis of all ethnic backgrounds who work professionally in the mountains as "climbing-Sherpas." The climbing-Sherpas themselves propose an even broader definition, suggesting that there can be Pakistani-, Indian-, and Chinese-born climbing-Sherpas.

the mountain was a tacit acknowledgment that some kind of hierarchy did exist. Subtly, it drew a line between Pemba's actions and those of the others on the mountain—most notably, the four Nepalis employed by the Korean team. It also hinted that because Pemba was not acting as a guide, no one else on the mountain was indebted to his skills. Was there a fundamental difference in the actions of the Sherpas who were "equivalent climbing partners" on K2, I wondered, and those who were up there for money?

Twenty-first-century Sherpas turned out to be prompt and courteous e-mail correspondents. Chhiring Dorje and Pemba Gyalje immediately answered my queries. Their written English was a little rough around the edges, but plenty good enough to convey the critical information.

On one point, however, Pemba was frustratingly hard to pin down. "Our expedition was properly non-guiding style expedition," he wrote. "I participated as a member with the Norit team, not a guide or high altitude worker. . . ." But then he added, pointedly: "They decided to give me some bonus because they understand well that I gave up my work in the spring season in Nepal."

Chhiring, meanwhile, wrote that climbing K2 was his "life dream." The first time I heard that a rescue party had succeeded in reaching the stricken Koreans was in a note from him on August 26:

> Pemba gyalje also went up to rescue Marco and he was [at] 8000m. Pasang bhote rescue jumic and koreans from 8350m but Pasang bhote, jumic bhote, Park Kyeong, Hwang Dong, Kim Hyo and Gerard (irish man) swept by serac avalanche in cuiler 2 pm and this I heard from Pasang Lama in kathmandu.

The cynic in me couldn't help thinking that Pemba was somehow being taken advantage of—Norit claimed Pemba wasn't guiding on K2, and yet he was getting paid. And on the morning of August 2, while almost every remaining Western climber in Camp IV rejected the idea of searching for survivors and made the prudent decision to descend for their own safety, it was three climbing-Sherpas who charged up into the Bottleneck: Pasang Bhote and Tsering Bhote from the Korean team, supported by Pemba Gyalje behind them.

In the annals of Himalayan climbing, Sherpas were so often lauded for their cheerful attitudes, loyalty, and selfless devotion to their employers that their behavior, more often than not, was just accepted as an innate cultural characteristic. Academics have proposed other explanations— that their "cheerfulness" was a result of their Buddhist religion, or their background in mercantilism and trade. Certainly both had something to do with it, as did that most painfully obvious factor that many Western climbers were loath to admit: They were earning good money.

Desperately short on manpower, did they really have a choice?

What the hell, I thought.

I'll be in Kathmandu anyway. I might as well look these guys up.

7

CONTACT

L and at midday, during business hours, after an overnight flight from Europe or North America, and the first thing you notice on leaving Tribhuvan International Airport is the noise and condition of the road: a fusillade of horns—blapping, tapping, popping, poking—in chaotic crescendos as the traffic weaves back and forth between potholes and pedestrians. Kathmandu is situated in the middle of a broad, terraced valley surrounded by jungle hills. It is forty-five hundred feet above sea level, and roughly the same latitude as Fort Lauderdale, Florida. There are palm trees, banana trees, monkeys, and dozens of emaciated, sullen cows wandering the streets and idly sniffing at garbage.

Ask a shopkeeper, taxi driver, or streetside huckster where he is from, and he will give you the easiest answer.

Kathmandu, of course.

But be careful. Kathmandu Valley is at once a civilization centuries old, and a city still in its infancy. Before 1950, Nepal was ruled by a tightly controlled Hindu aristocracy. Understandably weary of the imperial presence to their south, they kept the borders of their mountain kingdom mostly closed. At the same time, the Ranas enjoyed such a lavish lifestyle that, during the first half of the twentieth century, the economic gap between Kathmandu's elite and its poor widened. There was little business to lure the rural inhabitants of Nepal to the city; anyone who chose to seek their fortune in a far-off city moved to India. The people around Kathmandu Valley rebelled in 1950, and King Tribhuvan, a Shah, was annointed ruler the next year. The first motor road linking Kathmandu to the outside world was opened in 1956. In 1974, Tribhuvan brought regularly scheduled international air transport to the country. The population of Kathmandu tripled in twenty years.

And so, there is always a second answer to the question. You just have to rephrase the query: *Where is your village home?*

It was the last week of September: high season in Thamel, the tourism capital and red-light district of Kathmandu. I sat in a corner of the lobby of the Hotel Marshyangdi, watching as a party of German trekkers clad in matching fleece jackets assaulted the concierge.

"But my luggage is missing. Lufthansa has lost it," one exclaimed at a decibel level that was impossible to ignore. "How can I trek to Mount Everest base camp with no trekking equipment?"

I knew Chhiring Dorje the moment he walked through the door.

He wore a sleek soft-shell jacket, a cleanly pressed T-shirt tucked into Schoeller hiking pants, and a pair of Salomon trail-running sneakers.

Chhiring shook my hand aggressively, laughing as he did so, and said in broken English: "*Namaste*, Fredrick! How are you? You like we can go get some tea?" He stood perhaps five feet, eight inches tall, but had broad shoulders and a thick torso. My first reaction was that of my inner climber, sizing him up: *This guy is built like a brick shit house.*

I had suggested over e-mail that we meet up for a beer or coffee. Nodding toward the door, Chhiring immediately began to retreat from the bustling hotel lobby, motioning me to follow. I almost tripped into a thickset kid with a mop of dark hair that flopped over his forehead, almost touching the wire-rimmed glasses he wore.

The one-lane street was flooded with motorbikes and early evening shoppers. I skipped a half step to catch up with Chhiring. The Asian kid was following close behind. Chhiring glanced over his shoulder.

"This is my brother, Ngawang," he said by way of introduction.

Five minutes later we had found a quiet table at the Rum Doodle Bar & Restaurant. The Rum Doodle is a Thamel institution, the traditional venue for Western climbers and trekkers to engage in a little pretrip debauchery or gorge on well-prepared, Western-style meals after returning from the hills. It was not quite six p.m., however, and the place was still deserted. A waiter approached and Chhiring ordered tea for the three of us.

"K2 is very dangerous," he told me immediately. "A very dangerous mountain . . ." He and Ngawang giggled nervously, nodding their heads in unison. Humor seemed an odd emotion given the serious subject matter, but there was no mistaking it. Chhiring seemed very cheerful indeed. "I have a rule before I take people to a mountain," he continued. "I always ask, Have you spoken to your family, your wife and children, and made sure it is okay for you to climb this mountain with me?"

The waiter, a fine-boned Hindi man, returned with a tea set, placed a saucer in front of each of us, and poured from a pot. Chhiring took a sip and nearly spit out the liquid. He issued a rapid burst of Nepali directed at the waiter, who immediately scurried off to the kitchen.

"This tea," Chhiring said, puckering his lips. "It's no good." I took a sip myself and immediately understood what he meant: The drink was lukewarm at best. We sat for a moment, and then Chhiring returned to the conversation. "That's what I tell everyone. First, you talk to your family. Only once their permission is given, then it's okay to take you up the mountain. . . ."

Not only had Chhiring Dorje been one of the few climbers on K2 who had successfully down-climbed the Bottleneck without fixed ropes, but he had done it with another human being hanging from his harness. Though it was never mentioned in the first wave of press covering the disaster, the feat was so extraordinary it almost bordered on legend. As Ed Viesturs would later write: "That's pretty astonishing, but I can just imagine how you might pull it off: kick each foot in solid, plant the ax, then tell the other guy to kick with his own feet and even punch holds with his hands. Don't move until he's secure." Nevertheless, in the annals of high-altitude mountaineering, there was nothing quite like it. But Chhiring Dorje wasn't interested in talking about his rescue of Pasang Lama.

The first thing he wanted to tell me about was his home.

Chhiring Dorje was not from the Solu Khumbu. His home was the village of Beding, in the Rolwaling valley, west of Namche Bazaar, separated by the fifty-seven-hundred-meter Tashi Lapsa Pass. Beding, the highest permanently established village in the Rolwaling valley, is tucked under 7,145-meter-tall Gauri Shankar. Anthropologists believe that the first Sherpa inhabitants of Rolwaling came from the Khumbu in the middle of the nineteenth century. This theory is supported by the fact that the oldest settlement in Rolwaling, the seasonal habitation of Na, is also the highest in elevation, and the closest to the Tashi Lapsa and the Khumbu. Its name is a simple homage to the agrarian lifestyle that supported the Sherpas for centuries. *Na* means barley, the traditional Sherpa crop before the potato arrived in the 1880s.

But Chhiring didn't tell me any of this as we conversed.

His birthplace, he says, is a sacred place. It was made by Padmasambhava, the Guru Urgen Rinpoche, the Indian holy man who first brought Buddhism to Tibet. *Rolwa* means furrow, and *ling* means place. Local lore has it that in the seventh century, Padmasambhava created the valley, plowing through the brown earth and Himalayan stone with his spiritual power. Ever since, it has always been considered by its inhabitants to be a *beyul*, a place that was created as a refuge for Buddhists in time of war or upheaval. This belief is reinforced by Rolwaling's geographic landscape. Unlike the Khumbu, a north-south valley that runs straight to the Nangpa La and Tibet beyond and has naturally been a conduit for trade, the Rolwaling is oriented east-west; any convenient access to Tibet is blocked by Gauri Shankar's hulking mass.

The first recorded Western visitor to the Rolwaling Valley was Edmund Hillary, who passed over the Tashi Lapsa in 1951 on the British Everest reconnaissance expedition. His view would have been much the same as Rolwaling's original settlers', except stone fences and rock shelters now dotted the landscape. As Hillary descended into the valley, he was setting foot into a place that still moved to the timeless rhythms of life untouched by the industrial age. In 1974, anthropologist Janice Sacherer visited the Rolwaling and undertook the first ethnological study of the Sherpa community there. She estimated the population to be two hundred individuals, and noted that battery-powered transistor radios had only recently arrived. "The most remarkable divergence from the social pattern of Khumbu," Sacherer wrote, "was the very large number of celibate monks." Rolwaling's historic religious sacredness was reinforced in modern times by a charismatic lama, who had converted many of Beding's young men to a monastic life. This was the same year Chhiring Dorje was born.

Chhiring's memories of childhood are of walking and hard work. Sherpa subsistence agriculture depends on exploiting the changes in altitude to support a variety of crops—potatoes could be planted first in Ramding, the lowest village, at three thousand meters, in late winter, then in Beding at thirty-six hundred meters in early spring, and then finally Na at forty-one hundred meters. Yaks could be grazed as high as five thousand meters. In many ways, the Sherpa farmers who cultivated the Rolwaling followed the same patterns that characterized medieval Europe, or worse: They lived in roughly built houses of dry stone masonry and hand-hewn timbers, and had no animals with which to till their fields (yaks are universally notorious for their animosity to the yoke). Small wonder that Chhiring tells me, "I didn't like being a farmer."

In 1990, at the age of sixteen, Chhiring took his first portering work in Solu Khumbu. With an uncle, he visited Kathmandu, then traveled to the Khumbu and trekked from Lukla to Namche to Island Peak, on to Everest base camp, then over the Cho La Pass into the Gokyo Valley, and finally back down to Lukla. His pay for carrying loads that often reached an excess of seventy pounds? A hundred and fifty rupees a day, or just over two dollars at the exchange rate at the time. After a month of backbreaking labor, Chhiring had earned perhaps seventy dollars. From Lukla, after the tourist portering work was done, Chhiring trekked all the way back to Kathmandu. Prices were cheap then, as Chhiring remembers: "One plate of dal bhat, from Lukla to Jiri, was twenty-five rupees [about thirty cents]." The next year, Chhiring got more work as a cook and porter on the trekking circuit around Annapurna. And that fall, he went to Everest.

Chhiring's uncle—his mother's brother—Sonam Tshering, had summited Everest with a French expedition on September 26, 1988. He was the first Sherpa from the Rolwaling to summit Everest, and became a pivotal figure not only in Chhiring's life, but the life of the entire village. Within two years, five more Rolwaling Sherpas had claimed the top of the world.* "He was a good guy—he taught me the technical systems; he said, 'Do this like this'"—Chhiring mimes with two hands tying a knot—"and also don't drink too much."

Sonam Tshering took young Chhiring Dorje under his wing and brought him on his Everest first expedition.

Everest *did* play an integral role in laying the foundation for what would happen in Pakistan—in every case, it was there that the relationships formed between the Sherpas and their Western counterparts. If it hadn't been for Everest, Chhiring Dorje, Pemba Gyalje and Jumik Bhote would never have been invited to K2.

In traditional Sherpa culture, there was a concept of a *zhindak*—a wealthy or powerful patron who takes a "small" person under his or her wing. As Sherry Ortner explains it, ". . . *zhindaks* do not directly bestow success—wealth, position, and so on—but only facilitate achieving it, helping the hero to help himself." The notion is tempered by the highly egalitarian nature of Sherpa society. Ortner goes on: "The junior part is not positioned as a child or a social inferior, but rather something more like a talented but disadvantaged protégé. In folktales, for instance, the junior party is usually a bright young man who is down through no fault

---

* Twenty years later, by the spring of 2010, the number of Rolwaling-born Everest summiteers has increased more than tenfold, to fifty-one.

of his own, but who needs some extra help and power to come back strongly and defeat those who are illegitimately besting him." For Chhiring, his uncle Sonam Tshering might have played the role of a *zhindak* through his adolescence. Sonam Tshering, in turn, benefited from his own close relationship with the up-and-coming Kiwi guide Rob Hall. In part, it was networks of personal contacts and friendships embodied by the notion of a *zhindak* that provided the means for whole villages like Rolwaling to evolve so rapidly from the near medieval conditions that Hillary observed in 1951.

In 1993, both Chhiring and Sonam Tshering returned to Everest. Sonam Tshering would be climbing on an all-Nepali team organized with the goal of getting the first Nepalese woman, Pasang Lhamu, to the summit. He got Chhiring a spot on the team as well. On April 22, Pasang Lhamu, Sonam Tshering, and three other Sherpas left the South Col bound for the summit. They succeeded, with Pasang Lhamu becoming in one stroke both the first Sherpani and the first Nepali woman to reach the top of Everest. It was Sonam Tshering's fifth Everest summit. Pasang Lhamu was extremely tired and possibly feeling the effects of altitude-related illness when she left the summit; it took her five hours to descend to the south summit (the distance normally takes only one hour). Now facing a crisis that would bear eerie similarities to the situation his mentor, Rob Hall, would face three years later, Sonam Tshering and another Sherpa bivouacked on the south summit with the stricken Pasang Lhamu while their two other companions descended to get help. The next morning, Sonam Tshering evidently sent the third Sherpa down with desperate orders to send up fresh climbing-Sherpas with oxygen bottles. Neither Sonam Tshering nor Pasang Lhamu was seen alive again.

Pasang Lhamu's success and subsequent death elevated her to the status of national hero in Nepal. Accusations that she was unprepared and inexperienced for Everest, that she was motivated by competition (there was a rival expedition composed of Indian and Nepali women also on the mountain that same season), that they had attempted the summit too early in the season (the typical summit window is late May)—all were swept under the rug in a national outpouring of pride. She was posthumously awarded the Tara Award by the king, had her face immortalized on a national stamp, and became a household name in Nepal. But today few remember Chhiring Dorje's uncle Sonam Tshering, the first man of Rolwaling to conquer Everest.

The years after Sonam Tshering's death were hard for Chhiring Dorje. He was still young, with a paltry mountaineering résumé, and it was difficult to find work. He was thrilled when a Norwegian team hired him the following autumn to attempt the West Ridge of Everest, but the expedition was abandoned when another Sherpa from Beding was killed. By then, one thing was clear to the aspiring mountain guide: To find regular employment, he needed to go where the work was. The original generation of Sherpa guides was culled from the ranks of coolies in Darjeeling, but now the work was in Kathmandu.

"The Sherpas of the Rolwaling," an anthropologist wrote in 1984, "who are in the first phase of adjustment to a tourist dominated economy, have not yet begun to establish households in Kathmandu and to spend the greater part of the year outside Rolwaling." Chhiring was a member of the very first generation of Rolwaling Sherpas to leave home.

In Kathmandu the year after the Norwegian expedition, Chhiring stopped in at a small Sherpa restaurant in Bhoda, the traditional Buddhist neighborhood in the city. He noticed an attractive young Sherpa woman who worked there, serving pots of steaming tea and making yak momos in the small kitchen. Her name was Dawa Phuti and she was from Namche. Chhiring began to visit the same restaurant as often as he could. They married in March of 1996, and later that same year welcomed their first child, a baby girl they named Namdu. In 1998, at the age of twenty-four, Chhiring reached the summit of Everest for the first time.

As the years passed and Chhiring became more established, the work slowly grew easier to find. Chhiring went to Manaslu, Cho Oyu, Shishapangma, and the south face of Lhotse with Japanese teams, and Pumori, Island Peak, and Ama Dablam with German expeditions. Then, on Everest in 2004, he met an American. His name was Eric Meyer.

Meyer remembers Chhiring clearly. "He was always smiling. . . . His connection to the mountain, to the life of being up on Everest, he just had this enormous self-confidence." Part of Chhiring's cheerfulness may have been due to the fact that he was not on Everest that year to work as a guide. Rather, he had been paid a small fee by a Western team to independently search the mountain for the camera that was carried by George Mallory and Sandy Irvine on their final bid to reach the summit in 1924. (Neither Englishman returned, and the mystery over whether or not they actually reached the top has endured ever since.)

Back in Kathmandu, after the expedition was over, Eric met up with Chhiring for dinner one night. He had become close friends with another Sherpa, Tenzi, as well, and now the American doctor told them both that if they ever wanted to come to the United States, he would help them any way he could. Chhiring told Eric that he was busy for the next year or two, but he would love to visit Steamboat Springs.

Three years later, after the Everest season was over, Chhiring and Dawa cleared customs and walked into the general arrivals hall at Denver International Airport. Eric clearly remembers the moment: Chhiring's eyes were wide; he pushed a luggage cart and scanned the waiting crowd with a look of growing apprehension. Then the Sherpa found Meyer waiting for him, and he broke into a wide grin.

Meyer had arranged for Chhiring and Dawa to stay at an affluent friend's second home. He also set him up with work on a concrete crew owned by a local schoolteacher, outdoorsman, and Everest summiteer, Matt Tredway.

By any standards, concrete is especially hard work: a double-walled structure of forms weighing forty-five pounds each must be carried and joined together to hold the wet material inside while it dries. Chhiring Dorje was one of Tredway's best employees ever. As he tells it, "At the time, it was the big boom. These kids, and I call anyone thirty and under a 'kid,' they didn't want to work hard. They could make seventeen bucks an hour at McDonald's. Chhiring, he full-on embraced it. . . . It was obvious he was intensely smart. After his first time building a footer or a slab, he knew what to do. He took ownership."

So Chhiring Dorje ended up on a blue-collar work crew of American climbers, doing what he had always done: trade sweat equity for high pay. When he flew home in November, five months after he arrived, Chhiring had bankrolled four or five times what he would have made in a typical Everest trip. There is a similarity here. Just as the Sherpas of Rolwaling had traditionally spread their economic activities over a wide swath of altitude and terrain, exploiting the changes in the landscape, Chhiring realized, as the millions of people applying for U.S. visas each year know, that a well-paying working-class job in America could afford his family an upper-class lifestyle in Nepal. By the summer of 2007, he and Dawa had two daughters: Namdu was eleven years old; Tenzing, seven. Both attended the Little Angel's School in Kathmandu—one of the premier boarding schools in the country.

One evening that summer, Chhiring visited Eric Meyer. Meyer looked at his friend and told him that he wanted to plan an expedition for the next summer to Pakistan, to K2. He asked Chhiring to join him.

At thirty-three years old, Chhiring had come farther in his life than his parents or anyone of their generation—even Sonam Tshering—might have imagined. With a formal education that ended when he was twelve years old, he now spoke Sherpa, Nepali, Tibetan, English, and Japanese, plus a smattering of Hindi and German. In a country where the average income was less than five hundred dollars, he was earning an annual income of more than fifteen thousand dollars, enough to provide for his family and educate his children.

Chhiring Dorje knew that he could make more money guiding on Everest. In fact, Meyer wasn't trying to hire Chhiring at all. He offered to help find sponsorship to pay the Sherpa's share of costs for the expedition, but Meyer didn't want Chhiring to be responsible for leading him. They would be equal partners, and Chhiring would get no guide's salary. But something else festered in Chhiring's psyche, something that maybe he didn't even completely understand. It was the same trait that many had noticed in Tenzing Norgay.

Matt Tredway, Chhiring Dorje's employer in Steamboat, remarked on this same hidden quality in his character. "I did get the sense that somehow he's got something to prove. . . . He wants to be a part of history." In a word, Chhiring Dorje shared with Tenzing Norgay a sense of destiny—a drive to achieve, to be successful and well-known, to become a "big" person, as a Sherpa might say.

"Yes," Chhiring said. "I want to go. But first, I need to talk to my family."

Pemba was away guiding, and the day after meeting Chhiring I left Kathmandu on my own trip to the mountains. It wasn't until I returned to the city five weeks later that I had the chance to finally meet him. Pemba insisted on inviting me to his home for dinner, though we had never met. He arrived at my hotel at six o'clock in the evening. He was right on time.

I watched as a man in stylish jeans, a puffy red down jacket, and a black helmet pulled into the courtyard of my hotel on a motorcycle. He gunned the engine, turning the bike in a tight circle so that it was facing out before coming to a stop. The helmet flipped off to reveal a square-cut, handsome face, skin the color of milky coffee, his hair jet-black and cleanly cropped. Pemba was leaner than Chhiring, but beneath the puffy jacket I could sense an extremely athletic build. The engine idled as he reached out to shake my hand in a casual greeting.

"Yes, it is good to meet you," he said. "I am Pemba." With no further introduction, he abruptly put his helmet back on, kicked up the bike stand, and motioned for me to get on behind him.

It was a twenty-minute ride to Pemba's house, a modest concrete duplex owned by his uncle beyond the Ring Road, northeast of the center of Kathmandu. As soon as we stepped inside the threshold of the door, a giggling blur streaked toward Pemba's leg. That, as I soon learned, was Lhakpa, Pemba's four-year-old daughter. Moments later, Pemba introduced me to his wife, Jammu, a lithe woman of thirty. I shook her hand, thanking her for having me for dinner, and presented her with a box containing four oversize pieces of chocolate cake I had bought at a Thamel bakery that afternoon. She eyed them curiously. "For dessert," I explained.

As Pemba motioned for me to take a seat on the living room couch, I noticed it was unusually dark inside their home. The living room was lit solely by two candles, while a kerosene lantern provided more working light in the kitchen. Jammu returned from the kitchen and set two beers down on the coffee table in front of us. A summer monsoon had destroyed a key hydroelectric plant in Nepal, Pemba told me, and months later the government still imposed thirty hours of rolling blackouts per week to conserve electricity.

I sipped at my beer and watched Lhakpa rampage around the living room, cheerfully throwing anything she could get her hands on at the floor. First to go was a runner of woven climbing rope that sat on the coffee table, then an empty candleholder and a stack of DVDs next to the TV. Then she reached for my glass. "Lhakpa!" Pemba raised his voice in consternation, but then he stopped, leaned back on the sofa next to me, and took a sip of beer. There wasn't a single crease on his forehead, or twitch in his eye, or any other trace of parental angst. Pemba seemed completely at peace with the world.

So this was the man who was responsible for rescuing both Marco Confortola and Wilco van Rooijen, the only two survivors of the eight who bivied above the Bottleneck. This was also the man who had allegedly assumed de facto leadership of the advance rope-fixing team on summit day, and made the decision to rope fifteen summiteers together at eighty-five hundred meters on the descent in order to safely lead everyone to the top of the fixed ropes.

Pemba's English is excellent, but unlike with Chhiring Dorje, whom you could almost describe as a chatterbox, I found it hard to make small talk with him. An air of calm dignity surrounded the Sherpa as he sat playing with his daughter in the candlelit room and his wife prepared supper in the other room. I was hesitant to interrupt this quiet life to ask him to tell the story of how eleven men met their deaths. Pemba, for his part, didn't press me on why I was so interested in K2, or what the purpose of my visit was. Other journalists were in contact with him, I knew, and so I assumed this was just part of the drill. Or perhaps he knew better than to jump right to the matter of interest. Chhiring Dorje talked about it with such ease—even humor—but K2 was not a subject for family dinner conversation.

Instead, I awkwardly pulled out my digital camera and showed him pictures from my most recent expedition. I knew Kangtega was not far from where he had been born. His eyes lit up. "Ah, Kangtega," he said, nodding his head with interest. "And you made the summit?" Yes. He let out a low whistle. "Very difficult, no?" He edged closer on the couch to see some of the photos.

Pemba Gyalje met Gerard McDonnell in 2003, on the south side of Everest. It was Gerard McDonnell's first expedition to Nepal, and he was part of an all-Irish team organized by a professional adventurer named Pat Falvey. Pemba Gyalje had worked with Falvey before, and now he was hired on as sirdar of the expedition. As Gerard approached Everest early that spring, following the well-traveled trekking route north from Lukla, he observed with fascination modern Sherpa culture.

"It was the first time I'd ever had anything done for me," McDonnell would recall later. "These porters—it was the first stage I had to get used to somebody carrying my stuff." Later in the expedition, while climbing on the mountain, Gerard noticed that one of his teammate's boots had come unlaced. He bent down to tie it for her, only to have a Sherpa rap him firmly on the backside. The message was clear, but Gerard ignored it and continued to tie the knot. The Sherpa hit him again, harder. "He said, 'Come on, move along. That's my job,'" Gerard would say with a disbelieving chuckle. "The Irish sense of humor and the Sherpa sense of humor seem to work well together," he added.

Gerard, Pat Falvey, and two other teammates left Camp IV on the South Col in the middle of the night, but a fierce plume of snow raked the summit pyramid. They turned back and returned to camp by dawn. They chose to wait a day, the wind subsided, and they went for the top. Just above the Hillary Step, only an hour from the summit, Gerard and another Sherpa, Pemba Rinji, meet Pemba Gyalje, their sirdar. Pemba Gyalje was on his way down, having been on the advance rope-fixing team that morning, and then escorted another client, Mick Murphy, to the top. At that moment, as they stood waiting for the line of climbers on the Hillary Step to clear, Gerard decided to switch to a fresh oxygen bottle. An obvious and disconcerting hiss came from the seal when he screwed the regulator hose to the cylinder. Somehow ice must have formed between the threads.

Pemba Gyalje immediately took over the situation. Gerard McDonnell watched as Pemba Gyalje issued several rapid-fire commands to Pemba Rinji. Pemba Rinji protested at first, and then begrudgingly did as he was told: He passed over his functioning system to McDonnell, assumed the Irishman's faulty set, and descended immediately. "It was obvious it had developed into an argument. . . . Pemba Rinji, to my mind, he was on the summit. But he didn't actually stand on the summit," Gerard recalled. Instead, Pemba Gyalje turned around and accompanied the Irishman to the top.

On the summit, Gerard was distracted by the fact that Pemba Rinji had been given the malfunctioning oxygen system. He and Pemba Gyalje spent only a few minutes on top, and hurried down. "Sure enough, when we caught up to him he was climbing very slowly," Gerard said later. "I took off my mask and said, 'Look, let's share. . . .' He point-blank absolutely refused—there was no way he was going to take it. That's when I insulted his mother." Pemba Rinji finally relented.

Through his goggles and face mask, Gerard McDonnell observed with incredulousness the spectacle of Everest's summit ridge on a busy day. "Another thing that struck me was the amount of people who looked to be in trouble, moving slowly and stopping to rest. I was struck by all these people who looked like they needed to be rescued. I was like—who do we help here?" Then Gerard and Pemba Gyalje spotted Pat Falvey descending in front of them. "Pat was in a bad way," Gerard later said. Pemba Gyalje tied a rope to Falvey and short-roped him over the south summit. Then Gerard took over the task of helping his altitude-impaired teammate down safely. Always conscious of the people around him, Gerard knew that Pemba must have been exhausted from leading the advance team that morning. "Pemba Gyalje had a big day under his belt," Gerard said. "I knew he had to be getting pretty tired." Working together, Pemba Gyalje, Pemba Rinji, and Gerard McDonnell were able to get Falvey back to Camp IV, though they were almost stopped by an unexpected bank of clouds that washed over the South Col, reducing visibility to three or four meters.

The minor incident with Gerard's oxygen system was quickly forgotten, but at the time each man perceived a slightly different reality. To Gerard, the decision to send Pemba Rinji down so close to the summit seemed a little cruel. To Pemba Rinji, not being allowed to continue with his client to the summit was a slight from his sirdar—perhaps complicated by the issue of who would receive a summit bonus at the end of the expedition. For Pemba Gyalje, it was just another day at the office. Each time he was presented with a problem—a malfunctioning oxygen system at the top of the Hillary Step, or a failing client at 8,750 meters—he knew he had to take decisive action. Above eight thousand meters, Pemba Gyalje knew that the clock was ticking. It may not have been fair, but it aptly illustrates a controlled, conservative guiding style.

Gerard was impressed by Pemba's climbing skills, and Pemba was more than a little surprised by Gerard's own sense of responsibility and partnership. By the end of the expedition, they had become especially close friends.

Dinner at Pemba's was traditional Nepali fare: thick lentil broth, stewed buffalo meat, steamed vegetables, and a bowl overflowing with fresh white rice. The four of us sat down at a small table in the kitchen, and Jammu made a show of serving me first. I waited for everyone to get their plate and then lifted my fork to begin. Pemba, I suddenly noticed, had rolled up his sleeves and was busy mixing up the food on his plate with his right hand. There were no utensils set in front of him.

I rolled up my sleeve, picked up a handful of rice and a piece of meat, and raised my hand to my lips. A few kernels of rice fell onto the table, and a trickle of juice from the meat dribbled down my chin.

Jammu's face reddened in horror, and she immediately got up, went to the kitchen, and brought me another set of utensils. "Please," she said, "you may use these." Pemba and Lhakpa watched with interest.

"No, thank you, Jammu," I said. "I am happy to eat with my hands, thank you." Jammu sat back down, still looking slightly mortified that her American guest wouldn't behave like an American. Pemba shrugged at no one in particular.

Lhakpa, who seemed more interested in piling her food into small mounds on her plate and trying to spill my beer, kept the three of us on our toes throughout the meal. Jammu periodically leaned over the table to clean errant food from her daughter's dimpled cheeks, while Pemba gently scolded in Nepali. Lhakpa would merely laugh and push a handful of rice under Pemba's nose. None of his commands had the slightest effect on the kid, and I suddenly realized that this mighty mountaineer, a six-time Everest summiteer who had dragged injured men down mountains like sacks of potatoes, was putty in Lhakpa's grubby little hands.

Halfway through dinner, the lights came back on. Lhakpa could be contained no longer and exploded from her chair to raise havoc in the living room. Pemba watched her leave, smiling to himself, and Jammu rose to prepare dessert. Pemba turned to me. "And do you like to rock climb?" he asked. Throughout dinner, it was the first time he had broached the subject of climbing.

"Absolutely, yes," I replied.

Jammu placed a plate of apple and pear slices on the table between us. There was no sign of my sticky chocolate cake slices. "We have two rock-climbing cliffs, here in the Kathmandu area," he said. "They are equipped sport-climbing destinations. One is nine kilometers from Thamel. Would you like to go?"

From Pemba's home village of Karikola, a day's march south of Lukla, it is a week to ten days of hard trekking to reach Beding, where Chhiring Dorje grew up. Both men had moved to Kathmandu as young adults, accumulated significant Everest experience over the years, and possessed solid language skills. They also had had the chance to travel and train in Europe and North America. They were among the top Sherpa sirdars of their generation, and made top dollar. Both were thirty-four years old when they arrived in K2 base camp in the late spring of 2008. And incidentally, the mountain had not been climbed without supplemental oxygen by a Sherpa.

On May 29, Pemba Gyalje and Gerard McDonnell dropped their packs on the pocked surface of the Godwin Austen Glacier. In one week since leaving Skardu, they were already filthy, sweat stained, and badly in need of a fresh round of laundry. Above them, the pyramidal south face of K2 loomed in silence, its features highlighted by the growing afternoon shadows. Their teammates meandered around the uneven glacial surface, searching for flat spots where they might pitch their tents; they could see a broken line of porters stretching back across the Godwin Austen Glacier toward the Broad Peak base camp. In ones and twos they arrived, adding their loads to the growing mound of dust-blasted duffel bags and equipment that lay in a heap. No other tents were pitched on the lateral moraine that would be their base camp home for the next three months. The Norit expedition was the first team to reach K2 that year.

In his well-worn duffel bags bound for base camp, Pemba carried several tightly wrapped packages of brightly colored prayer flags. According to the Tibetan lunar calendar, it is bad luck to begin anything serious on a Saturday. Pemba borrowed Gerard's sat phone and dialed Jammu in Kathmandu. Jammu, in turn, had talked to their lama, requesting instructions on behalf of her husband. The information was relayed to K2 base camp: Thursday, June 5, between eight and ten a.m., would be a favorable date and time to begin.

One week later, at the appointed hour, Pemba knelt at the newly constructed stone altar. He removed his MP3 player from a pocket, pressed play, and then slipped it between two stones in the foundation. A collection of crampons, ice axes and helmets lay in bundles against the cobbled altar. Out of a small speaker, calming Tibetan chants rose through the morning air. Head bowed forward, Pemba silently asked for blessings. Gerard McDonnell and his teammates looked on solemnly.

The prayer flags, hanging from a central flagpole, whispered above their heads.

An hour after the puja was over, Pemba, Gerard, and a third teammate, Court Hagens, were hiking toward the start of the SSE Spur on their first foray up the mountain.* Wilco, feeling it would be a shame to waste such good weather, had begun fixing rope and already established Camp I.

Chhiring Dorje, Eric Meyer, and the American team did not reach the mountain until June 26. By then, small clusters of tents dotted base camp, and more were being set up every day. A team of four personable Norwegians arrived a day or two behind them. Among their luggage was a small muddy goat with tightly twisted horns. It walked on four legs, still very much alive, with a leash that attached it to one of the cooks.

In base camp the porters were paid and then a crowd of onlookers—most of them Pakistani—circled around the creature. A word was muttered and Rolf Bae ran off to fetch his own knife. He handed it to one of the cooks. Fred Sträng trained his video camera on what transpired next. The blade glinted in the mountain light and then it plunged into the beast as another man held it down. Everyone would be eating meat tonight.

The first couple of days in base camp were hard for Chhiring Dorje. The slaughter had upset him. "This was not polite to the mountain," he told me, shaking his head. Most Buddhists are squeamish about taking an animal's life, even slaughtering livestock for food. Chicken, yak, and mutton are part of Sherpas' traditional diet, but they try at all costs to avoid being party to any killing themselves, normally by purchasing butchered meat from Tibetans or neighboring Nepali tribes. But in the Rolwaling Valley, the Sherpa community took the Buddha's teaching particularly seriously. In 2002, the Lama Nawang Chokling of Beding gompa went so far as to issue the following statement in a public letter to visitors:

---

* Court Hagens would later leave base camp to return home before the start of the summit push.

We Sherpas of Rolwaling are proud of our heritage as a
"beyul"—a sacred valley established by Guru Rinpoche
himself. One of our most important traditions is the
absolute prohibition of hunting and slaughter in our
valley. However, some trekking groups have been buying
livestock from our villagers and killing them right here.
Of course, the purchase price is a big temptation for a
few of our poor people, but the killing is extremely
offensive to most of us. We would request that all
agencies please instruct your staff not to purchase any
livestock in Rolwaling.

Chhiring also faced some awkward situations as he tried to establish
a rapport with his teammates. Soon after they arrived in base camp, all
members of the American international expedition pitched in to erect
their mess tent. As usual, Chhiring was working harder than anyone,
excavating a flat floor and cobbling rocks together into rough walls. Born
and raised in a village built predominantly of dry-stone masonry, Chhiring knew a thing or two about working with stone. Then Mike Farris, the
American leader, barked an order at him—"Chhiring, no, don't do it like
that!"

It was a tiny spat, the sort of minor personality difference that occurs
every day on an expedition. But Chhiring didn't know what to do. He
didn't even know his own feelings about being on K2. When Eric Meyer
went and knocked on Chhiring's tent fly later that afternoon, he found
his friend dismayed, feeling sad, and ready to quit the climb before it
even started. It cheered him up a little to be able to visit with Pemba and
the four climbing-Sherpas working for the Korean expedition. Just having the chance to speak a little Nepali felt good. The Korean Sherpas—
actually not Sherpas, but Bhotes from the village of Hungong below
Makalu—were nice guys, young, strong, and eager to make names for
themselves as competent guides.

"They were . . . very hungry," Chhiring would say.

The morning after dinner at Pemba's, I dashed off a quick story to the *Huffington Post* praising both him and Chhiring for their bravery and quiet humility. "It is clear that both men are far too humble to consider what they did that extraordinary," I wrote. "Even so, the cynic in me couldn't help but think that if these guys were from Europe or the States, they'd probably have big-money endorsement opportunities, get invited on *Oprah*, and have their faces on the cover of *People* magazine. As things turned out, you have to read the fine print to hear about them."

While walking back to my hostel, dodging rickshaws and an extremely persistent street vendor hell-bent on selling me either tiger-balm salve or a pocketknife, I spotted a familiar face on the street. It was American climber Steve House and his Slovenian partner, Marko Prezelj, two old acquaintances from base camps past. We chatted casually for a minute about our respective trips that fall. They had been just two valleys away from Kangtega, attempting the west face of Makalu, a truly futuristic objective on the world's fifth highest peak. We agreed to meet up for drinks later that evening.

Around nine p.m., Marko, Steve, and I piled into a dimly lit reggae bar located on the second floor of a concrete tenement building. We were soon joined by two more American guides, Fabrizio Zangrilli and Vince Anderson, and British climber Nick Bullock. Two sets of speakers six feet high were ludicrously crammed into the small room, which lodged the typical collection of Thamel characters: a pair of British trekkers in rugby shirts talking with a gaggle of Australian girls taking their gap year before university; a hippie woman in a hand-sewn dress dancing by herself; a dreadlocked bartender with a constantly wandering eye. We removed our shoes and crawled awkwardly around a table placed on top of a recessed bed of raised cushions. I ended up sitting next to Marko.

Steve ordered double tumblers of blended scotch on the rocks, and we settled in. It didn't take me long to start talking about the K2 disaster. Marko took a swig of his drink and glared at me. Fabrizio had attempted

K2 twice himself, and knew many of the climbers on the mountain that year.

"Hugues—he was a great guy," he told me, shaking his head, "but he was . . . *so slow.*" In 2007, Fabrizio had shared the SSE spur with Hugues D'Aubarède, who had hired two Pakistanis to accompany him. As Fabrizio described the odd relationship between the Frenchman and his two employees: "He was really tied to them on the mountain, not in a literal sense, but because they set up the camps and carried the heavy loads. Hugues liked to brag about all the climbing he had done in the Alps with big-name guys like J. C. Lafaille, but that was all a guide-client relationship. He wasn't part of the decision-making process. But on K2, from what I saw, he was trying to play that role and make the decisions and strategy for his team."

Marko leaned forward. "This eight-thousand-meter collecting," he said, half shouting above the thumping Bob Marley remix, "it is boring climbing. There is no imagination."

If anyone was entitled to think that what happened on K2 that summer was the most absurd, silliest boondoggle of a climb, it was Marko Prezelj. In 1991, Marko reached the south summit of Kangchenjunga, the world's third-highest peak, in a pure alpine-style climb. The ascent launched a remarkable Himalayan career, one defined by the difficulty of the objectives he chooses and the means by which he then tries to climb them. Marko has summited a few eight-thousand-meter peaks, but he has no interest in attaining Messner's eight-thousand-meter crown for its own sake. What's most important to Marko is that he climbs alone, with one or two partners, on steep technical ground without relying on fixed ropes. The well-choreographed summit-day routine on Everest weighs against Marko's state-of-the-art ascents like the World Wrestling Federation stands up to a back-alley knife fight. Marko, I knew, would never be caught dead clipped to an ascender climbing the Bottleneck.

"Sherpas, eh?" Marko asked, his Slavic brow furrowed. "You cannot trust them." He spoke with the finality you acquire only after twenty years of expeditioning, the tone beneath his curt Eastern European accent telling me the issue was not up for debate.

I demurred, saying something like they were the only ones I could trust.

"No," Marko said, throwing back his drink and setting it down hard enough that the ice cubes rattled in the glass. "You cannot trust them because they will only tell you what they think you want to hear."

8

A CRITICAL SITUATION

The second week in July, the winds came.

A high-pressure system settled over western China to the north of the mountain; warm air from the seasonal monsoon low above the Indian Ocean set up to the south. The opposing systems met along the high divide of the Karakoram Range. Like tightly drawn lines on a contour map, the pressure gradient steepened. Pemba's prayer flags fluttered and snapped above the rippling base camp tents as day after day hurricane-strength winds beat across the upper mountain.

For the men and women hoping to reach K2's summit, the bad weather served to realign their schedules. By the beginning of July, only the Koreans and the Norit team were sufficiently acclimatized to mount a summit push as soon as conditions cooperated. Other expeditions, like the two international groups, had more recently arrived and still needed time to properly prepare. But as the days ran together into weeks of impotent ambition, nearly every team in base camp decided they would go for the summit the first chance they had.

The details of the "base camp meetings" have been one of the most talked-about aspects of the disaster. Minor discrepancies and differences among the different published accounts make knowing exactly what was decided—and, more important, what was understood by all parties—almost impossible. But most of those who were present in base camp recollect that it was Kim Jae-su, the leader of the Korean expedition, who first organized a meeting with the other teams who would be going for the summit.

Throughout that summer, Kim had been an enigmatic personality in base camp. He carried himself with a rigid air that was frequently interpreted by his neighbors as being standoffish or somehow disdainful of others. Kim's projected persona was certainly complicated by his incomplete command of English, but there is no doubt he believed he was most qualified to lead the advanced team. In a translated interview conducted after the climb, he would say, "When it comes to equipment, we were the most well equipped team among all the teams . . . and more particularly, I was the one who had the most experience among [all] climbers at that time." Asked by one of the Americans when they would pack up and head home, Kim responded that they planned to stay as long as it took to reach the summit.

Kim did have a practical reason to feel that his team should be in charge. The Korean's climbing-Sherpas had already single-handedly fixed the Abruzzi Ridge as high as Camp III. Though relations between teams in base camp that summer were almost entirely friendly, many would mention an occasional, unspoken sense of condescension from Norit or the Koreans. On the other side of the coin, it is also fair to say that both Wilco van Rooijen and Kim Jae-su, whose expeditions had invested by far the most time and energy in preparing the SSE Spur and the Abruzzi Ridge, respectively, felt a little chagrined that now a host of smaller teams were going to piggyback on their hard work all the way to the summit.

Such was the subtext of the crucial base camp meetings, which began the second week in July, in preparations for a predicted weather window on the eighteenth of July. Kim's position from the outset was that his team should lead the advance party, tasked with the all-important job of fixing rope up the Bottleneck and the Diagonal early on summit day. He planned to provide four men, Hwang Dong-jin, his deputy leader, as well as his next-best man, Park Kyeong-hyo, and two of their climbing-Sherpas, all using supplemental oxygen, to form the nucleus of the group. The Serbians' lead Pakistani guide, Shaheen Baig, who had summited K2 in 2004, was also instrumental in forming the plan and was to be the other acknowledged leader of the advance party. Baig spoke excellent English and many of the other climbers looked to him to help answer the numerous logistical questions involved in planning the climb. As Chris Klinke remembers it: "Mr. Hwang was nominally the leader, but that was because the Koreans seemed big into official titles. Shaheen was the one we all trusted to really be in charge."

On July 16 they meet again in the Serbs' base camp tent for what would be their most in-depth discussion to date. Team leaders present were Wilco van Rooijen, Marco Confortola, Mike Farris, Kim Jae-su, and Milivoj Erdeljan. The Serbian liaison officer called the meeting to order with a brief prayer and salutation. By rough consensus, it had been decided prior to the meeting that each of the other expeditions would contribute its strongest man to the advance team.

The Italians, Marco Confortola and Roberto Manni, indicated that they would be sending their Pakistani HAP. Though they did not say so in the meeting, they were beginning to have serious misgivings about the capabilities of their employees. Before the meeting, Marco had approached Kim and requested help from their climbing-Sherpas carrying the Italians' rope to Camp IV because their own hired Pakistanis seemed weak and unreliable. Karim Meherban, another Pakistani who had been on the mountain the year before working for Hugues D'Aubarède, and was back with him in 2008, also agreed to join the advance team on behalf of the French international expedition. Pemba Gyalje made seven—the Sherpa knew he was the strongest of the Norit team and the most experienced in these matters. It was, he said later, "the polite thing to volunteer."

Most present at the meetings believed that the American international expedition would likewise contribute Chhiring Dorje to the advance team—an assumption that belied the fact that Chhiring Dorje, like

Pemba, planned to climb without oxygen and was an equal team member, not a paid employee. "Chhiring sort of said he'd do it, then decided he wouldn't do it, then said he'd decide once he got up there," Mike Farris remembers. For his own part, Chhiring says that he decided he would prefer to climb with his other teammates.

It was Sheehan Baig's recommendation, as well as the general consensus in Norit and among most of the other teams, that six hundred meters of line was adequate to fix the Bottleneck and the Diagonal. American Chris Warner, who summited in 2007, agrees that amount should do the job. According to the notes of the July sixteenth meeting, the agreement hashed out was that each expedition would provide a portion of the equipment: four hundred meters of rope from the Dutch team, two hundred meters of rope from the Italian team, and two hundred meters of rope from the Korean team for reserve purposes. The Koreans and the Italians would each supply fifty bamboo wands, and the Americans would bring ten ice screws and several spools of fishing line to tie between the wands, making it easier to navigate on the low-angle Shoulder.

But then Kim Jae-su spoke up. The Korean leader said that he would prefer to use more rope—at least an additional two hundred meters above what the others deemed to be the critical technical section of the route to the summit, and possibly more below, too. Several other expedition leaders, including Wilco, expressed the opinion that they didn't think that much was needed. It was finally decided that the Koreans could fix as much additional line as they wish, *so long as they transported the extra supplies up the mountain.* According to records of the meeting, Kim said that was fine by him, so long as his expedition's climbing-Sherpas fixed from Camp IV to the summit, and the Pakistani HAPs were responsible for fixing the route from Camp III to Camp IV, which had not been fully prepared prior to the final weather window.

During the meetings, other details were discussed as well: who would be responsible for collecting the gear at Camp IV, and fixing each portion of the Bottleneck and the Diagonal. Later, Pemba said he expressed some dismay that they assumed they could micromanage the decisions within the advance rope-fixing team—deciding every last question while drinking tea in a base camp tent. "We must decide only in Camp IV. We need flexibility," he urged. "With eight members of the trailbreaking party, the leaders should be changed every fifty meters, to keep men fresh, always. The advance trailbreaking team must all meet and speak to one another."

These words, the advice of a seven-time veteran of advance rope-fixing parties on summit day of Mount Everest, went largely ignored. Pemba knew from experience that the ultimate success of the plan would depend not on strategy but on the tactics: how quickly and efficiently the advance team knew their jobs and could work together. Yet none of the Korean climbing-Sherpas, nor Chhiring Dorje nor Shaheen Baig, for that matter, were physically present for all of the meetings; the plan for summit day was mostly crafted and agreed upon by the expedition leaders—who would not personally accompany the advance team.

Nevertheless, it appeared to be a sound strategy on paper, assuming everyone held up their end of the bargain. "No one was to blame," Mike Farris said later. "But different people came away from the meetings with different assumptions. . . . It was good to have a plan, but it seemed like it might be hard to execute."

In the following ten days, several more meetings were held, but never in my own research did I find a single confirmed instance where the entire advance team met together.

At ten p.m. on July 31, 2008, Pemba Gyalje emerged from his tent in Camp IV. It was pitch-black and the snow crunched underfoot. It was time to get going.

But where were the other members of the advance team? Success hinged on efficiently preparing the route ahead of the mass of climbers who would shortly follow behind them. The 1996 Everest disaster was precipitated in part by the failure of the advance team to finish fixing line above the south summit. On K2, according to Pemba, the plan was to meet at ten and leave no later than midnight, while the main body of climbers would depart camp around two a.m.

Pemba trudged around camp, knocking on ice-wreathed tent flies, the halo from his headlamp searching for coils of rope, ice screws, and snow pickets among the packs scattered outside. "It's good weather; let's go," Pemba called. A few voices answered in broken English, but everyone was still in their tents, still waking up. The minutes ticked past. Pemba shouted louder. One by one, the other members of the advance team assembled outside. Pakistani Muhammad Hussain of the Serbian team eventually appeared from his tent, then Mohammad Ali from the Italians. They were joined by Jumik Bhote, the young sirdar of the Korean team, and Pasang Lama, his teammate.

But the two men who were expected to lead the group, Shaheen Baig and Hwang Dong-jin, had still failed to show themselves. From one of the Pakistanis, Pemba learned distressing news: Shaheen Baig had become sick at Camp II, and returned to base camp. And Hwang Dong-jin and Kim Jae-su, who had adamantly claimed the leadership of advance team, lay incommunicative in their tent.

The folly of their plan, which had been designed with academic precision during the base camp meetings, slowly dawned on Pemba. "The Koreans said our climbing leader is very experienced, and he can do everything," he would ruefully remark. "And so we designated Hwang as team leader for the trailbreaking party. Everybody said, 'Yeah, if he is a good climber, then okay.' But that is completely wrong. It was very, very difficult, because in base camp all the majority of people said, Why not? They can do it; the Korean climbers, the Pakistani climbers said, 'We are strong—why not?' But when everybody got to CIV, everybody was . . . flat."

Multiple factors had laid the groundwork for the near total breakdown in leadership among the advance team. The expedition leaders who attended the planning sessions took Kim's and Hwang's qualifications at face value, a dubious decision that was augmented by the language barrier and the fact that the Norit team, ascending a different route until Camp IV, had no chance to observe their abilities on the mountain prior to summit day. Likewise, no one had stopped to critically assess whether the Pakistanis had the necessary experience to follow through with their obligations, though they had outwardly seemed eager to take charge. There was an underlying sense that both Koreans and Pakistanis were anxious to participate in the advance team to win the respect and recognition of the Westerners whom they shared the mountain with, some survivors would observe later. And those Westerners, knowing that summit day would be a grueling trial under the best of circumstances, appeared only too happy to let them have the job.

On balance, the advance team was marginally qualified from the start for the task at hand. Combined with two more unanticipated developments—the illness that forced Shaheen Baig to descend, and the freak windstorms on the ascent to Camp IV, which delayed the climb by a day and sapped everyone's energy more than they were willing to admit—it was enough to nearly sabotage the summit climb before anyone had even left high camp. If he hadn't woken everyone up, according to Pemba, no one would have left camp.

As the Sherpa searched for the necessary men and equipment, another headlamp appeared. A voice speaking in lilted English called out, "Hello—I am Alberto, from the Spanish expedition." Pemba had never seen Alberto Zerain in base camp. His team held permits for both K2 and Broad Peak, and spent most of the summer acclimatizing on the easier mountain. With a promising weather forecast, Zerain switched objectives at the opportune moment. After two days ascending the lower Abruzzi Ridge, he left Camp III at ten p.m. and, climbing in lightweight style without so much as a backpack, arrived in Camp IV only two hours later. Zerain was eager to continue, but waited for the advance team to organize themselves.

Even counting the welcome addition of the Basque alpinist, the advance team was still short on manpower. Thrust by circumstance into taking charge of the group, Pemba knew he needed help. Who he turned to reveals where his trust ultimately lay. Pemba went straight to Chhiring Dorje.

For the past week, Chhiring had vacillated over whether to join the advance team. Mike Farris had broached the subject in base camp, but it was clear none of the other members of the American international team planned to participate. Like Pemba, Chhiring was going to climb without supplemental oxygen, which would severely curtail his capabilities on summit day. Moreover, Chhiring wanted to be with his friends. On July 25, the day of the last meeting in base camp before the summit push, Chhiring had decided not to go with the advance team. Now Pemba pressed Chhiring to join them.

"We're missing two members of the trailbreaking party, and rope, too," he said, crouched next to the door of the tent Chhiring shared with Eric Meyer. "I need some help."

Both Chhiring and Pemba had come to K2 as equal members of their teams. But now, on far and away the most important day of the climb, they both found themselves pressed into doing the same thing they were paid handsome wages to do on Everest, using supplemental oxygen. Only this was K2, and they would be climbing with only their own lungs to propel them.

Chhiring sat up in his sleeping bag and began to get dressed.

Pasang Lama is slightly built, five-foot-six in height, with a peach-fuzz mustache, a broad face, and searching eyes. He's twenty-six years old, and he is not married.

The first time we met, he had not seen any of the feature articles about the disaster that were plastered across newsstands across Europe and North America. I showed him the *Men's Journal* article, watching as he stared at the glossy images and delicately flipped through each page. His fingers traced across Chris Klinke's photo, and I pointed out the second dot from the top that was most likely him. The interview quietly unraveled into unanswered silence. I suggested he take the magazine to read, and we could talk later.

A week had passed by, and now he earnestly returned the magazine to me. Pasang Lama's English is quite good, and I asked him what he thought of the story.

"It is okay, but there are some things," he told me, flipping to page seventy-one.

The Koreans and their porters were next on the summit.

"They call us porters," Pasang Lama said. "That's not right."

Like Pemba and Chhiring, he was stylishly outfitted in jeans and a black puffy down coat. I noticed an MP3 player tucked into his pants pocket, and headphones snaked up underneath his jacket and hung loosely around his neck. He would easily fit in at the local brew pub in any ski town across North America or Europe.

Pasang Lama was born in Hungong, a village of four thousand people, situated in the Arun river valley. That's two valleys to the east of the Solu Khumbu, right beneath Makalu. He moved to Kathmandu when he was eighteen years old, and, like Pemba Gyalje and Chhiring Dorje, he told me that he was brought into the mountain tourism industry by a sympathetic uncle and aunt. They took him on a job to Manaslu in 2002, which was where Pasang Lama got his first taste of what happens on a mountain expedition. He spent several years doing general portering and trekking jobs, and finally broke into the serious high-altitude work in 2006.

That same year, he summited Everest for the first time. It was practically the first time he had worn crampons. He was twenty-three years old. In the two years leading up to the K2 expedition, Pasang Lama climbed Everest again from Tibet, plus a few six-thousand-meter peaks, and attended a two-week mountaineering course held annually at the Khumbu Climbing Center in the village of Phortse each February.

"At the Khumbu Climbing Center, we try not only to promote skills that are important for professional guiding work, but also to inspire Nepalis as their own personal climbers," says Conrad Anker, the director of the program, which is funded by the Alex Lowe Charitable Trust. "It's a blast to go out climbing with our students, just for fun. You'd be amazed to see how quickly their abilities progress."

"Since the Khumbu Climbing School, I have good ice-climbing technique," Pasang Lama said confidently, and in his voice I heard something more. It was the casual, self-assured echo of any young mountain guide the world over, who knows he is fit and strong and does not believe he can fall.

Sometime between twelve thirty and one a.m. (recollections vary), the advance team shouldered their packs and departed Camp IV. Eight tiny splashes of light began to inch up the Shoulder toward K2's final defenses. Under any circumstance, climbing by headlamp is a surreal experience. The breathtaking panoramas and staggering relief that are a climber's constant backdrop during daylight hours disappear, while objects at close range appear in curious detail. Time moves slower. Shadows spiral and twist across the surface of the snow with each movement of the head.

For the first hundred meters, there were several bamboo wands that Marco Confortola had placed the afternoon before to guide them. But they ended pitifully close to camp. Rolling hillocks of névé stretched endlessly on. The cumulative result of the windy, predominantly dry weather pattern of the preceding month was that large portions of the route—virtually everything that was exposed to the wind—was blasted into a glassy sheen of hard névé snow and alpine ice. Come what may, summit day would be played out in particularly unforgiving conditions.

Conferring among themselves before they left camp, the team had agreed that Muhammad Hussain, the Pakistani guide who worked for the Serbian expedition, should lead the first section of the climb. Hussain had summited K2 in 2004, and presumably knew when to begin fixing rope, and where existing anchors among the rocks on the edge of the Bottleneck couloir might be found. Only half an hour above camp, he stopped to fix the first rope.

Pasang Lama, who was following closest to Hussain, believed that the crevasse danger on the moderately sloped area warranted the protection. And hadn't his employer, Mr. Kim, specifically stipulated that they begin fixing ropes below the Bottleneck? Pemba and Chhiring, who were slightly farther behind, could only stop and hope that Hussain knew what he was doing. Moreover, in the pitch-black of the moonless night, it was impossible to judge how much distance they had covered and how much more terrain remained before the start of the Bottleneck. They kept hiking, and more ropes kept appearing out of the darkness.

Meanwhile, back at Camp IV, the first climbers of the main group were beginning to pile out of their frosted tents, strap on their crampons, and follow behind. Less than an hour separated the leading elements of the main party from the advance team.

The beam from Pasang Lama's headlamp softened in front of him. He noticed the gray stain of predawn light seeping into the sky as the advance team arrived at the base of the Bottleneck couloir. The usable light brought clearer focus to their predicament.

Both Pasang Lama and Jumik Bhote were under the impression from their employer, Kim Jae-su, that they should fix most of the route—not just six hundred meters of line in the Bottleneck and the Diagonal, but also additional rope above and below the most critical section, as Kim had asserted in the base camp meetings. Indeed, as was agreed, the Korean team had carried extra line up the mountain for that purpose. The problem began the day before, on the climb up from Camp III to Camp IV. As had also been decided during the base camp meetings, and is confirmed by Pasang Lama, the responsibility for fixing this portion of the Abruzzi Ridge was delegated to the contingent of professional Pakistanis involved in the summit push. But as the Korean team ascended toward the high camp on July 31, they found the route only minimally equipped. Part of the issue was that the terrain on this section of the mountain is glaciated snow climbing—depending on one's comfort level with an ice ax and crampons, it should have been safely navigable without fixed lines. This evidently had been the Pakistanis' judgment, and so the route was left almost entirely unfixed. The Koreans embraced a far more conservative approach, and promptly told their climbing-Sherpas to fix this portion of the route. Thus, the additional line they had brought with them for summit day was used before getting to Camp IV.

When the advance rope-fixing team regrouped at dawn, Chhiring Dorje estimates that Hussain had fixed more than four hundred meters of line; only two hundred meters remained for the Bottleneck and the traverse. It was clearly not enough. Pemba and Pasang took over the lead while Chhiring and Jumik turned around and descended to remove rope from below. Pasang Lama carried in his pack one section of line he had planned to save in reserve, but now he uncoiled it and began to lead up the beginning of the couloir. Now the first rays of direct sunlight caught the top of the serac wall looming overhead, and the summit of Broad Peak glowed behind them.

Pemba stretched two more rope lengths up the gully. As the Bottleneck steepened, the conditions deteriorated. Climbing moderate ice is a technically easy though unforgiving process. With one ax, Pemba moved deliberately, placing the front points of each crampon carefully. He could not fall. Now the golden hues of alpine light washed over them, and a line of more than twenty climbers was clearly visible, stretched between Camp IV and the bottom of the couloir.

Nearing the top of the couloir, Alberto Zerain arrived at the belay shared by Pemba and Pasang. "I can lead now," he told them, and the Basque tied into one end of a rope that Chhiring had just sent up from below and led through the Bottleneck itself, belayed by Pemba. Alberto climbed so fast, stretching the rope out its full length, that he created another problem for those who would follow. The rope wasn't fixed to any intermediate stations; it was difficult for more than one climber to be attached at once. As Pemba and Pasang Lama awkwardly ascended behind Alberto, Pemba had to stop to arrange a halfway station. Time slipped by. Now the first few climbers were ascending beneath them, climbing up the pitch immediately below where Pemba and Pasang stood as Alberto led another pitch, traversing to their left directly under the wall of ice.

Pasang Lama heard calls from anxious climbers below. "Go up! Keep moving!" There was no place to stand, no room for more bodies. In an effort to accommodate them, Pasang unclipped from the anchor and climbed up and to his right, moving off route, searching for a place to wait on top of the distinctive heart-shaped rock that forms the right-hand border of the very top of the couloir. Directly above him, the serac curled forward, blotting out the bright blue sky. They heard Alberto's voice calling to them. He had built an anchor—the rope was fixed. "I must continue now," he shouted across.

Pasang Lama's expedition leader, Mr. Kim, appeared at the belay just below the untethered climbing-Sherpa. "Pasang," he cried, "we must change oxygen!" Pasang looked down at the growing line of climbers stacked at the top of the couloir; he looked up at the serac wall, its surface beaded with droplets of water by the startling warmth of the mid-morning sun.

"It's time, but not now," Pasang called back. "First we get through the traverse safely; then we change the oxygen."

Already other climbers were beginning to follow the line Alberto had fixed. Mr. Kim clipped his ascender and began to make his way across, his crampons stepping on black rock that protruded from the icy skin of the mountain, Kim occasionally swinging his ax with his right hand in the ice overhead.

Pasang Lama down-climbed toward the fixed line. A thin crust of snow covered the hard ice at the top of the couloir. Pasang felt his feet find purchase beneath him. Just as he was transferring weight, his crampons ripped through the crust and his weight fell onto his ax, which was securely sunk into the mountain. Pasang gathered himself, reached the fixed line, and began to follow Kim across the traverse. Pemba still remained at the top of the Bottleneck. He let other climbers pass, and waited for Gerard.

Chhiring Dorje, having passed up several sections of rope he had retrieved from below, was now waiting in the line of climbers some fifty meters below. Wilco, the Dutch leader, was directly in front of him when suddenly his crampons cut from underneath him and his body slammed into the ice, hitting Chhiring a moment later. The sharp points of crampons sliced into the Sherpa's high-altitude suit, as the leash attached to

Wilco's ascender and Chhiring's body arrested the fall simultaneously. Down feathers fluttered in the air. Now more climbers, one by one, reached the anchor where Pemba waited and began the traverse.

Cecilie Skog, the Norwegian climber, was climbing just in front of the Serbian Dren Mandic. The Serbian momentarily unclipped. There was a muted noise, a flutter of fabric, and then Cecilie was screaming and a body cartwheeled down the gully, thrown into a savage, looping orbit that only gravity and the mountain's geometric form could control. He finally came to rest next to some exposed rocks on the eastern edge of the bottom of the couloir.

From his stance midway across the traverse, Pasang Lama watched it happen. He saw Dren fall and the broken human form far below, and noticed several climbers on the fixed line in the Bottleneck still looking upward, moving higher. He thought he saw Dren Mandic move.

What kind of job is this? he thought. *Why isn't anyone even looking?*

But helping his clients get to the top of K2 *was* Pasang Lama's job, and he still had work to do. He helped Go Mi-yeong and Kim Jae-su change their oxygen cylinders, collecting the empty bottles and hanging them from an ice screw at the far end of the pitch Alberto Zerain had helped to fix.

Then he heard his name being called from above. "Pasang, Jumik is tired! Go!" Pasang tried to hurry, stepping in front of Go and Kim and scurrying around a half dozen other climbers who were in front of him. When he reached Jumik at the head of the line, he was lying in the snow next to the anchor. They were halfway across the Diagonal. Jumik didn't say anything and it was obvious to Pasang Lama that he was exhausted. The younger Sherpa tied in to the rope and began to ascend the final section to the top of the serac.

The snow conditions varied widely on this section of the mountain: in subtle lees protected from the wind by the serac wall to his right, Pasang Lama found deep, unconsolidated snow. Other spots were windblown and hard. He quickly realized he needed a second ice ax, and reached back to grab a tool offered by Jumik. Then he continued. Pasang Lama had only three years of true mountaineering experience, and two weeks

8:27 a.m. on August 1, 2008: More than thirty climbers from seven different expeditions push for the summit of K2. American Chris Klinke snapped this shot as the main body of climbers neared the Bottleneck. Directly in front of him is Italian Marco Confortola. Note the fixed line he is ascending. Chris Klinke/goalexploration.com

Norwegian couple Cecilie Skog and Rolf Bae. Chris Klinke/goalexploration.com

The American International Expedition's summit team just before departing base camp: (*left to right*) Chhiring Dorje, Chris Klinke, Fredrik Strang, and Eric Meyer. Chris Klinke/goalexploration.com

Roeland van Oss, a young member of the Dutch Norit Team, was a crucial communication link in base camp during the summit climb. Chris Klinke/goalexploration.com

This composite image, made from two photos taken by Chris Klinke, captures the main body of summiteers traversing the Diagonal snowfield at 12:08 p.m. Alberto Zerain, the Basque soloist, can be seen resting under the small ice feature above the serac; Pasang Lama, the next-highest climber, is fixing the last section of the Diagonal. The aborted body recovery of Dren Mandic can be seen in the bottom right corner.

At 7:06 p.m., Pemba Gyalje Sherpa and Gerard McDonnell unfurl a world-peace flag on the summit of K2.

Gerard McDonnell Family

Exhausted from days of effort at high altitude, Wilco van Rooijen and Cas van de Gevel rest in the Norit mess tent as Dr. Eric Meyer treats their frostbite injuries.

Chris Klinke/goalexploration.com

Wilco is carried to the helicopter for evacuation to Skardu.

Chris Klinke/goalexploration.com

Tuesday, August 4: Marco Confortola arrives in base camp, the last survivor of the summit push.

Confortola collapses in front of the chorten on arriving in base camp.

Jumik Bhote (*pictured in front*) celebrates his return to Kathmandu after a successful autumn trip to Shishapangma with Go Mi-yeong and Kim Jae-su. His younger brother Tsering looks on. **Virginia Oleary**

Pasang Lama, who lost his ice ax while fixing the hand line on the descent from the summit, only to be rescued by Chhiring Dorje. **Freddie Wilkinson**

Pemba Gyalje in Kathmandu, November, 2008. **Freddie Wilkinson**

Chhiring Dorje, with his wife, Dawa, standing in the kitchen of his Kathmandu home.

Freddie Wilkinson

The upper mountain on August 2 at 9:59 a.m. This photograph, taken with Gerard McDonnell's camera by Pemba Gyalje, captures the locations of the missing summiteers. *1* indicates the Korean group at the top of the fixed lines; *2*, the climber on top of the serac believed to be Karim Meherban; *3*, the climber at the bottom of the Bottleneck Couloir believed to be Marco Confortola; *4*, Big Pasang Bhote and Tsering Bhote.   Gerard McDonnell Family

Close-up of the 9:59 a.m. photograph: This image shows the stricken Korean team at the top of the Diagonal being attended to by the rescuer believed to be Gerard McDonnell.

The Gilkey Memorial, with 2008 additions.

Wilco van Rooijen in April 2009, after surgery removed parts of eight toes.

of technical ice instruction. And yet it fell to the twenty-five-year-old climbing-Sherpa to fix the top section of the traverse, while more than a dozen mountaineers—all older, with far more experience, many of whom claimed to be elite mountaineers—waited below.

A patch of exposed ice waited just below the top of the serac. Pasang Lama was essentially soloing, but could see the faint line of steps Alberto Zerain had kicked an hour before, and noticed that an old rope stretched across the exposed lip. He headed in that direction.

The old rope was so tight that it was difficult to tie a knot to connect Pasang Lama's rope to it. Finally, he succeeded in clipping a carabiner through two loops of rope twisted against each other—something named a clove-hitch knot he had been taught at the Khumbu Climbing Center. Then he continued on top of the serac. The slope lessened in angle, but the snow grew deeper and deeper, until he was sinking in up to his thighs with each laborious step. Behind him, the long line of climbers had already begun to ascend the rope he had just tied off. Ahead he could see Alberto Zerain, a small human form toiling up the final snow slope in the bright sunshine. Pasang Lama put his head down and followed.

By then, a few climbers had decided the summit wasn't worth it. Chris Klinke articulately explained his own rationale for dropping out of the line near the top of the Bottleneck: "It came down to personal responsibility. . . ."

I didn't ask, "Who's got all the rope," "Who's in charge?" That's why I made the decision to turn around. . . . Pemba tried to step up, but you had thirty people at Camp IV who were supposed to work as a team, and nobody had communicated before; no wonder stuff went wrong. The level of personal responsibility for fixing rope was passed off to the fixing team. Discussing something and making it happen are two different things.

Chris and his teammates Eric Meyer and Fred Sträng returned relatively early to Camp IV, along with Nick Rice and Jelle Staleman. At the same time, a second wave of climbers arrived from below, including a second group of Koreans and the other two of their climbing-Sherpa team, Tsering Bhote and Big Pasang Bhote, from the Abruzzi Ridge, and Norit member Mark Sheen from the SSE Spur. It seemed odd to them that more people weren't descending before nightfall.

Above the top of the fixed lines, the last hours of the ascent existed as eighteen solitary struggles. Each step was a painful trial, a private victory, a new creation.

Pemba Gyalje remembers that nobody was speaking. Alberto Zerain, who had already reached the summit and was on his way down, would say basically the same thing to *Men's Journal*: "As I descended, everyone stopped to ask me how far to the summit. Did I tell them to turn around? No, you can't. There are a lot of people, and they are all going up together. It's the majority against you."

Only Rolf Bae, the Norwegian, hung back a little below the summit. He stood there and watched the line of climbers that included his wife inching closer to the sky. He paced back and forth, and Pemba recalls that he was the only one who expressed any worry about the sunset that was fast approaching. Of the twenty people who reached the top of the fixed lines, only Rolf and his teammate Lars Oystein turned around before the summit.

Fifty meters below the summit, Pasang Lama passed Alberto Zerain on his way down. Other than the thin marks of Zerain's crampons etched into the crown of hardened snow, Pasang Lama had the summit to himself. He took off his pack, turned off his supplemental oxygen, and planted his ax firmly into the mountain. Then he stood there, a little numb, looking down at the jagged teeth of the Gasherbrum group, the furrowed ripples of the Baltoro Glacier, the browned, lifeless hills of western China stretching away to the horizon. He turned around in slow, disbelieving circles, shooting a few photos and video clips with his camera and exclaiming to himself over again: "K2 summit! K2 summit!"

The Norwegians, Lars Nessa and Cecilie Skog, joined Pasang on the summit next, followed by Jumik and four of their Korean clients. Flags were unfurled and photos taken. Below, they could see a staggered line of more climbers inching closer. Everyone sat down and rested for a while. Kim Jae-su smoked a cigarette. Their shadows swept past the crest of the ridge, far beyond it, and they were bathed in shades of amber sunlight.

Pemba Gyalje was on top a little ahead of Chhiring Dorje. But they were not far apart. Chhiring had a video camera and did some quick filming on the final stretch of snow. Other than Zerain, they were the first to summit that day without using supplemental oxygen. They were also the first two Sherpas to climb K2 without oxygen, ever. It is a measure of Chhiring Dorje's strength that in his backpack was a full oxygen bottle, mask and regulator. Even though he carried the gear, which weighed approximately eight pounds, all the way to the summit, Chhiring felt no need to use it himself. It was for emergency use only.

The intermittent train of climbers continued to arrive, separated by only five or ten or fifteen minutes: Hughes D'Aubarède, Karim Meherban, Wilco van Rooijen, Cas van de Gevel. Marco Confortola was just below the true summit, still plodding upward, when the others began to descend.

If the old media rivalries between Peary and Cook, the *Times* and the *Herald*, set the gold standard for adventure media controversy, the modern benchmark was reached in the aftermath of the 1996 Everest disaster. Jon Krakauer's bestselling narrative *Into Thin Air* unsparingly dispatched criticism at various climbers involved in the disaster, including himself. He was particularly unforgiving of Anatoli Boukreev's decision to guide Everest without bottled oxygen. After summiting early in the day, Boukreev had nearly run down the route, arriving back in camp well ahead of his paying clients. The rest of the group slowly disintegrated in a fierce and unexpected storm. To his credit, Boukreev did return out into the storm several times that night to rescue two lost teammates, while Krakauer, who had arrived in camp after dark, lay exhausted in his tent. In response to *Into Thin Air*, Boukreev, allied with a coauthor named G. Weston DeWalt, produced his own book titled *The Climb*.

The linchpin to Krakauer's argument was the fact that when climbing without supplemental oxygen, a high-altitude mountaineer is particularly susceptible to the cold. This forces the climber to constantly keep moving in order to stay warm. Krakuaer pointed out that when Ed Viesturs summited without oxygen later that same year, he was scheduled to shoot several short film sequences with an IMAX movie team, but found stopping and waiting for them impossible because of the cold. He kept climbing to keep warm, and broke trail all the way to the summit. Boukreev, Krakauer asserted, was fundamentally hamstrung from performing his job as a guide because he simply could not stay warm at his clients' plodding pace.

Pasang Lama passed off the rest of his oxygen to a client just below the summit. Chhiring Dorje and Pemba Gyalje had been on their own all day, and even those who were using oxygen, Jumik Bhote, the five Koreans, Hugues, and Karim, had at most an hour or two of gas left. And yet they all stopped, just below the summit, in the total darkness, and regrouped one final time.

The descent from the summit to the top of the fixed lines was one of the most important pieces to the story of what happened on K2. Somewhere in that stretch of two hundred and fifty vertical meters of terrain, the group became completely fragmented. None of any of the survivors who spoke to the media publicly described this portion of the climb in any detail. In fact, none of them seemed to even be aware—as they lampooned the advance team in the press after the tragedy for bungling their job by running out of rope—that the climbing-Sherpas had decided among themselves that morning that Jumik Bhote, who was climbing on oxygen, would carry a section of Kevlar rope all the way to the summit. Yet all three surviving Sherpas are certain that the entire summit party did share a rope above the fixed lines.

In an e-mail Chhiring wrote: "On the descent from the summit to 8,450 meters everyone was tied on one rope since it was a little steep."

Pasang Lama elaborated on what happened, explaining in a taped interview that he, Jumik Bhote, and their five Korean clients had left the summit well before the Europeans, with still an hour or so of usable daylight. But they were moving slowly, and several of the Koreans struggled to maintain the motor skills necessary to avoid tripping on their crampons. Jumik and Pasang Lama began to hastily fix a hand line with the cord Jumik carried.

"At that time I had one ice ax, Jumik had one ice ax, and then with his ice ax we fixed the rope, and then he was the last one before sending [everyone down], and I was the first one to receive the clients," Pasang Lama described the system to me. They executed several pitches of descent in this manner: Pasang going first to secure the bottom end of the rope by stabbing his ice ax into the surface of the mountain, and then collecting the five Koreans at the anchor as they descended behind him. Jumik, coming last, removed the top anchor and then downclimbed to join the group, with no real belay and no margin for error.

Sometime just after dark, the eight climbers who had been last to leave the summit began to catch up with the Korean group. Chhiring Dorje, Pemba Gyalje, Gerard McDonnell, Hugues D'Aubarède, Karim Meherban, and Wilco van Rooijen left the summit slightly spaced out, but no more than a half hour apart, and so joined the Korean team in ones and twos. Marco and Cas, who had kindly waited a few extra minutes for the Italian to take his summit photo, were the last to reach the group.

There is no doubt in Pemba Gyalje's mind that everyone was together just below the summit. "Around eighty-five hundred meters we regroup everyone on the descent, except the Norwegians and the Spanish [Lars Nessa, Cecilie Skog, and Alberto Zerain]," he says. "All Koreans, Dutch, French, Pakistanis, Chhiring, and all Nepalis regroup. . . ."

We found a critical situation because some Koreans, Hugues, and Wilco, Gerard, and Marco, they are trying to sit down. And also they cannot descend same line. Some people going like this, some people going like this [zigzag motion]. And I found it is too dangerous because of slab avalanche. Then I talk with Jumik because Jumik has eighty meters Kevlar rope. I said, "Jumik, now we have to use the rope, and everyone put together on the rope, then try descend same direction. Otherwise everybody on their own trail on the slope is too dangerous." Finally he agreed and we use the rope and we connect all people together.

And so they continued to use the rope (variously described by the three surviving Sherpas as being fifty to eighty meters long). Some of the others probably walked down beside it, choosing to remain beyond its grasp, but according to the Sherpas, the lower they got, the more and more of the exhausted summiteers availed themselves of the hand line the Sherpas were temporarily fixing and then leapfrogging down the mountain. Pasang Lama remembered doing eight or nine pitches in total. "For seven people it was enough rope," he says. "But later you know all the people, everybody used it. Everybody was inside [on] the rope. Everybody."

Eventually they reached a section of slightly lower-angled terrain, just above the top anchor of the fixed lines. Again, Pasang Lama stabbed his ax into the snow to anchor the bottom of the rope, and then he was joined by Pemba Gyalje. The Koreans began to appear behind him.

Pemba unclipped from the anchor and moved forward on his own, following the circuitously long trail that switchbacked to the east, which Alberto Zerain made that afternoon, on his ascent. More than anything else, Pasang Lama recalls that at the last anchor he was beginning to feel seriously cold. He also had been the one to anchor the highest fixed line, which he had clove-hitched to the section of exposed old line. He knew he could find it again, even in the darkness.

"I thought, 'Now it's a flat area, and then there's fixed rope . . .'" Pasang Lama told me later. He turned to Mr. Kim, who had just arrived at the end of the hand line. "I talked to Mr. Kim [and said], 'First off there is a flat area; then the rope is fixed'; then he told me, 'Okay.' Just, 'Okay.'"

Pasang Lama took the direct path down to the top anchor of the fixed lines, arriving a little before Pemba Gyalje, who had taken the more indirect switchback. He was in such a hurry he forgot his ice ax was still plunged into the snow, securing the bottom end of the rope and anchoring everyone else who was coming down behind him.

Later, I would have the chance to ask four of the five other surviving summiteers about this episode. Kim Jae-su responded affirmatively, stating: "When descending, we had to all descend one by one and we were a big party; it was impossible to get all people together at the same place and time, so that was the reason we were separated. Yes, all four Sherpas set up the fixed rope." Both Wilco and Cas could only vaguely recall using a rope in one place, but readily conceded that it probably happened as Pemba said. And to my specific question asking if he had any memories of a rope being used above the fixed lines, Marco Confortola replied: "Honestly, I don't remember these details."

The only person I never had the chance to directly ask was Go Mi-yeong. She died in a fall while descending a section of mountain that had been stripped of fixed rope after summiting Nanga Parbat, eleven months after she survived K2. But immediately after the disaster on K2, in base camp, the Swedish climber Fred Sträng approached Go and Kim and asked if they would make a statement for his video project. They spoke awkwardly in English for a few moments, clearly frustrated, and then Sträng told them to just go ahead and say how they felt in Korean, their native tongue. The ensuing testimonies entirely validated the Sherpas' story.

Of the three Sherpas who would ultimately survive, only Chhiring Dorje expressed having any specific reservations at that time about the decision to continue descending without waiting for the others. Both Pemba Gyalje and Pasang Lama left the party expecting the others to follow very quickly behind them. They were thinking like guides, in a sense. Trying to keep a large group of people moving down mountain terrain means you have to multitask by thinking one step ahead. As soon as Pemba and Pasang Lama realized that the terrain had moderated to the point that they no longer needed to use the hand line, they focused on the next obvious job: finding the top anchor of the fixed lines. But they were both exhausted from their efforts on the advance team that morning—enough that once they broke contact with the group, reclimbing back up to them would be nearly impossible. And they both were getting very, very cold.

When Pemba and Pasang Lama left the bottom anchor to look for the top of the fixed lines, Chhiring was still at the top anchor, it being his job to remove the anchor and descend last. He down-climbed to the rest of the group at the lower anchor, and began heading toward Pemba Gyalje's and Pasang Lama's lights below. At the moment of reckoning, Chhiring's thoughts turned to his family, to the network of people whose lives he saved every day from the ruin of third-world poverty by virtue of his strange and dangerous profession.

> Nobody was moving. And I'm looking down, too much deep snow . . . and I said, "Hey, everybody move! Let's go down now!" And everyone said, "Okay, okay." And I'm thinking, "Uh-oh." Look at this situation, and I think I could die today. It looks like not so nice a situation: now is no rope, too dark, deep snow, too much shaking is going . . . maybe avalanche. And I'm thinking, "Okay." I think of my two daughters, and my family and wife, you know? I think I'm crazy, if I die, how to grow them—my daughters? And I'm thinking, now, maybe I go down. If good luck, maybe I arrive in Camp Four, if bad luck, I fall down.

Chhiring Dorje knew he must unwaveringly focus on saving his own life for those who depended on him.

He made his decision, continued down, and caught up with Pasang Lama at the top of the Bottleneck, at the bottom end of the fixed line Lars Nessa and Cecilie Skog had placed after the initial avalanche that took Rolf Bae. Compared to the separation of the summit team, which Chhiring spoke of with great solemnity, his decision to short-rope Pasang Lama down the couloir didn't seem to occupy too much of his thoughts at the time.

9

PEMBA'S CHOICE

Most of the world's population gets around on low-capacity, four-stroke motorcycles. Pemba rides a Honda Hero 100cc bike, which itself may be the single most widely used machine for land transportation in the world. It certainly is the vehicle of choice for negotiating the underpaved streets of Kathmandu. But Pemba was not the sort of rider content to go with the halting current of third-world traffic.

He showed up at my hostel two days later, at nine a.m. on the dot, wearing a large backpack filled with climbing equipment. I offered to contribute some of my own gear, but instead he passed his rucksack to me. "No, for you I have packed extra shoes and harness," he said. "Okay—we go now." I shouldered the pack, hopped on the bike, and we were off.

We sped through the narrow, tourist-clogged streets of Thamel, weaving between groups of European trekkers and local shopkeepers. Pemba relied on his horn less than other riders; rather than force a hole in the traffic, he would patiently wait for openings to appear and then decisively cut to exploit them. Just as I was adjusting my hat to ensure it wouldn't be blown off, he made a quick jog left to avoid colliding with a brightly clad Hindu baba who was hustling a pair of young travelers, then turned right onto the main road leading out of the city, nearly throwing me in the process.

Pemba accelerated into fourth gear, pulling left to dodge several bikes putting along at a pedestrian pace. I felt my own body slowly relax, and I realized I trusted my pilot. We were out of Thamel now, and the shops lining the road were just getting set up for a busy day of commerce. Hardware stores and fruit stands, motorcycle repair shops and department stores roared past. The crowded sidewalk offered flickering snapshots of life in Nepal's capital city: uniformed children with backpacks walking to school, long-faced Sikh men haggling over a partially rebuilt car engine, Hindu women in bright robes, striding purposely through a morning of errands, beggars searching the road for a bit of discarded food or something to sell, teenagers in Britney Spears T-shirts loafing around to watch the scene, the occasional cow sniffing at a piece of trash, thin-mustached shopkeepers waiting for the next sale. People were everywhere, and yet all were reduced to a passing blur by the Honda's straining engine and Pemba's lead foot.

The cliff was in Balarjun forest, a thickly vegetated jungle hill that was once the home of a royal palace and is now designated a city park. We stopped at the gated entrance, where Pemba showed a soldier in the sandbagged guardhouse an ID card and paid a thirty-rupee entrance fee (about fifty cents; Pemba wouldn't let me pay). The soldier opened the gate, and we drove another two kilometers down a dirt path until a scruffy-looking escarpment seventy feet tall appeared through the trees.

At the base of the cliff, Pemba opened his neatly packed rucksack and handed me a harness and a pair of rock shoes. I uncoiled the rope while he tied into one end and scampered nimbly up the first feet of the climb.

Through the nearly hundred-year history of Western mountaineers and Sherpas climbing together, the sahibs interpreted the Sherpas' perceived cheerfulness as an indicator that they were motivated by feelings of joy and self-fulfillment similar to their own, rather than financial gain.

One expedition leader wrote in 1929 that their Sherpas "followed us to the last man into desperate places, with . . . no thought of payment, but . . . purely from ethical motives from noble natural instincts."

"No less than the Western mountaineers who employed them, they were doing what they wanted to do, what they were born to do," another opined in 1963. "They were not hired help but companions in adventure."

But in the depressed economies of the Himalayan states, it was a fact of life that most could not afford to climb mountains for pleasure. That didn't mean that Sherpas didn't take pride and find occasional enjoyment in their work, but despite the Westerners' views, it was primarily all about the money. I had cynically presumed this to be the case with Chhiring and Pemba—even if they weren't considered paid guides, I thought they must have been motivated by some kind of financial reward.

But as I watched Pemba climb, my own cynicism began to melt away. Because I knew as soon as he started up that first climb: Pemba was not just a guide, but a hell of a good climber. And it was obvious he loved climbing for reasons that transcended pay, too.

The Sherpa tiptoed his way up the climb, carefully placing each foot with the precision of a well-rehearsed ballet dancer. Efficient climbing technique is a complex subject; the minute details in kinesthetic movement and neuromuscle memory that define the best climbers are studied by physical trainers and Ph.D. sports scientists. Books have been written about it, carefully analyzing the myriad different movements and body positions necessary to scale a rock face. But suffice to say, climbing skill is a quality that is easier recognized than it is explained or taught.

Beginners often place undue focus on their hands, frequently pawing the rock above their heads in a frantic search for the next hold. Experienced climbers learn that it is far more efficient to rely on their legs to *push* them up a cliff, rather than try to use their arms to *pull* them skyward. Pemba, I noticed immediately, rarely looked at his hands. Rather, his gaze was fixated downward, carefully studying the texture and grain of the rock below his waist.

The cliff itself was a crudely hewn limestone conglomerate, its surface glassy smooth and frequently dirty. Tufts of grass sprouted from small ledges and cracks. It was not the kind of crag a rock climber would willingly choose to practice his craft, but it did make for challenging and deceptive climbing. If each foot was not positioned perfectly, for the maximum friction, it could easily slip. A classic mistake on this kind of nebulous terrain is for the climber to try to compensate by making bigger moves, reaching very high from one foot to the next in an effort to bypass the insecure placements in favor of bigger footholds. The drawback is that this kind of motion requires much more power, and will frequently throw the climber out of balance.

Pemba made no reckless moves. Each step was short and controlled, his overall pace steady and measured as he worked his way higher up the vertical climb. His progress was interrupted only when he paused to clip the next protection bolt. It was readily clear, however, that Pemba wasn't in the least bit worried about falling—he was in complete control.* As he neared the top of the cliff, a soft, sliding melody wafted through the air. I looked around momentarily, thinking other climbers must be nearby, before I realized what it was. Pemba was quietly singing to himself.

I seconded the climb, safely belayed by Pemba from an anchor on a ledge near the top of the cliff. As I joined him at the stance, I realized we had made a mistake. Now that both of us were on top, it would be necessary to descend back down the climb. Normally, the procedure would be to thread the rope through the anchor in a retrievable rappel, so that each of us could descend the rope independently, using our own separate friction devices. But, because I was borrowing gear from Pemba, I didn't have a device of my own: We had to figure out a way for two people to descend the climb with one device.

This type of problem is a classic guiding challenge, one that aspiring

---

* The short sixty-foot climb was a pre-equipped "sport" climb, meaning that a half dozen masonry bolts had been drilled into the rock at regular intervals. By clipping his rope through each successively higher bolt with a carabiner and sling, Pemba safeguarded himself in case of a fall. Were he to slip, it would be my responsibility, as his belayer, to secure the rope, which would catch his body weight through the highest bolt.

guides who are training to pass their exams and gain international certification will almost certainly be asked to perform by their instructors. What counts isn't so much which technique you choose to solve the problem, but how quickly and efficiently you can effect the solution.

Pemba, I had noticed when I reached the top of the climb, was belaying me through a large carabiner, using a specialized knot called a munter hitch. Also known as an Italian hitch, the knot allows slack rope to be pulled through as the climber ascends higher, yet will pinch down on itself, creating enough friction to easily hold the force of a fall, should the climber slip. As I reached the top of the climb, Pemba had quickly secured me by tying off the belay into a complex variation of the munter hitch called a munter mule. This is not an easy knot to master; even experienced guides will occasionally flub it. Yet Pemba tied it with the practiced ease of a rescue expert.

We exchanged some pleasantries about the route we had just completed, and the fact that it was good to be out climbing together. Then I leaned back, weighting the tied-off friction knot as I looked over the edge. I nodded to Pemba, and he released the mule knot so that he could feed slack into the rope. Pemba steadily lowered me back down the climb to the base of the cliff. We never spoke a single word of discussion about the minor predicament—Pemba dealt with it as easily as one might run back into the house to retrieve a pair of absently forgotten car keys.

The rest of the morning passed in a rush of sweaty enjoyment as Pemba showcased his home crag. There were only a dozen or so routes, each of them fifty to sixty feet tall and equipped with a series of protection bolts. The first several climbs we warmed up on were relatively moderate, despite the rock's cryptic nature—perhaps 5.9 or easy 5.10 in American grades.* Pemba's cell phone seemed to be constantly ringing, but he hummed and sang softly to himself as he floated up each route.

---

* Rock climbers use an open-ended grading system, beginning with the easiest grade of 5.0 and running to the hardest, currently 5.15. Anything 5.10 or higher is generally considered an expert climb.

Then we approached a difficult route with a fierce-looking sequence to gain a ledge some fifteen feet off the ground. I eyed the line cautiously. Pemba would have to use a small, sharp-looking solution pocket to make a long reach across a four-foot section of overhanging blank wall. The footholds were polished smooth. It would be like sticking two fingers into a hole the size of a bottle cap and trying to do a pull-up off of it. And even worse, the first bolt was positioned so high that he would have to make the moves without the benefit of a belay. If he fell, he would hit the prow of a boulder at the base of the cliff, which would send him cartwheeling down the hillside below.

Pemba spit out three quick gulps of air. The middle finger and ring finger on his right hand wiggled into the pocket. He pasted his foot high on a glassy ledge, and pulled the weight of his hips over it. The next handhold, a bottoming crack, which one second before had seemed impossibly far away, suddenly rocked into his reach. He grabbed it decisively, made another move to a large bucket hold, and clipped the first bolt. I watched his body instinctively relax, as he hung straight-armed and rested, secure in the knowledge that now he was on belay.

By now, an internal alarm that is hardwired into the psyche of every veteran climber was beginning to register in my subconscious. It dawned on me that Pemba had pulled off a near-flawless sandbag, a sandbag being a subtle game of one-upmanship that is sprung on an unsuspecting partner. In climbing parlance, the climb Pemba had just fired was a greasy 5.11 in the no-falls zone. I decided I'd top-rope this one.

After he had completed the climb and lowered back to the ground, Pemba's cheeks were flushed and he was panting slightly from the effort. In between breaths, however, the skin around the corners of his eyes was pinched in a few wrinkles and the corners of his mouth wrapped up ever so slightly toward his ears. He was smiling.

"I did not want to go rescue Marco . . ." he said unexpectedly. "I did not want to even go to the summit. Three times I said, 'Let's go down.'" He spoke quietly, his shoulders slumped and his body language perfectly neutral. But his gaze met mine steadily and without impediment.

On the evening of July 30, two days before they would summit, Pemba shared a cramped tent with Jelle Staleman and Gerard McDonnell at Camp III on the South-southeast Spur. The wind crackled and snapped outside, beating the tent fabric in low, humming vibrations. As the night went on, the poles began to flex and bend, strained by the force of the air to near breaking point. Fearing that their tents would soon be destroyed, the climbers spent the last hours before dawn lying fully dressed in their down suits, waiting for calamity to strike. And strike it did—but for their neighbor, the soloist Hoselito Bite. Sometime in the middle of the night, the hapless man lost his tent. Immediately naked at seven thousand meters in the midst of sustained sixty-mile-an-hour winds, the soloist may well have perished were he truly alone. As it was, Gerard, Pemba, and Jelle immediately accommodated him in their cramped tent. No one slept. Sometime later that night, as he lay in the darkness, listening to the freight-train force of the gusts outside, Pemba decided the summit wasn't worth it.

"We must go down!" he yelled to his tentmates. Though the forecast models had predicted high pressure with relatively calm skies, the team had been getting pounded by hurricane-force winds for close to forty-eight hours. "The weather forecast is completely unreliable," Pemba shouted over the storm.

Gerard listened earnestly to his friend's advice. Jelle, who was younger and less experienced than his tentmates, also took the Sherpa's words seriously. All three were unnerved by the wind's ferocity. Just as Pemba convinced his friends to call off the summit bid, he yelled across to Wilco van Rooijen and Cas van de Gevel in the other tent, "We must go down; the wind is too much!"

"No—we wait until eight a.m. for a new forecast!" Wilco suggested. Two days before, at Camp II, it had almost been too much to convince the driven Dutch leader to take a rest day, rather than push on to a higher elevation in the unsettled weather. Now, one step closer to the summit, he wasn't ready to retreat yet. Pemba halfheartedly consented to wait, but insisted that if the forecast was bad, or the winds didn't begin to decrease, he would descend. As if on cue, at eight a.m. the winds abated. The climbers packed up their equipment and continued on to Camp IV under clear skies.

Again, on summit day, right after Dren Mandic fell, Pemba urged the group to descend. He was waiting at the top anchor in the Bottleneck for his teammates as the line of twenty-five tightly spaced climbers laboriously ascended the fixed rope in single file and set off across the traverse. A frantic motion caught his eye. A muted cry rang out above the chorus of breathing. And then Dren Mandic was falling. It was the first fatality of the day.

The shocked climbers stood panting at the top of the Bottleneck. No one was quite sure what to do. The gaping maw of the serac hung overhead. Pemba could feel the collective drive of the summit party waning into indecision. "It is too late in the day," he said, breaking the silence, "and we move too slowly to make the summit with safe time for the descent. We should descend."

But then the Italian Marco Confortola spoke up. "The first men to climb K2 summited at six p.m., so we must continue; we must move!" Group momentum surged forward again, and the long train of climbers continued their ascent.

And again, just moments later, as the other climbers continued through the Bottleneck and across the traverse, Pemba turned to his friend Gerard and tried to convince him it wasn't worth it. "This is not a good situation," Pemba said, rattled by the Serbian climber's death. "I am not good psychologically. Let's go back down."

"But it's good weather, Pemba," McDonnell responded. "We have to at least *try*. . . ." For all the instinct that was quietly urging him to go down, Pemba could not bring himself to turn back alone, while his friends climbed on. The Sherpa reluctantly agreed to continue.

Twenty-four hours later, Gerard McDonnell and ten other men were dead.

Now, three months after the disaster, as we enjoyed a low-key morning of sport climbing on the outskirts of Kathmandu, Pemba was clearly haunted by those moments. It was the first information he had volunteered about K2. Pemba stared off into space, then shook his head slowly, thinking about how easily they all might have turned around and returned safely home to their loved ones. He recalled Gerard McDonnell on summit day—the impish, youthful smile coated in a thick, frosty beard, his eyes alight with a mixture of determination and joy.

I kept saying we should go down. But Gerard, Wilco, and Cas, Chhiring Dorje, Marco—all of them decided to keep going up. And so did Pemba. "Gerard . . ." Pemba said, his voice momentarily tapering off as he searched for the right words to capture his best friend. "He was . . . too optimistic. We were like brothers." Pemba was quiet for a while. Then he continued. "It was very dangerous to go into the Bottleneck. I told Pasang Bhote and Tsering Bhote not to go, but they said they must find Jumik and the Koreans. . . ."

As Pemba went on to tell me the story of how he rescued Marco Confortola and Wilco van Rooijen, I understood at last his reticence to speak of the disaster. Pemba was an exceptionally gifted mountaineer. His instincts had warned him to descend. His long experience of working summit days on Everest must have told him that the plan on K2 had no margin for error, and the errors began before they even left camp. If Pemba had the authority—if Pemba had been working as a guide—he would have turned the group around long before they reached the summit. And everyone might have lived.

But those decisions were not his to make. And while Pemba's judgment as a guide gave him the perception to see that trouble was coming, his skill as a climber helped him to personally survive the darkened descent. But he did not get the entire group down. The bravery of his choice to return into the serac's line of fire the next day is self-evident. But the final story of what happened next does not make Pemba a hero. He only watched as the nightmare unfolded around him, and did what he could.

———

On the morning of August 2, 2008, Pemba Gyalje woke just before dawn. His face was swollen and his lips parched dry. He was in Camp IV. The memory of the blackened descent from the summit came rushing back to him a second later. The struggle to find the top of the fixed lines. Down-climbing the Bottleneck amid a torrent of small avalanches. The group of stationary headlamps at the top of the serac, distantly burning like a fire's last embers.

Pemba vaguely remembered someone returning after him in the night. He sat up, looking around the tent. The down baffles of Gerard's sleeping bag were crumpled and folded inward. It was empty. Pemba heard other climbers stirring in the tents around him. He hastily put on his boots and crawled outside.

Someone was in the other Norit tent. He could hear the person breathing. Pemba unzipped the door. It was Cas. The Dutchman was passed out cold, fitfully snoring. He must have made it down the Bottleneck after him. Wilco was not in the tent.

Pemba stood up. In the blue-hued landscape before the sun's rays hit the mountain, he saw a cluster of dots. They were near the top anchor of the fixed lines, on the left side of the serac. It was roughly the same location of the headlamps the night before. They didn't seem to be moving. The dots were very small compared to the hulking serac wall nearby.

Pasang Bhote and Tsering Bhote were standing by the Korean tents, adjusting their harnesses and readying their packs.

What's happening? Pemba asked.

We're going up the Bottleneck. Pasang Bhote was bent over, buckling his crampons on each foot.

The Bottleneck? What? It's too dangerous up there.

Pasang Bhote stood up suddenly. *Only two Koreans came down last night after you. Two Koreans and one of the Dutch. Three members of our team are missing with Jumik, and Mr. Kim told us to go help them.*

Don't go under the serac. The Bottleneck is too dangerous.

Pasang Bhote and Tsering Bhote didn't reply.

It's too dangerous up there, Pemba said one more time.

We have to try. We have a job to do, Pasang Bhote ruefully spoke at last. *Keep your radio on.*

A half hour later, someone knelt outside the vestibule to Chhiring and Eric Meyer's tent, searching for the zipper. Pemba crawled inside. He looked like he had aged ten years in the four and a half days of the summit push.

Pemba didn't say anything for a moment. Then the awful reality of the situation shuddered through him. "Wilco and Gerard are missing. . . . I . . . I don't think I have anything left to give. We have to go down. We've all been at eight thousand meters for too long."

He put his head on his arms, sitting cross-legged in the threshold of the tent, and sobbed uncontrollably. Chhiring and Eric watched Pemba. They were quiet, mostly because there was nothing to say. After a moment, they passed him a hot-water bottle and lit their stove to make more breakfast. As they waited for a pan of snow to melt, Meyer reached into a stuff sack and pried the cap off a small bottle. First he handed Pemba a Dexamethasone to ward off cerebral edema, then a Provigil for alertness. Pemba looked down at the circular off-white tablets cupped in his hand, pausing for a moment; then he tossed them into his mouth. The small bowl of hot tsampa cereal seemed to perk him up.

Both Chhiring and Pemba went out of their way to acknowledge and thank Eric Meyer for helping them survive when they arrived in Camp IV after the summit. As Chhiring volunteered in one of his earliest e-mails to me: "If eric wasn't there at camp 4 then its difficult for me and also pemba gyaljen. eric gave me medician after arrived at camp 4 and also gave medician to pemba gyaljen next day 2nd august [*sic*]."

The use of drugs in high-altitude climbing is a rarely mentioned yet pervasive—and troubling—phenomenon on the eight-thousand-meter peaks. The genuine problem is that it is impossible to draw the line between using them for safety, only after someone has shown symptoms of edema, to get the climber down alive, and taking them prophylactically, as a performance-enhancing drug, to get the climber to the top. In one sense, any time a human being is at eight thousand meters, they are acutely at risk for developing one of these illnesses, and should take all precautions that are available to them.

It's impossible to know how much drugs are being used on the busy "regular routes" on the eight-thousand-meter circuit, but I asked Swiss alpinist Ueli Steck about it recently. Like Marko Prezelj, Steck specializes in technical, alpine-style ascents, with no trace of fixed ropes or hired support. But while attempting these sorts of once-in-a-lifetime challenges, he frequently acclimatizes on the easier trade routes. "At six thousand meters, on Gasherbrum II, everyone was walking around like zombies. And I thought, 'If they are like this here, how will they be at eight thousand meters?' But they went up; I saw them higher. How can you be stronger at seven thousand meters than at six thousand meters?" I asked Ueli in his estimation what percentage of climbers on the normal routes were using dexamethasone to get to the summit. His answer didn't skip a beat: "Ninety-five percent."

The use of drugs is far less pervasive in Eric Meyer's opinion. "It's a really hard thing to speculate about percentages," he says, "but I think it's really low. Maybe on Everest—if you separate the demographics—there are certain climbers like the seven summiteers types, who are willing to do drugs to get to the summit." Of course, both Chhiring Dorje and Pemba Gyalje had already summited without them, and by the morning of August 2, everyone in Camp IV had one basic goal: get down as safely and quickly as possible. "It was in my best medical decision making to selectively use drugs to help people who were in a perilous situation physiologically, to help everyone get down safely," Meyer explains. "It followed from my own sense of wilderness ethics."

Pemba and Cas searched the area immediately around camp for survivors. Then, sometime after ten-thirty a.m., Roeland radioed from base camp. He had just heard from Maarten van Eck who, incredibly, reported that Wilco had just called his wife in the Netherlands. The Dutch climber was below the Bottleneck, but clearly disoriented and in need of help. Pemba immediately tried calling Wilco himself on Gerard's sat phone. It rang for a moment, and then his teammate answered.

"Stay to your left-side, going down," Pemba told him. "We will go right side, coming up to meet you." Pemba and Cas marched slowly uphill, retracing the route they had followed only a day before toward the base of the Bottleneck. The Shoulder of K2 is really a series of flat, rolling knolls of snow. As they climbed higher the weather worsened; silent whisps of cloud that seemed to appear from nowhere began to obscure their view. Pemba and Cas traversed back and forth, trying to look down both sides of the broad ridge, calling Wilco's name, over and over again.

They returned to Camp IV unsuccessful. By then, a half dozen other climbers were out of their tents, talking in measured tones. Present were Eric Meyer, Chhiring Dorje, Fred Sträng, and Paul Walters from the American team, and Mark Sheen, another member of the Norit team. Everyone had seen the stationary cluster of dots that morning, but all were in agreement that it was simply too dangerous to try to reascend the Bottleneck. "There'd been no significant movement up there that morning," Eric Meyer would recall later. "Then the weather started to deteriorate and we decided that we had to be moving down the mountain by noon."

At eleven thirty a.m., the haggard band of climbers was ready to leave Camp IV. By then, a thick band of clouds had enveloped the upper mountain. "Part of you wants to go into your tent and sleep and become a reptile," Meyer says. "The cognitive part of you that's still working is telling you you need to get down. And it's only going to get harder and harder." Seeing safety in numbers, the hodgepodge group from different expeditions decided to travel together down the Abruzzi Ridge. Mark Sheen, who had ascended the SSE Spur, chose to join them and descend the Abruzzi as well. Meyer offered each man a Decadron and a Provigil—anything to help get them all safely off the mountain.

Pemba watched as they departed. Other than a handful of Korean climbers, including Go Mi-yeong and Kim Jae-su, who lay nearly unresponsive in their tents, and Marco's two Pakistani high-altitude porters, he and Cas were now the only climbers remaining in Camp IV. Eric

Meyer had left him with a small supply of drugs and the unused bottle of oxygen Chhiring carried to the summit, but the Sherpa knew he too had to descend soon. He could feel the insidious effects of the high altitude. His movements were getting slower and growing more labored; fine motor skills, like the coordination necessary to light a stove, demanded total focus. And he was constantly cold. They needed to get to a lower elevation that afternoon. He had nothing more to give.

They would wait a few more minutes, Pemba thought, and then start down.

The radio crackled to life at noon on August 2. Pemba was in his tent at Camp IV, the yellow fabric casting a jaundiced tint on his surroundings. Cas lay next to him. The Abruzzi team had departed camp only a half hour ago, and the two men were preparing to begin their descent down the SSE Spur in a matter of minutes. Two of their teammates, Gerard and Wilco, were still missing, but Pemba knew they had to descend to a lower altitude as soon as possible to save themselves. The decision had already been made.

Pemba, Camp Four, Pemba, are you there? It was Pasang Bhote and Tsering Bhote.

Yes, Pasang—what is it? Pemba responded.

There is a person lying in the snow.

Who is it?

We do not know. . . . He is asleep. He is wearing a green-and-black climbing suit.

Pemba thought for a moment. *That . . . that is the Italian. Marco. He is the only one with a green suit. Where are you?*

We are at eight thousand meters, at the bottom of the Bottleneck.

Can you come and bring him to camp?

We must continue to find our own team, to find Jumik and the Koreans. Can you come and get him?

It is very dangerous in the Bottleneck. You should bring him down to camp and we will regroup. The Bottleneck is too dangerous; there are too many avalanches.

Silence. Then—*We're going higher. Can you come and get him?*

Pemba was quiet for a long moment. He looked at Cas. The Dutchman didn't have much energy left in him. The static from the radio filled the tent. Pemba thought of how he, Chhiring Dorje, and Pasang Lama had descended the Bottleneck the night before, how lucky they had been to make it through without being hit by another avalanche from the serac. He remembered the sound the falling ice made in the darkness around him. At that moment, other people were fighting their way up through that same terrible gauntlet.

Okay, Pemba said at last. *I'll come.*

In 1986, seven climbers, all exhausted after long summit climbs, were caught on the Shoulder in a prolonged storm. They were stormbound for five days, and when the weather finally broke, only two of the seven had the strength to complete the descent. Likewise, the underlying reason for Dudley Wolfe's demise in 1939 was the extraordinary amount of time he spent above seven thousand meters. By August 2, Pemba had spent five nights above sixty-seven hundred meters, and just endured a twenty-four-hour summit day. As the Sherpa and Cas left Camp IV and yet again trudged up the windblown Shoulder toward the upper reaches of K2, Pemba knew that each step higher was only bringing him less oxygen in return. Each step carried him closer to death.

Clouds now raked across the mountain; the visibility reduced to near whiteout conditions. In his pack, Pemba carried the oxygen bottle and mask from the American international team. The most experienced mountaineers remaining on the upper mountain, both Pemba and Cas were keenly aware that they now walked a perilous line between their ability to help others and the possibility that they might run into serious trouble themselves.

A short distance above high camp Cas stopped. He turned to Pemba.

"I am tired," he told him. "I have to stop. I'll sit here and be a lighthouse for you to find Camp IV." Pemba nodded. It was a sign of the depth of Cas van de Gevel's mountaineering experience that he recognized his own physical limit. The Dutchman's decision to stop was another opportunity for Pemba himself to turn around. By any conservative mountaineering standard, carrying on solo into the shrouded gloom was a significant risk.

But Pemba continued. He was now completely alone. Above him, he knew that Tsering Bhote and Pasang Bhote had entered the Bottleneck couloir, but he could not see them—he could not see anything in the clouds, nor did anyone respond to occasional shouts and whistles. There were only the sounds of his dogged breaths and his crampons gnawing into the surface of the mountain with each step and the wind blowing beyond his goggles and hood.

A shape appeared out of the colorless murk. It was a block of ice. Pemba realized that he was walking on smaller cubes of frozen debris. He had reached the bottom of the couloir. He stopped and looked around, then took a few more steps onward. Above, a spot of color smudged the limit of his field of vision. He trudged toward it. Green. Like a stormbound apparition a human body lay on the ground. Pemba climbed higher. It was Marco.

He was prone on the cement-hard avalanche cone, his arms and legs splayed out in a position of utter defeat. His harness was loosened to below his knees. In advanced cases of hypothermia, the victim often experiences the perverse feeling that he is *overheating*. Marco's down suit was unzipped to his chest, and he had even removed his own gloves. The Italian was, in Pemba's own words, "completely disassembled."

The Sherpa shook him. Marco responded groggily, struggling to bring his eyes into focus. He did not speak. It took a minute to get him sitting up, pull his suit back on, and thrust a mitten over each of his stiff hands. Then Pemba pushed the oxygen mask to his face. Marco held the mask and breathed in deeply. As the Italian slowly regained consciousness, Pemba looked around. It was already after two p.m., and he was alone with an incapacitated victim to attend to, in a whiteout, at eight thousand meters.

This was not the first time Pemba had revived a comatose climber. He turned the valve on the canister to the maximum flow rate. Marco had not used supplemental oxygen during the climb and there was a good chance that the sudden rush of oxygen to his system would get him back on his feet, so he could descend under his own power. It was his only chance. The compact Pemba knew he couldn't move the strapping Marco by himself.

They sat together and Pemba waited as Marco breathed deep gulps of the thick, life-preserving gas. After a few minutes, he began to perk up.

The Motorola radio Pemba carried squawked to life.

Pemba, we are at the top of the Bottleneck. We have Jumik and the Koreans.

It was Big Pasang. Pemba unzipped his suit and reached inside.

What is the condition of everyone? Marco, Pemba noticed as he held the radio to his ear, was beginning to move.

They are fine, but with some frostbite. Jumik needs to have a helicopter ready as soon as he arrives in base camp for transportation to a hospital.

There was a pause, and then Pemba heard Jumik's voice come on the radio. He spoke for a moment to Nawang Dorje, the Korean team's Nepali cook in base camp. Then Big Pasang came back on the radio.

We are bringing them down the couloir now.

Okay, come quickly. It is dangerous. Marco stood up.

We have also seen one person hit by serac fall. They were coming behind our group. We don't know who it was but he was wearing a red suit with black patches.

Come quickly down now.

Marco, still on oxygen, took a tentative step, and then another. It was time to start down. In the recesses of his altitude-numbed brain, Pemba knew what he had just heard was important. But first things first. Once everyone was out of harm's way, he could get the full story directly from Big Pasang. For the time being, he shoved the conversation aside and focused on getting Marco out of the debris zone. They took a few steps together.

And then he heard the distinct clap of pieces of ice colliding with rock like a volley of gunshots fired somewhere in the cloud above. In an instant, Pemba knew with primordial certainty that the serac had let loose again.

A split second later refrigerator-size pieces of ice tumbled into view to his left. Smaller pieces flew overhead. Pemba crouched, helpless to dodge the icefall that rained down like frozen shrapnel around them. Out of the corner of his eye, to the left in the main flow of the slide he recognized a patch of color, the unmistakable shape of a human body rolling past. There was more than one.

A small piece of ice struck Marco in the back of the head. His legs instantly buckled forward. As he fell, Pemba instinctively reached out to try to keep him on his feet, but his hands could not find purchase on the synthetic shell of Marco's suit. The Italian was being swept away, drawn into the avalanche like a drowning man swept out to sea. Pemba's gloved hands finally found the Italian's neck. His grip tightened. Ice was everywhere. The Sherpa held on.

Silence returned to the mountain. Clouds continued to slip over the Shoulder, hiding all but their immediate surroundings. The avalanche was over. Pemba and Marco stood up.

To their left, a little below them, they could see a macabre form of two human bodies. Pemba went closer. Big Pasang and Jumik lay together. Farther to the left, Pemba could see two Korean bodies. He took out his camera.

A voice called out from above. It called out in Nepali.

Hurry down! Pemba yelled back, but he did not wait. He turned his back on the Bottleneck and led Marco to safety.

Pasang Lama was also searching the Shoulder that afternoon with two Korean teammates. His companions were on supplemental oxygen but nevertheless moved slowly. Pasang Lama heard the radio call from Big Pasang and continued higher up the Shoulder, expecting to locate his teammates and help them down. As he climbed on, he heard a voice calling out from inside the cloud. Pasang Lama asked one of the Koreans to pass his oxygen mask to him. The climbing-Sherpa sucked down several deep breaths of the enriched air, and then hurried ahead, pushing himself as fast as he could go through a little break in the visibility. He cramponed farther to his left, rounding a vague, convex slope. The mountain seamlessly merged with the sky in a befuddling gray snowscape, and then there was Tsering Bhote, twenty-five meters away. He sat in the snow, lying there motionless and staring at the ground.

What happened? Pasang asked as soon as he reached him.

They're dead. Tsering Bhote was talking, almost to himself. *There was an avalanche from the top and it swept them away. What happened I don't know.*

Pemba's account of what happened in the Bottleneck couloir on August 2, 2008, was a wild departure from the mainstream version of events. It left little doubt that after Wilco and Marco passed the stricken Koreans at the top of the traverse, Jumik Bhote and at least two of his clients had somehow become ambulatory, freed themselves from their entanglement at the top of the fixed line, and traversed two hundred meters into the top of the Bottleneck. However improbable, it was confirmed not only in the last radio call from Pasang Bhote, but by the final resting place of their bodies in the debris field at the bottom of the Bottleneck. Had they fallen from the location where they were last seen by Marco and Wilco that morning, their bodies would have tumbled to the south, over the rock slabs near Wiessner's attempted route and been funneled into the snowy wastes of the south face. The horizontal distance involved is simply too great. Yet Pemba and Marco specifically recalled seeing the four bodies tumbling out of the Bottleneck in the midst of the final serac fall.

Dead men tell no lies.

It is also worth considering the brutality the mountain had released in little more than twenty-four hours. Most often, death comes softly in the high mountains: on Everest, climbers expire like David Sharp, lying down to rest along the trail, feeling the inevitable ebb as their core temperature drops, perhaps enduring a few cycles of Cheyne-Stokes breathing. The process can take hours, and is occasionally beaten back at the last possible moment, as proven by the survival of Seaborn Beck Weathers on Everest in 1996, and Lincoln Hall on the same mountain ten years later. In the midst of a storm, climbers frequently disappear, swept away in unseen falls or avalanches, never to be seen again. Occasionally their corpses appear after the tempest, shoulders hunched over or lying on their side beside the trail.

But K2 in 2008 was a different affair. Virtually every man to perish on the mountain suffered a fall, or was struck by icefall. Pemba himself witnessed five traumatic deaths—five human beings reduced to corpses in a matter of a few seconds. As he was returning to Camp IV, those bodies occupied his thoughts. By now, Pemba's mind had entered an alternate place. Under the most advantageous circumstances, summiting K2 is a grueling physical and mental effort; accomplishing the climb without supplemental oxygen pushes the experience further. Not only had Pemba done that, he had led the advance team, fixing a sizable section of the Bottleneck himself, and then spent most of the next day searching the Shoulder as the weather deteriorated and a full-blown storm seemed imminent.

Pemba and Marco met Cas and then the two Korean climbers as they were descending toward Camp IV. The Sherpa's mind latched onto one basic thought process, the same logic that Maarten van Eck had struck upon back in Holland. Whom could he personally account for? Pemba had not seen the remains of Gerard McDonnell, Karim Meherban, and one of the Koreans—he didn't know which one. Pemba also knew from Cas that Hugues D'Aubarède was in all likelihood gone. But he was most preoccupied with trying to find Wilco van Rooijen, who he knew was probably still alive, wandering lost in the general vicinity of the Shoulder. Two more times Cas and Pemba searched the area immediately around camp while Marco recovered in his tent.

At five forty-five p.m. in base camp, Chris Klinke, the ruddy financial manager from Michigan, noticed that the cloud cap that hid the south face down to Camp III had begun to lift. Chris trained a high-powered optical scope on the mountain. A tiny, orange dot winked at him from the wilderness of snow and ice. At almost the same time, Roeland spoke to Maarten van Eck again on the Thuraya. Maarten had the coordinates for Wilco.

Roeland raised Pemba and Cas in Camp IV. "He's below you guys, somewhere between Camp Three and Camp Four," he said. "Look to your right on the way down; he's somewhere off to the right."

By the time Pemba and Cas left Camp IV, it was completely dark. Pemba kept the sat phone on, in the inside pocket of the blue Feathered Friends one-piece suit Gerard had gotten for him. He kept shining his light, turning to look right across the open slopes of the concave bowl that arched toward the steep rock buttresses of the Magic Line. Cas was behind him, moving a little slower, lingering at the transitions at each anchor station. Pemba plowed ahead, looking to his right, as base camp had advised.

Camp III was pitched in a small snow basin that feeds one of the large seracs on the southeast face to the south of the SSE Spur. As he neared the top of the open snow bowl, Pemba tried once again to call Wilco using Gerard's phone. He immediately heard something, a noise foreign to K2's natural sounds. It was a phone, ringing somewhere in the darkness to his right. The Sherpa called out, but got no response. His weakened headlamp beam shone feebly against the mountain. The snow basin, Pemba knew, was the perfect pitch and aspect to hold wind slab, making for threatening avalanche conditions. Pemba would not leave the fixed lines. No one answered the phone. He descended to Camp III alone.

The next morning Cas woke him. They raised Roeland in base camp on the radio. "Start calling Wilco's name—he's to your west, to the left," Roeland said immediately. Cas, who was still dressed from his unplanned bivouac on the fixed lines between Camp III and Camp IV, departed at once. Pemba put on his boots to follow.

Soon they had Wilco inside the tent. Their missing leader seemed in surprisingly good condition, considering it had been more than fifty hours since he departed Camp IV for the summit. He spoke lucidly on the radio to Roeland, and seemed capable of descending under his own power. There was only one thing Pemba noted as being out of the ordinary: Wilco was convinced they were in Camp I. It was a disappointment when they informed him how far they still had to go. They melted water and prepared to descend.

"Don't send a rescue," Pemba said to Roeland when Wilco handed the radio off to his teammate. "It will only make it a more dangerous situation."

I saw Pemba again only a few weeks after I left Nepal.

That autumn he had quietly participated in several different media projects about the disaster, including two documentaries, one produced by the Discovery Channel and the other by Pat Falvey, Pemba and Gerard's longtime friend and expedition mate. Now, *National Geographic Adventure* magazine decided to give him the "Adventurer of the Year" award. They bought him a plane ticket and arranged an expedited visa to the United States. Pemba had been to Europe several times, but it was his first journey to America. A close-up portrait of his face splashed across the cover of the November issue of *National Geographic Adventure* magazine.

I picked him up in Queens early one gray, late-autumn morning. I got lost trying to find the address of his friends he was staying with. Block after block of impersonal brick dwellings with leaves rotting in the gutters flashed by as I circled through the neighborhood. Then, trying a different side street, I hung a right and something flashed gold and promising against the drab cityscape ahead. It was a large stupa, two buildings wide, with a pageant of prayer flags stretching down to the sidewalk. Down the hill and across the river, faint glimpses of the Manhattan skyline were barely visible.

Must be in the right neighborhood, I thought. The occasional pedestrian I passed was clad in the impersonal garb of cities in winter: caps and scarves, hoods cinched down, perhaps a set of headphones playing.

I circled once more and there was Pemba, his jacket zipped tight, shoulders hunched to protect his neck from the wind, not wearing any hat. He had caught a cold. The Hudson River Valley slipped quietly past as we drove north. Pemba pulled out his camera to shoot a video clip of the traffic jam at the toll plaza before we crossed the Tappan Zee Bridge. Leading up Directissima, one of the Shawangunks' classic climbs, I over-placed a cam and Pemba had to hang on the rope to get free when he followed behind me. It was windy on top and we hurried to the rappels.

His story was just really breaking. The *National Geographic Adventure* article declared him "the savior" of the storm. The complex series of events and decisions that had happened throughout the course of the climb that placed him in position to be able to rescue Marco, the conflicting emotions and ravaging fatigue of five days' intense effort above sixty-seven hundred meters, the whole story was neatly summed up in a couple of column inches:

> With his team in shambles, Pemba had to act fast. He heard over the radio that Confortola had been spotted midway up the Bottleneck. "I thought, Okay, if we are lucky, I can rescue Marco," Pemba says. So he began to climb, soloing through swirling snow up the couloir. "It was very scary, but I knew Marco was still alive," he says. "I could not turn back."

The author of the article took a few minor liberties in embellishing Pemba's own experience, while ignoring the most crucial part of his story. There was no mention of Tsering Bhote and Big Pasang, who had gone even farther into the Bottleneck that day to rescue Jumik, Hwang, Park, and Kim, other than to mention the gruesome detail of four more bodies falling out of the couloir.

History is written by the victors—in mountaineering, it might be said that history is written by the white man with the satellite phone. Likewise, the rescues that are remembered are the ones that are successful. That had been one of my main motivations for talking to the Sherpas in the first place: They were simply the best surviving sources of information as to what happened on K2, and that also probably explained why *National Geographic Adventure* put Pemba on its cover. But if it wasn't for the malicious timing of the serac's final releases, five more climbers might have escaped from K2. The real tragedy, I realized, was that they had almost pulled off one of the great rescues in the history of the mountain—surely an effort on par in terms of sheer guts and determination with that of the American team led by Charles Houston and Bob Bates—*and no one even knew about it.*

For his part, Pemba never once seemed proud or expressed any satisfaction at the accolades that were coming in. On the contrary, I felt he was just going through the motions of media celebrity—silently burdened by the weight of things the living must carry.

The ground quite literally changes beneath your two feet the moment you realize that you are no longer a detached entity from the subject of interest. In experimental research, this is known as the observer effect, or the Hawthorne effect, and is used to describe the changes that the act of observing will have on the phenomenon being observed. In physics, the closely related Heisenberg uncertainty principle states that pairs of physical properties, like position and momentum, cannot both be known to arbitrary precision. That is, the more precisely one property is known, the less precisely the other can be known. And not long after Pemba and I climbed at the Gunks, I was reminded of my own culpability in helping to produce the next generation of mountaineering hero.

The reminder came from an unlikely place—the Internet, in an anonymous response to the blog I had written about Pemba and Chhiring.

Pemba Gyalje was NOT a guide on K2. He was a full climbing team member of the Norit Team. He was a good friend and climbing partner of Gerard McDonnell's. They had finally fulfilled their dream of climbing K2 together as partners. It is also incorrect that Gerard McDonnell abandoned the Koreans that day. Pemba Gyalje's account has confirmed that Gerard was seen descending BEHIND the Koreans on the traverse toward the top of the gully before he was hit by serac and fell. Gerard did not abandon the Koreans that day, he continued his rescue efforts until his tragic death.

This was all true, at least according to Pemba's full version of the story, which I had finally heard after I had written the piece. The commenter knew what she was talking about. But as I read the reply, one mischosen word bubbled to the surface; indeed, the word seemed to encapsulate and, perhaps, explain the overwhelming emotional response the tragedy had evoked from the very beginning. In my piece praising Pemba and Chhiring, I had contrasted their efforts with the media's focus on the Western survivors:

> *Outside* and *Men's Journal* recently published feature-length pieces on the K2 disaster. Both stories led with the tale of three European men, Wilco van Rooijen, Gerard McDonnell, and Marco Confortola, who bivouaced at nearly 28,000 feet after the catastrophic serac avalanche stripped the Bottleneck Couloir of its fixed ropes on the evening of August 1st. The next day, they were forced to down climb the Bottleneck unroped. Along the way they passed a party of distressed Korean climbers; the three abandoned them to continue their own descents to safety. Two of them made it, but McDonnell was swept to his death in an avalanche.

"Confortola and van Rooijen can hardly be faulted for not doing more," I had added, almost as an afterthought, but the one word must have lingered with the acerbic taste of a festering wound.

Abandoned.

The poster's screen name was Starkey, and it took me two heartbeats to figure out who that must be.

PART THREE

*T*here are no available witnesses to what happened from the time Marco Confortola separated from Gerard McDonnell and the Korean group at the top of the Diagonal to the moment he and Pemba Gyalje saw four bodies falling in the midst of the last icefall at the bottom of the Bottleneck. Not one man survived. The thick cloud that enveloped the mountain from midmorning to late afternoon made it even impossible to watch the unfolding drama from a distance. For all of the people in and around Camp IV during that time, and the state-of-the-art communications technology they had collectively brought up the mountain, K2 was effectively closed off to the outside world, and the final hours of seven men were obscured.

Conflicting realities and disparate accounts are part of the historiography of every recorded human catastrophe. Prior to the Internet, personal journals were the primary form of documentation in expeditionary mountaineering. Visual images were captured on slide film. And, until very recently, video cameras were too bulky to be carried on any serious summit climb. Not only did this mean there was less documentation, but the information was also more centralized. Fritz Wiessner's disastrous 1939 K2 expedition, for instance, produced a flurry of letter writing, correspondence, and criticism afterward, but all of the firsthand information came down almost entirely to two personal diaries: that of Wiessner himself and a young American medical student named Jack Durrance. The high-water mark of media censorship was undoubtedly the 1950s, the height of the golden age, when the world's highest peaks finally succumbed to great national efforts. Back then it was the expedition leader's prerogative to write the official history of the climb—and it was common for each team member to be required to sign a legal document promising not to produce any competing accounts. The adulatory public had no idea at the time, but divisive arguments and controversy most certainly festered between the mountaineers they collectively lionized as national heroes.

Maybe modern technology, the democratization of media, blogs, etc., simply provided people with more opportunities to publicly share their stories. To create more information. And the more stories that were out there, the more opportunities for conflict and controversy. At the same time, if there was a greater volume of documentation to draw from, it also felt like all that information was more fragmented. Thirty-three individuals were present in Camp IV the night of July 31—how many sat phone calls, digital photos, video clips, and blog reports did they produce?

Even Pasang Lama, Chhiring Dorje, and Pemba Gyalje—the three guys I felt were the most lucid—hadn't truly pieced everything together. Most often they shrugged, spoke a few brief generalities, and proved awkwardly circumspect when I asked about events beyond what they had personally witnessed. But there were clues—tantalizing loose ends that just didn't make sense to anyone with big-mountain experience. Not only the particulars of Pemba's and Marco's stories, but other details buried in the flood of information. A few pixilated images, the confusing chronologies of hypoxic memories, the technical minutiae of high-angle rescue. At the same time, I had to keep remembering not to turn into a conspiracy theorist myself. I was torn between wanting to arrive at total understanding, and knowing rationally there was no neatly packaged explanation to what had occurred on K2.

There was only one person whom I hadn't spoken to who might possess new firsthand knowledge of the incident. He was the voice calling out from *inside the cloud—Tsering Bhote, the highest man, higher than even Pemba Gyalje, to survive the Bottleneck on August 2. Tsering and Big Pasang were assigned to the Korean "B" team, a second wave of climbers who arrived in Camp IV on August 1 as everyone else was already going for the summit. They spent that night searching the upper Shoulder for their teammates descending out the bottom of the Bottleneck. Sometime before dawn Tsering and Big Pasang returned to Camp IV. Four of their teammates were still missing: Kim Hyo-gyeong, Hwang Dong-jin, Park Kyeong-hyo, and Jumik Bhote, the expedition sirdar. Big Pasang and Tsering, Jumik's younger brother, were Kim Jae-su's rescue party.*

Twenty-six years old, Big Pasang was known among his friends as being especially strong. As they ascended the couloir, he surged ahead. It was Tsering's slow pace that saved him. He was just outside the path of the final serac fall when he saw his brother, cousin, and two more men sweep past him to their deaths.

But Tsering had eluded me while I was in Kathmandu for my Kangtega expedition, and then, over the winter, the story took an unexpected turn: The media spin began to circle back around toward Kathmandu. Hollywood, such as it was, came knocking—the names of big players like National Geographic, *the* Discovery Channel, *the* New York Times, *were all rumored to be circling around the K2 story. In moments of vanity, I wondered if it was partially my own doing, for publicizing their deeds in the first place. And if anyone should profit from the disaster, wasn't it the climbing-Sherpas, who had sacrificed so much?*

By the beginning of the twenty-first century there was lengthy precedent for Sherpa celebrity. Both Tenzing Norgay and Ang Tharkay were the subjects of biographies written in the 1950s. Those two, and a handful of other tigers in the intervening years, had visited Europe, met heads of state, done public glad-handing of the highest order. Tenzing Norgay's nephew Nawang Gumbu, who summited in Everest 1963 with Jim Whittaker, even gave JFK a Kharta scarf in the Rose Garden. Two more recent examples of Sherpa celebrities are Babu Sherpa and Jamling Norgay, son of the original Everest summiteer. Jamling costared in a highly successful IMAX movie about the 1996 Everest season, while Babu became famous and earned international sponsorship for setting records on Everest, becoming, among other things, the first person to pitch a tent and spend the night—without oxygen—on the very summit.

From the point of view of the climbing-Sherpas, K2 had the potential to pay off their mortgage, send their children to school in the United States, maybe even let them quit high-altitude guiding and begin climbing as a sponsored pro. After all, as everyone knew in the back of their minds, no Sherpa to date had completed all fourteen eight-thousanders, an achievement that was bound to happen sooner or later. Surviving K2 could be leveraged into a lucky career break by the climbing-Sherpas just as easily as it could by the Western mountaineers.

Annie Starkey's comments, meanwhile, pointed me in a new direction. If there were answers to what happened in the Bottleneck couloir that day, they couldn't be found by a close analysis of the empirical data alone. Other missing pieces of the story were tucked away in the lives of those who bore witness to the tragedy, and its unsettling aftermath—those who had kept vigil around eleven different living rooms and kitchen tables, scattered across the globe. The realization pushed me toward an even greater body of evidence that might help explain what happened, though it was evidence of a different kind.

I knew a considerable amount about the survivors, not only their stories from K2, but also their backgrounds as climbers and their temperaments as people. But to understand those final hours, I needed to know not only the living, but also the dead—Jumik Bhote, who was last seen alive with his three Korean clients near the top of the fixed lines, Big Pasang Bhote, who climbed the Bottleneck the next morning despite Pemba's warnings, to try to rescue them, and Gerard McDonnell, who could have descended with Marco Confortola, but for some reason didn't.

As I pondered each iteration of what might have happened, one image would not leave my mind. It was taken by Pemba Gyalje, documenting the remains of two of the Bottleneck's final victims. The two bodies came to rest together. They were dressed in thick down suits, gloves, goggles, face masks, and hoods, so that no human skin was visible, save for a single outstretched hand. They might as well have been two mannequins, except for the streak of bloody snow stretching out of the frame. Tattered lengths of old fixed rope bound the two bodies together. They seemed to hold each other, as if in an embrace.

Beneath the grotesque imagery, there was an incongruous dignity to the scene. Something had happened up there. Those corpses—still warm when Pemba snapped the photo—quietly insisted that the story continue, even if it crossed the fuzzy threshold from fact to theory. The more I learned—the closer I got—the more I discovered the true reach of the tragedy, how the pain continued, splintering away from the mountain like a pane of fractured glass, slicing into the lives of those who survived.

10

THE HOUSE OF BHOTE

"*H*ow *did you find me?*" *Virginia O'Leary asked when we spoke on the phone. "Of course," she replied, after I told her. "That damn blog." I heard Virginia let out a split-second sigh, a wordless note that communicated her personal feelings quite clearly.*

Virginia was guarded at first. It was obvious from our first e-mail exchange that what happened on K2 was, for her, just a piece of the puzzle, only part of some bigger dynamic. "I was a good friend of Jumik and his family," she wrote, "but the tragedy on K2 was not the only tragic occurrence that year involving the Bhote family." Her blog was intended to be a private affair, a letter addressed to interested friends and family back home, detailing her adventures while she was gone. "Letters from Kathmandu," she called it. Virginia couldn't have known what she was really chronicling when she began making regular weekly posts in 2007.

Much later, she decided to take the blog down altogether.

Virginia still remembers the first time she read about Maurice Herzog on Annapurna. She was twelve years old. The mystery of the Himalayas captivated her as she followed the Frenchman's epic battle to summit the world's first eight-thousand-meter peak. Her youthful fascination with the mountaineering tale slowly evolved into an adult passion for the country of Nepal, though it took many, many years before she finally managed to visit the country. Life got in the way first. Soon after she had earned a Ph.D. in social psychology, Virginia lost her husband, a well-regarded journalist, in a small plane accident. She was pregnant with their first child. Virginia resolutely went on to become a successful career academic, the chair of her department at Indiana State University and then Auburn University in Alabama. All the while she raised her son as a single mother.

At last, in 1993, she finally arrived at a point in her life where she had the time, the money, and the freedom to fulfill her dream of seeing the Himalayas. Having no idea of how to go about organizing a mountain trek, she and several friends booked spots on a commercial tour with an American guide. She was fifty years old, and it felt a little adventurous just to be going to such an exotic place as Nepal.

The trip was a turning point in her life: Virginia returned to the country at least once every twelve months for the next fifteen years. Having focused on industrial-organizational psychology, Virginia had by training a keen eye for the subtleties of workplace dynamics. She immediately realized, when she counted the number of laborers associated with a first-class trekking operation, why the trip was so expensive. "We had a Western guide, a sirdar, a cook, an assistant cook, and then the ordinary porters," Virginia recalls, shaking her head. When she wanted to go on another trek four years later, in 1997, Virginia contacted Patrick Kenny, the American leader of her previous trip, and asked for a recommendation for a good Nepali guide. "I told him I wanted to go trekking in the Solu Khumbu, but didn't want to pay top dollar," Virginia says. After all, she reasoned, if she was going to see the Himalayas, why not see them with a real local as her guide? That was how she met Pemba Bhote.

Like the Sherpas, the Bhotes, or Bhotia, is the name of a specific tribe of people of Tibetan descent living within Nepali borders. Unlike the former title, however, being called a Bhote in general Nepalese society often carries a derogatory connotation. For centuries, upper-caste Hindis used the term to refer to any poor villager from the mountains, with much the same intention as a poor rural farmer might be called a hillbilly or a redneck in the United States. Most Tibetans who settled in Nepal were originally poor immigrants, but even purebred Sherpas, who were among the early waves of Tibetan migrants to relocate to Nepal, looked down their noses at the impoverished Bhotes and Khambas who struggled over the Nangpa La pass centuries after them.

Hungong, Pemba Bhote's village home, is a large city by Himalayan standards, at one point boasting a population of over four thousand people.* It's just east of Makalu, in the Arun river valley, and the closest portal to the outside world is the airstrip in Tumlingtar, a week's trek to the south. The people born in Hungong follow virtually the same traditional pattern of life as the Solu Khumbu Sherpas, growing potatoes and other high-altitude crops, raising yaks, perhaps engaging in a little regional trade. The difference between the Sherpas of Solu Khumbu and Bhotes of the Arun is that the latter were born two valleys away from the most popular trekking region in the Himalayas. Almost no Western tourist dollars made it to Hungong. It was, in Himalayan terms, a neighborhood on the wrong side of the tracks from the enchanted villages of the Khumbu. Younger generations of Bhotes found no other options than to join the stream of other rural Nepali ethnicities and move to the city in search of work. Such was the case with Pemba Bhote, the oldest brother in a family of ten children, who came to Kathmandu in the early 1990s.

That first trek together was a magical experience, and Virginia found Pemba a charming young man. What he lacked in English skills he made up for in his friendly enthusiasm in conversing with his clients, and the sheer gusto with which he approached his job. With her son Sean, they did a sixteen-day trek that began in Lukla and took them north into the Sherpa heartland. With Pemba, Virginia spent two days crossing steel-reinforced but still plenty rickety suspension bridges across the Dudh Kosi and strolling through bustling villages made of cobbled river stone.

---

* By contrast, Beding, Chhiring Dorje's home village in Rolwaling, had well under a thousand residents at its peak population.

Then they made the long, switchbacking climb to Namche Bazaar. And then—there it was. Everest. Just standing there at the head of the valley, its lower flanks guarded by the fierce wall of Nuptse, a regal snow plume blowing from its summit.

Virginia began learning Nepali. During the trek, she noticed that Pemba, like many young trekking guides, tried earnestly to affect a sense of worldliness while in the company of his American clients. He never passed up the opportunity to mention that he had visited the United States three years ago, with his friend Tom. Evidently a previous group of American trekkers had paid for Pemba to come and visit them in America.

"He kept talking to us about his friend Tom—'my friend Tom'—so one day my friend Adrienne said, 'Pemba, do you have any photos from the U.S.?' And the next day Pemba brought his pictures in a packet envelope. We looked and our mouths fell open." Photo after photo showed Pemba—back then nothing more than a young cook—smiling back at the camera with his friend Tom. Virginia knew that face instantly, the eagle eyes, boyish features, a face that had looked out at the country and reminded generations of Americans of a thousand ongoing catastrophes in the world beyond their borders.

Pemba's friend was . . . *Tom Brokaw?*

While visiting the Khumbu in 1994, the famous American newsman and several of his friends had apparently taken a liking to Pemba, who was at the time still in his early twenties. They chipped in and flew him to the United States for a monthlong visit. Pemba stayed at Tom's ranch in Montana. The incredible thing, Virginia realized, as Pemba eagerly showed them photos of his travels, was that he was clueless as to his friend Tom's celebrity. "He wasn't watching the nightly news. He was a cook's helper," Virginia remembers. "Pemba had no idea who Tom Brokaw was. We were astonished." So far as Pemba Bhote understood it, every American had a thousand-acre ranch tucked away in the high Rockies.

By the end of their trek together, she was as captivated by the country as ever, and felt especially close to the young man who was her guide.

Pemba was, in Virginia's estimation, friendly and sharing, strong as a horse, and committed to providing for the rest of his family, all of whom were still living in Hungong. When she left Nepal, she gave Pemba an unusually large tip: enough money for him to make a down payment on a used car that he could drive as a taxi. They had discussed it on their trek, that the taxi business could be a good means for him to provide more regular income to his family instead of his being completely reliant on trekking jobs.

Virginia began to lead study-abroad programs to Kathmandu for interested college students. She'd pay Pemba a small fee for hosting a traditional dinner for her group at his home in Bhoda, the Tibetan district of Kathmandu. They would all sit together, eating dal bhat served from his kitchen, completely enthralled by the experience. The feeling was mutual: Virginia even noticed cute neighborhood children spying back at them through the windows. Pemba Bhote, meanwhile, began to move his siblings from Hungong to Kathmandu. To start with, he chose one brother and one sister—his brother Jumik and his sister Bhutti.

The conflict between staying in school and entering the workforce pervades countless families in the developing world. In 1990, the anthropologist James Fisher observed that entry-level salaries for schoolteachers in the Khumbu were the same as or better than for entry-level trekking and mountaineering jobs, and with better job security. As Fisher explains it: "Sherpas . . . think not just of trekking jobs but of trekking careers, and the capstone to a career in trekking is the position of sirdar. The hope of achieving this position draws the younger generation out of the schools and into tourism in large numbers." Indeed, the salary ceilings, for what one might hope to earn at the pinnacle of the two respective careers, don't compare. At the time of Fisher's research, an experienced sirdar could expect to clear more than thirty thousand rupees (forty-five hundred dollars) for a two-month Everest expedition, while a skilled high school teacher would make less than sixty-six hundred rupees (nine hundred dollars) in the same time frame. But Pemba Bhote's dream for Jumik when he brought him to Kathmandu was for his little brother to stay in school while Pemba worked trekking jobs and drove the taxi.

For the time being, the financial security of the family would rest on him; the family's future hopes would rest on Jumik.

Pemba had three younger brothers, and Virginia once asked him why he had chosen Jumik to be the first to join him in Kathmandu. She remembers his answer to this day.

"I chose the one who loved me best," Pemba told her.

The same year Virginia O'Leary met Pemba Bhote, a dusty, mud-speckled motorcyclist made his way north through the barren wilderness of the Canadian Yukon. The bike had a small trailer attached behind it that was neatly packed with camping and outdoor gear. The traveler was youthful and powerfully built, and he spoke with a strange, sonorous accent. He was Gerard McDonnell, twenty-six years old, and he had come a long way from his home of Kilcornan, County of Limerick, Ireland.

It would be tempting to see parallels in Gerard's life and those of the Sherpas I had spent so much time researching. Gerard was raised on a dairy farm in the country. He grew up outside, was taught the value of working hard and doing your chores on time, and had an agriculturalist's special appreciation for the value of every living thing.

Dogs were always a favorite of his. One oft-told story in his family concerns the time young Ger found an abandoned dog wet and shivering in the rain. He wrapped his coat around the animal and made sure it found a cozy nook in a dry barn. His coat smelled for months afterward. He spent so much of his youth exploring and playing amid the lush pastoral landscape of fields, hedgerows, creeks, and barns that his mother frequently had a hard time locating her son. She eventually learned to call for the family dog, Princess; whatever direction it came running from indicated where she could find Gerard. A few years later, it was raining again, and Gerard was on a date with his girlfriend in Cork City when they came upon a homeless person on the street. Gerard stopped and struck up a conversation with the man—listening to others was turning out to be one of the young man's greatest strengths. Before long Ger had given the luckless fellow his coat, and, somewhat to the consternation of his girlfriend, was escorting him to a shelter where he could get a warm night's sleep.

When he enrolled in Dublin City University to study electronic engineering, Gerard was passionate about hurling—the peculiar Gaelic sport played with wooden sticks and a ball similar to field hockey. But during his university years he discovered a new pastime. "I remember vividly my first rock climb," Gerard would explain later. "It's my belief that everyone has a love of climbing inside of them; it's kind of almost belted out of them as children—'Get off the stairs; get down off the tree.' The first thing a child or toddler wants to do is climb something." Gerard joined the Dublin City University Mountain Club and then took a technical course in Scotland. Hurling began to fall by the wayside. Reminiscing about the change in hobbies he would joke that he gave up hurling because it was too dangerous. "It's easier to control circumstances on a mountain than it is on the hurling field," Gerard quipped.

Toward the end of his undergraduate studies, a chance event occurred that changed the course of Gerard's life. He walked into the dining hall one day to find a group of friends frantically filling out sheets of paper. "What are you doing?" Gerard asked, oblivious. He was informed that the deadline to apply for the Morrison's visa was the next day.

"The Morrison's visa—what's that?" Gerard asked. He was told that it was a lottery to win a green card to go to the United States. "I never had any interest in going to the States," Gerard said, but he decided on a lark to fill out an application as well. Several months later, an official envelope arrived in the mail. Gerard McDonnell had won an invitation to live and work in the United States of America.

The States didn't agree with him at first. He flew first to Virginia to validate his visa, and wound up working as a software engineer in Maryland. But it wasn't long before what he perceived as the artificial anxieties of the suburban East Coast began to grate. When his boss took a new job in Norway and invited Gerard to join him, he jumped at the opportunity. His only condition was that he get a few months off between commitments, to tour the rest of America.

Gerard left Annapolis on his recently purchased motorcycle and rode it to Key West, Florida, then across the Mississippi to the Rocky Mountains and down into Mexico, trying to visit as many national parks and wilderness areas as possible along the way. Traveling solo, he would often park his bike at a trailhead and head out for a few days' hiking and camping—and he managed to do some technical climbing as well, whenever he had partners. Everything he needed was carried in the small trailer hitched behind the bike.

As the climax of his journey, Gerard dreamed of continuing on beyond the Colorado Rockies and Sierras, all the way north through Canada to see the most remote country the North American continent had to offer—Alaska. His original inspiration for seeing the fiftieth state was a *National Geographic* documentary, but soon the challenge of just getting there began to attract him as much as the wilderness. "I wasn't too sure what kind of condition the roads were in up there in northern Canada. Some people said, 'No, don't do it.' But I did some investigating, and the more investigating I did the more I wanted to do it."

By his own reckoning, the connection Gerard McDonnell felt with the Alaskan landscape was nearly instantaneous. Certainly, as he worked his way west and south on the two-lane road from the U.S./Canada border toward Anchorage, then weaved around the Talkeetna Mountains to the north and the Chugach to the south, it would have been difficult for any outdoor lover not to be captured by the untamed scenery. "It's definitely a place of extremes," Gerard later described Alaska, "but in many ways, those very extremes—they're addictive. . . . In those extremes, or with those extremes, comes extreme beauty."

If winning the Morrison's visa was the first major turning point in his life, reaching the Alcan Border crossing and entering into Alaska marked the next change. Gerard was still a young man in his twenties, unemployed, and single, with only a loose commitment to eventually move to Norway and begin a new job there. A passionate outdoorsman and proficient climber, he was nevertheless a novice when it came to big-mountain climbing. That began to change once he settled in Anchorage.

"Once I arrived in Alaska it was obvious to me that I needed to spend more time there," he said later, with characteristic understatement.

On June 1, 2001, the Crown Prince Dipendra—the great-grandson of King Tribhuvan—walked into a social gathering at Narayanhity Royal Palace attended by his father and mother, King Birendra and Queen Aishwarya, armed with an MP5 submachine gun and an M16 rifle. Witnesses would later recall that Dipendra had been visibly drunk earlier that evening and had a disagreement with one of the guests, and then been escorted out of the party by two siblings. The scuttlebutt around court held that Dipendra was enmeshed in a dispute with his father over potential marriage arrangements. An hour later, he returned to the party and opened fire. Nine people were murdered, including both the king and queen, and his brother Prince Nirajan. The last life Dipendra took was his own.

Much as the assassination of Archduke Ferdinand helped spark World War I, the royal massacre proved to be the flash that ignited Nepal's volatile political scene, especially in unstable rural towns like Hungong, into the conflagration of open civil war. After seizing control from the Ranas, Tribhuvan dabbled in a brief experiment in democracy during the 1950s, before his successor son, King Mahendra, abolished parliament and effectively instituted a constitutional monarchy in 1962. By the last decade of the twentieth century, the government's wayward economic policies brought escalating prices and repeatedly failed to provide basic services to many of the nation's rural citizens. Left-wing Maoist doctrine began to take hold among Nepal's neglected mountain populations. In 1996, the Communist Party of Nepal (CPN) formally adopted regime change from the old monarchy to a new people's democratic republic as official policy. The revolutionaries seized control over local governments in five districts, but the conflict largely simmered until Prince Dipendra's personal demons chased him to murder. The king's brother, who had been third in line for the crown, eventually assumed power of the monarchy after the massacre, but the communist insurgency went on the offensive.

Since the CPN first declared the "People's War" in 1996, Western governments, international journalists, and human-rights watch groups had warned that the situation had the potential to turn into a humanitarian catastrophe. In the year 2000, Amnesty International released a report accusing both the CPN, and the national police's heavy-handed response, of human-rights violations. The report summarized the situation after four years of simmering civil conflict.

> . . . grave human rights violations by the police and members of the CPN (Maoist) have since been reported on an almost daily basis. These have included hundreds of extrajudicial executions, dozens of "disappearances" and numerous incidents of torture and arbitrary arrests and detention on the part of the police. Members of the CPN (Maoist) have also been responsible for scores of deliberate killings and abductions of civilians and torture.

As the two forces skirmished, the Maoists began to quietly institute their social programs, which included destroying existing property records, redistributing land, threatening and beating local schoolteachers, and sending students to compulsory "political education" sessions instead. But most of the activity centered in a few districts of small agricultural villages in the middle west of Nepal, far from the Tibetan communities of the high Himalayas, or the eyes of Western tourists. Indeed, the late 1990s were a time of global prosperity, and good for the international tourism trade. On her visit to the Solu Khumbu in 1997, Virginia O'Leary saw little more than peaceful snow-clad peaks and squadrons of well-equipped Western travelers, blissfully unaware that anything was amiss in their mountain Shangri-la.

The 2001 royal massacre changed all that. With the monarchy nearly wiped out, the Maoists stepped up their activities, establishing "people's governments" in more than fifty districts. Peace talks then broke down in November, and the CPN launched a series of attacks that crippled the country's productivity. By April of 2002, ten months after the royal massacre, Amnesty International released a new report that declared Nepal a "spiraling human rights crisis."

In the spring of 2001, visitors to Makalu-Barun National Park, not far from the Bhote's village of Hungong, noticed few signs of open conflict other than some Maoist posters adorning village walls not far from vandalized government signs. By spring the next year, armed Maoist soldiers began stopping trekking and mountaineering expeditions to the area and demanding a ten-thousand-rupee (approximately a hundred-and-thirty-dollar) fee to be allowed to continue to base camp. For five thousand rupees, individuals could also continue, but the Maoists would force them to hand over their cameras and electronic gear. One expedition to the normal route on Makalu reported that though the Maoists were armed, they seemed nonthreatening to Westerners and were interested only in collecting revenue from their new tourist "tax." More ominously the report noted that "The Maoists are very young, nervous and heavily armed—who knows what discipline or organization they have. Armed confrontations are not friendly incidents." Two park rangers had allegedly been murdered early that year.

For most purposes, public schooling in the upper Arun Valley came to a stop. For Virginia's friend and guide, Pemba Bhote, there was no question. He had to bring the rest of his family to the relative safety of Kathmandu. Virginia promised to support their education, and three of Jumik and Pemba's sisters moved to the city in late 2001, followed by their mother and youngest sister in 2003. The Bhotes had always struggled with poverty, but in Kathmandu, the family became particularly vulnerable—rural poverty and urban poverty are two very different challenges. Financially, the fate of everyone hinged on the little taxi that Virginia had financed. But there was another problem—as the Maoist movement surged in the aftermath of the massacre, tourism took a nosedive. For Pemba, it was a one-two punch: Both as a trekking guide and cook, and again as a taxi driver, he depended on Western dollars. In Kathmandu, only Westerners regularly pay fares for taxis.

Jumik, meanwhile, was struggling with his academic career. The Nepali public school program finishes at the tenth form, a level of education roughly corresponding to ninth or tenth grade in the United States. At the completion of that year, everyone takes a standardized test. The highest-scoring go on to do two more years of studying, called "plus-two" years, after which successful students continue on to university or private college. Pemba Bhote and Virginia assumed Jumik would stay in school.

"He was a naturally smart young man," Virginia says, searching to describe his academic habits. "He was not undisciplined, but he wasn't studying all the time, either. Young men like him are like young men anywhere, the world over." If a somewhat carefree student, Jumik was a gifted athlete, and his greatest passion was playing soccer. Most afternoons and weekends small crowds gather on fields of rough grass thatched over browned earth in several public parks around the Kathmandu Valley. Jumik played on locally organized competitive teams.

It's possible the evening he finished his tenth-form leaving exam, Jumik went and played soccer. As he sprinted and kicked beneath the building monsoon skies, he would not have known that his exam, still ungraded, would ultimately deny him a place in Nepal's public education system to continue his schooling. He would not have realized that his life was about to drop into the great socioeconomic void that swallows up much of South Asia's youth.

"It was a big shock to everyone," Virginia recalls. The news that he'd failed his leaving exam was not only a personal setback for Jumik, but also somewhat of a collective defeat for the entire family. The Bhotes joined countless other families, displaced from their rural village by conflict and strife, surviving on a shoestring budget at the margin of urban poverty. By the time the civil war in Nepal finally began to wind down in 2007, Nepal's unemployment rate had climbed past 40 percent, while its literacy rate remained less than 50 percent. The per-capita income? Three hundred and eighty-seven dollars.

Pemba Bhote, meanwhile, decided to sell the taxi and buy a bus instead. He acquired a permit to drive a route along the busy Ring Road from one side of Kathmandu to the other. While Pemba drove, Jumik would collect fares and manage the passengers. They typically charged five rupees, about eight cents. So long as that bus—purchased with the capital from Virginia O'Leary's generous tip to her exuberant young guide—kept running, the Bhotes would survive.

Jumik worked for his older brother, continued to play soccer, and waited for something better to come his way.

11

RISK / REWARD

The job market for any ambitious young climbing-Sherpa is centered around a half dozen or so large logistics companies based in Kathmandu. These organizers consolidate the myriad expenses associated with a two-month Himalayan expedition—peak fees, food and provisions, domestic transportation, the salaries of paid expedition staff—into a single per-person price that normally includes all "in-country" expenses. Thamserku Treks & Expeditions, Arun Treks and Expeditions, Asian Trekking, High Altitude Dreams, and Explore Himalaya are a few of the biggest, each sometimes fielding as many as ten separate expeditions per season. There are dozens of smaller companies advertising the same services, but the biggest companies tend to attract the most labor-intensive gigs, large national expeditions and commercial teams with ten to fifteen climbers, that must field a small army of climbing-Sherpas to prepare the route. Everest expeditions are the most labor-intensive of all, because the reliance on bottled oxygen increases the number of loads that must be carried.

Asian Trekking, founded by Ang Tshering Sherpa, is probably the best-known trekking company in Nepal. The traditional business model for trekking agencies focused on forging alliances with Western guide services like Rainier Mountaineering, Inc., or Alpine Ascents International, and courting large privately organized expeditions. Ang Tshering decided, in effect, to skip the middleman, and sell spots on supported Everest climbs directly to paying Western clients. Though it seemed a novel idea at first, it was in many ways the logical conclusion of the Sherpa's gradual rise through the history of Himalayan mountaineering, and the more recent advent of guided climbing. Ang Tshering, for his part, was careful to remind everyone that he wasn't providing the Westernized services of a professional guide, merely the logistical infrastructure (tents, oxygen, and Sherpa teams to prepare the route) to help self-reliant mountaineers to reach the summit.

"In practical terms," says Phil Crampton, a longtime Himalayan guide with thirty Himalayan expeditions to his credit, "all of their services are relatively comparable. They're like any well-organized travel agency." The typical Himalayan trek or climb may be sold as a package deal, but in reality it will be led by a team of subcontracted cooks, climbing-Sherpas, and sirdars. "In the old days," Crampton notes, "it seemed like each agency maintained its own team of guides exclusively. These days, everyone seems to be working for everyone. There's not much loyalty."

Guiding work is seasonal. Every spring (premonsoon) and fall (postmonsoon), armies of trekkers and mountaineers invade Kathmandu for a few days, then embark for the mountains—more often than not accompanied by some kind of professional Nepali staff. Each winter and summer, hundreds of guides return to the city a few thousand dollars richer to visit their families and arrange the next spate of work. August and March are frequently the busiest months, as expeditions are finalized and employment confirmed. Because even the most bare-bones professionally supported Himalayan expeditions are expensive, even by Western standards, there are a good deal of last-minute cancellations and postponements. An aspiring trekking guide or climbing-Sherpa learns to never refuse any work, knowing that of a half dozen loose promises, perhaps one will materialize into actual employment. The final weeks of the off-season in Kathmandu frequently become a mad dash as some trips cancel, some trips hire, and everyone scrambles to find work.

In such an extremely fluid labor market, personal referrals are what ultimately win you the job. As in any trades business, each high-level sirdar, guide, and cook has his or her own network of partners, apprentices, and underlings they prefer to hire. A constantly shifting matrix of alliances and relationships decides what mountain and what kind of work, if any, a young cook or climbing-Sherpa might land for the next season.

Pemba Bhote was not interested in becoming a high-altitude climbing-Sherpa himself. On his one foray into technical mountaineering as a young man, he took a long, scary fall into a crevasse. After that, he decided to stick to the less lucrative but safer trekking groups. When he did land a trekking job, the family would hire another driver with a professional license to pilot the bus around Kathmandu while he was away. Occasionally, he arranged short stints of work for his younger brother as well, usually a position as an assistant cook or climbing-Sherpa on an expedition to a six-thousand-meter trekking peak. Then, sometime during the winter of 2006, Jumik landed a spot on an Everest expedition.

The invitation purportedly came from a relative from Hungong, Nawang Sherpa. Nawang was a generation older, established as a base camp cook, and held one peculiar qualification that distinguished him among the ubiquitously "qualified" cadre of Kathmandu cooks and trekking guides: Nawang had spent time in South Korea, and could cook excellent Korean food. The trekking agency that Nawang worked for, Windhorse Trekking, specialized in Korean expeditions, and for that spring they had booked a large expedition from South Korea to the North Col route. Jumik Bhote went to Everest, and at six thirty a.m. on May 16, 2006, he stood on top of the world, the first of thirty-one people to reach the summit that day, including ten Korean clients.

It was his first eight-thousand-meter summit. According to a résumé posted on Windhorse's Web site, prior to 2006 Jumik Bhote had summited Pumori (7,167 meters) once, in 2005, and participated in an expedition to Nanda Devi (7,800) in 2002. It doesn't specify whether he reached the top or not. Jumik also has a half dozen or so six-thousand-meter "trekking peaks" listed as well—mostly mountains that require a single day's effort climbing on snow with crampons. With nobody really paying attention, résumés like this are occasionally embellished. But even so, by climbing-Sherpa standards, Jumik was qualified enough to begin working on Everest. It was a step into the big leagues, but there was no reason to suspect he wasn't capable. He would simply learn on the job, the same as generations had before.

What is extraordinary is the trajectory of his career after 2006. A year later, Jumik was back on Everest with another group of Koreans. This team was officially titled the Korean "Flying Jump" expedition. That was how he met Kim Jae-su and Go Mi-yeong.

A year after that he would be sirdar on K2.

Virtually everyone who met him agrees that Gerard—or Ger, as he was known to many friends—had a unique ability to connect with people. It didn't matter who they were: musicians, outdoorsmen, tech-savvy computer programmers, vintage car collectors and motor-heads of all types, parents, grandparents, and especially small children. He could always look someone in the eye and appreciate them for their own individual personality. Alaska, his adopted home, is a place known for its individualism and quirky personalities. During his first years in Anchorage, Gerard would sign a twelve-month lease on a house, and then sublet the other rooms to friends of all persuasions.

"Ger got along brilliantly with his housemates," Hilka Korvola remembers. She had moved down from Fairbanks to Anchorage, and answered an ad in the paper that read "looking for roommate." "He was the leader of the household," Hilka says. "He paid the mortgage, was the natural leader. He always made people feel welcome to visit. . . ." After some searching, Gerard landed a software engineering job and quickly fell in with a diverse group of friends.

All the while, he kept his eye on the summits. An explicit part of Gerard's original decision to stay in Alaska was to pursue his love of the mountains. As he told it: "One of the reasons . . . why I made that phone call to my friend over in Norway and refused the job was I wanted to climb Denali." His goal was seven times higher than Ireland's tallest peak, he joked, and twenty times colder. A methodical planner, Gerard earnestly read all the books about mountaineering and Alaska he could lay his hands on. He researched the West Buttress, the most popular route to the 20,320-foot (6,194-meter) summit, and learned what equipment to bring, and what the likely hazards and challenges would be.

Jeff Jessen was working at the Anchorage REI equipment store when they met in 1998. Gerard regularly stopped in the shop to talk gear. They hit it off and soon were planning a Denali expedition for the next spring. Gerard's easygoing, lighthearted personality belied the fact that he was a disciplined and meticulous worker. He set out to climb Denali with the same mind-set an engineer applies to finding a solution to a complex equation. He practiced and experimented and looked at it from every conceivable angle. Jeff, Gerard, and a third friend, Mike Mays, began trying to spend as much time as possible in the Chugach Mountains, easily accessible by car from just beyond Anchorage city limits. For their final training mission, they planned to make an ascent of Mount Marcus Baker, the highest mountain in the Chugach.

"We cached our extra food and fuel, and then moved up to a high camp at ten thousand feet," Jessen remembers. "That was a mistake." A massive storm moved in from the Gulf of Alaska and lasted for nine days. The team of five (McDonnell, Jessen, Mays, plus two more friends, Mike Thompson and Jeff Young) hunkered down, facing winds up to fifty to sixty miles an hour and heavy snow. With the bulk of their provisions cached below and inaccessible, they began to have to ration what they had. In the midst of the storm, even a rescue was out of the question.

That week was a formative moment in Gerard's mountaineering apprenticeship. "We were doing a lot of shoveling," Jessen remembers. "Gerard ended up getting into my tent. We were rotating around the clock, shoveling, sleeping, cooking. Shoveling. Everyone was super low energy because we were conserving rations and fuel. Through it all, Gerard never lost his cool. He was a great guy to have that experience with."

Two months later, Gerard, Mike Mays, and Jeff Jessen were at the high camp on Denali. On their first summit attempt, Jeff began to have upper-respiratory problems a thousand feet below the top. Gerard and Mike escorted their friend safely back to camp, and tried again the next day. This time they were successful, but as they hurried down from the summit in deteriorating weather, Gerard and Mike met two Taiwanese women on the "football field," a small windswept plateau just below the summit ridge. Plainly exhausted, the pair informed them that they intended to bivouac. It was obvious their lives would be in extreme danger if they stopped for any length of time. Mike and Gerard tied the two fatigued climbers into the middle of their rope, and continued down. A bit lower they ran into a party of three South Africans, who also looked to be in trouble, and added them to their ad hoc team as well. All seven climbers arrived back in high camp together, physically exhausted but otherwise all right.

Afterward, the National Park Service recognized both Gerard and Mike with Denali Pro pins for their efforts, writing that their "sound decisions and selfless actions" had helped save lives. The collective experience Gerard accumulated on Marcus Baker and Denali that spring would stay with him through the rest of his mountaineering career—most of all, the lesson that you always kept the party together. Jessen sums up their ethos: "We stayed together as a team. We came as a team, and we went back down as a team."

After that year, Gerard was a committed expedition climber. "It didn't surprise me," Jessen says now. "The thing with Gerard that I really liked about him, whatever he put his mind or energy to, he did a hundred and ten percent." The attitude extended well beyond mountaineering, and also included playing music, tinkering with vintage cars and bikes, and orchestrating social outings of all kinds with his friends. One favorite winter activity was ice-skating. "I'll never forget ice-skating on this big lake—it was miles long," Gerard said. "We were skating at night and the moon was out and the northern lights were out, and the reflection of both the moon and the northern lights was on the ice. And the ice, because it didn't have any snow, it sort of looked like still water . . . the reflection was just perfect. It was like skating in space."

Hilka Korvola attended one such evening of revelry. "One night we went to Potter Marsh, and everybody had been drinking," she remembers. "We went out ice-skating, and Gerard said, 'No, the ice is too thin.' We all said, 'No, come on, whatever. . . .' Ger didn't make a big deal of it, but he and his girlfriend left and went home alone." For all his emphasis on the group, Gerard was someone very much capable of independent decisions, especially when it came to evaluating risk. "He was a guy confident in his own judgment," she says.

"I still see it on Everest all the time," eight-thousand-meter commercial trip leader Jamie McGuinness asserts. "Not only are they using their own members until they fall over; they're using their Sherpas too. . . . They just have no concept of rest, recovery. The Koreans drive their staff particularly hard. There's no sensitivity to them being sick or tired or anything else."

Practically every experienced big-mountain guide or climber has a story about a Korean team, and Jamie is no exception. "It's quite a bizarre tale, really," he says. "One Korean had found a rock in the Langtang region of Nepal that looked like Korean writing. . . . It was just the shape of a Korean symbol. They took that as a talisman, or something like that. It said for them to climb Everest. Their cook, who had lived in Korea and cooked Korean food, he lost the stone. They freaked out, got the staff to look for it. They looked for it literally for two or three days.

"So this set the Koreans off against the Sherpas. . . . Then—and I'm not sure what started it—one of the Koreans hit a Sherpa or one of the cook staff. I had to go in to tell them it's not acceptable to hit anyone or yell at them. They took severe offense at me admonishing them. . . . But in these things it's a game of chess. They knew I had the Sherpas."

Few Westerners who encounter situations like this realize mountaineering's place in Korean culture. In 2006, a survey found that mountain climbing was the most popular form of exercise in South Korea, with 13.2 percent of the population going on regular hiking excursions. Another survey conducted by the Korean Mountaineering Support Center found that the popularity of mountain climbing had increased nearly tenfold between 2000 and 2008, from 4.5 percent to 43.5 percent among men and from 5.5 percent to 35.6 percent among women. With South Korea's growing economic prosperity, there are more Korean expeditions to the Himalayas each year—and probably more stories floating around about them, too.

It just so happens that this tale told by Jamie took place on the north side of Everest in 2007, and concerned one group of Koreans named the Flying Jump expedition. The party was led by Kim Jae-su, and included Go Mi-yeong and Park Kyeong-hyo, as well as a young climbing-Sherpa from the Makalu region named Jumik Bhote. "I don't mean to make racial stereotypes," Jamie cautions. "But it seemed to me like they just push themselves to the max; the ones going to the top are the ones left standing, and all the rest are basically useless."

Seventy percent of the Korean peninsula is covered by mountains, though even the highest summits stand less than two thousand meters above sea level. For centuries, mountains have featured prominently in traditional murals and artwork; there are poems and fables told about them. Kim Jong-il, the despotic leader of North Korea, actively promotes the myth that he was born in a log cabin on the flank of a mountain (he was actually born in a Russian military camp). Traditional Korean society is heavily influenced by Confucianism, the quasi-religious code of ethics that originated from China around 500 B.C. Confucianism stresses the role of person-to-person relationships, loyalty, and filial piety, or *xiào*, which is described by analogy through five fundamental relationships. Notably, four of the Five Bonds are asymmetrical: ruler to ruled, father to son, husband to wife, friend to friend, elder brother to younger brother.

South Korea's modern history, like that of the former Eastern Bloc nations, is defined by the struggle to resist communism and totalitarian rule. From 1910 right up to the end of World War II, in 1945, Korea was occupied by imperial Japan. During this period, the Korean Alpine Federation and other climbing clubs provided a convenient cover for members of the resistance to organize. After the war, the United States and the Soviet Union hastily reached an agreement to cut the peninsula into two trusteeships divided along the thirty-eighth parallel. Despite massive bloodshed, the Korean War, fought between 1950 and 1953, ended in a stalemate, with an uneasy cease-fire agreement and two separate nations separated by a demilitarized zone.

A half century later, many South Koreans still think of themselves as being a nation at war. This is technically true: No formal peace treaty was ever signed with the North. All young men are drafted into the military for two years' mandatory service; conscription has profound effects on all aspects of Korean life. Business and social networks are built on contacts made while in the armed forces. Because university must be delayed until after military service, the typical Korean enters the workforce and begins his career only in his mid- to late twenties.

There is little time for Himalayan expeditions during a Korean's young adulthood, but much like in the tiny nation of Slovenia, mountain climbing in South Korea is an intrinsic part of mainstream culture. "Expensive North Face T-shirts bearing the name and cartoon of sponsored Korean climbers sell to even nonclimbers," says one American climber living in Korea. "There's a lot of national pride and international recognition wrapped up in mountaineering. Just getting invited on an expedition to an eight-thousand-meter peak is a pretty big deal." Hierarchical, competitive, somewhat militaristic, and largely male dominated, the Korean climbing scene mirrors larger Korean society—which makes Go Mi-yeong's personal life journey only more fascinating.

As a young woman and an aspiring climber, Go Mi-yeong was teased about her weight. It was the early 1990s, and sport climbing—a gymnastic discipline of high-level, bolt-protected rock climbing—was all the rage. Go was married to an up-and-coming climber in the Korean Alpine Federation, and resolved to become a top-level climbing "rock jock" herself.

"All the Korean guy climbers, in their typical blunt manner, told her,

'You'll have to lose weight, if you want to climb hard,'" says Sonia Knapp, an American who befriended Go Mi-yeong a few years later. "The first time she told me she had been more than chubby, I didn't believe her. I insisted she show me a photo, to prove it. . . . She did, and she was."

It wasn't long before Go was climbing very hard indeed. She became a topflight sport climber, specializing in international competitions staged on artificial walls, a seven-time winner of the Asian X Games. "She was unstoppable, but also super nice," Sonia remembers. "And not just to me, as the only 'foreign climber,' but to everyone. She was usually hanging out with the women, and was very encouraging." Sonia speculates that climbing became a subtle form of expression—or even rebellion—within the confines of her rigid culture. "She was unconventional, especially for Korea. She loved breaking boundaries for women, and she loved traveling." Go spent months abroad each year, training and competing in Europe and North America.

By 2004, Go's competitive career was winding down, and she turned more and more to ice climbing and mountaineering. She had divorced, and resolved to get a university degree, an achievement that is immensely important in Korea. Again she made waves, now by being a single woman in her thirties who was going to college and climbing frozen waterfalls; it was only perhaps natural that after she graduated she would gravitate toward high-altitude mountaineering. Her first eight-thousand-meter summit was Cho Oyu, in the fall of 2006. Then she went to Everest.

On the surface, Jumik Bhote and Go Mi-yeong, or Didi, as he came to call her, made an unlikely team. But both the older, independent Korean woman and the young, eager-to-please Nepali had turned to mountaineering, in a sense, to escape uncontrollable circumstances that might otherwise overwhelm their lives. When they stood on the summit of Everest together on May 16, 2007, Nepal had been in the grips of the Maoist rebellion for a full decade—virtually all of Jumik's adult life. Like his Korean employers, Jumik was the product of a society in conflict. During the last few years, things had been so bad that the men from Hungong living in Kathmandu sent their mothers or wives home to the village to see if their roofs were leaking. They were too afraid they would be conscripted at gunpoint and forced to fight if they returned. Compared to that, climbing mountains with Kim Jae-su and Go Mi-yeong must have seemed like pretty good work.

Pemba and Jumik picked Virginia O'Leary up at Tribhuvan Airport on July 31, 2007, and drove her to the apartment she would be renting while she taught the fall semester in Kathmandu. It seemed to Virginia that things had finally turned around for her Nepali family, as she had taken to calling the Bhotes. With the autumn tourist season just around the corner, Pemba had several treks lined up with European clients, while Jumik would be leaving soon for a postmonsoon expedition to Shishapangma.

Meanwhile, some of their other siblings were finding academic success. Three of the six Bhote sisters were enrolled in private school. "The youngest, Dawa Tuk Mu, is second in her class," Virginia proudly reported in the first of her weekly letters addressed to friends and family back home in the United States, which she posted on the Internet. And Tsering Bhote, the youngest of the four Bhote brothers, successfully passed his school leaving exam, becoming the first in his family to matriculate to college-level classes. "Tsering . . . will go on to get a BA in education in the fall," Virginia wrote. "As Jumik failed the exam when he took it Pemba is very pleased [he was furious with Jumik at the time he failed in part as he would not have done so had he had the opportunity]." With the help of a small group of friends from the United States, Virginia arranged to cover the cost of all four tuitions.

Kim Jae-su and Go Mi-yeong had chosen to attempt the South Face of Shishapangma—a steep, two-thousand-meter-high wall of ice fields and avalanche-prone couloirs. First climbed alpine-style in 1982 by three top British alpinists, it is far steeper than a normal eight-thousand-meter "walk-up" route. Its popularity has skyrocketed in recent years, however, in no small part due to the amount of fixed ropes modern expeditions have added to the climb. Despite his having two Everest summits under his belt, it would be a substantially harder undertaking than anything in Jumik's short career as a climbing-Sherpa.

"Pemba thinks that Jumik is the strongest climber in his group, which is worrisome," Virginia confided the week of August 17. "Apparently, the Koreans are notorious for attempting climbs that are beyond their abilities and ignoring the Sherpas' advice. This is especially troubling as the weather in the fall makes climbing much more dangerous than in the spring. Jumik will be back in mid-October, so do keep him in your thoughts. I know Pemba is worried."

Jumik departed Kathmandu for Shishapangma on August 28 with two other climbing-Sherpas, Tarke and Tshering Jangbu. Kim Jae-su and Go Mi-yeong would not arrive in Kathmandu for another week. To minimize their time on the mountain, they were sending their three climbing-Sherpas ahead to assess conditions and begin carrying loads and fixing line. "When I hugged him good-bye he said, 'See you soon, Mommy,'" Virginia wrote the day after he left. "He has always called me Mommy. Yes, I had tears in my eyes. I look forward to mid-October and his return. I promised him a party!"

Conditions proved especially unforgiving in the Himalayas that fall. Several unexpected storms blanketed the mountain with new snow, and when the weather cleared, the fickle currents of the jet stream raked the top of the mountain. One by one, the other expeditions attempting Shishapangma decided to throw in the towel. American guide Eric Remza was on Everest that spring and Shishapangma that fall, by happenstance exactly the same schedule as Kim Jae-su and Go Mi-yeong. "The summit [of Shishapangma] put up a fight. . . . Where we were, on the north side, there was significant avalanche danger. Our high point was about halfway between Camp Two and Camp Three. We stopped because we were really worried about avalanches. I would imagine it was just as volatile on the South Face."

"The weather has been terrible and all but the Koreans have left Tibet having failed to summit. The Korean group was scheduled to try to summit yesterday," Virginia wrote home after Pemba received a quick phone update from the expedition's cook. "They have had to fix the ropes three times due to avalanches. It is bitterly cold and very dangerous as it is a steep technical climb. We did not hear anything by dark last night and are worried. The cook said that the Koreans are hell-bent on summiting even if it takes two more weeks and the weather worsens each passing day. Arghhh."

Kim Jae-su, Go Mi-yeong, and their three climbing-Sherpas eventually summited on October 5. Unsettled weather dogged them all the way to the summit. "It was snowing lightly and the wind was strong," Jumik's teammate Tshering Jangbu Sherpa reported on their summit push. "Since we had to move ahead and fix the ropes, we had to concentrate very hard." This casual description is secretly revealing. Simply put, the Korean pair preferred fixed lines, a lot of them. Especially on summit day.

After the successful climb, Kim and Go raced back to Kathmandu. Jumik, Tarke, and Tshering Jangbu remained behind to pack up base camp, arrange for yaks to carry everything back to the road, and then take the bus home. A mix-up in transportation plans delayed them for more than a week; it was late October by the time Jumik returned, but the delay turned into an unexpected windfall. "Jumik has been asked to lead the Korean group on an expedition to Annapurna, K2, Makalu, and Lhotse in the spring and beyond. Apparently, the two Koreans are committed to climbing all eight-thousand-meter peaks across the next few years and were so impressed with Jumik that they are going to hire him to lead . . ." Virginia gushed.

Whatever had caused the transportation trouble, Kim Jae-su's response was apparently to fire Explore Himalaya and promote Jumik. "I don't know that story," Jamie McGuinness says, "but it's hard to make money from Koreans, and they are a hassle—I think it just might have ended up being more trouble than it was worth for Explore Himalaya." According to Jamie, Kim Jae-su tried to hire Tarke as well, who was a bit more experienced and a regular with Explore Himalaya. "We discussed it, going to K2 with the Koreans. We talked about the risks, and Tarke decided he didn't want to risk it for his family. He knew he had work with me every expedition I run. He was in a position to refuse the Koreans. . . .

"Jumik came to Explore Himalaya with good recommendations," Jamie remembers. "But he wasn't a regular—he was more like a free agent. He was a good guy, came across really well, worked really well. . . . Sure, he got promoted pretty quickly. But some people are ambitious."

On hearing the news, Virginia insisted that Jumik take a technical climbing course that winter. They even made a deal: In exchange for Jumik promising to go to the Khumbu Climbing School, she would buy him a set of Korean-language tapes. Jumik wanted the tapes so that he could surprise Go Mi-yeong the next spring by knowing a little of her language. Virginia paid for Jumik's class, as well.

The week after he returned from Shishapangma, Virginia went out to dinner with her whole Nepali family. "Jumik is now a real thulo manche (big man), having summited Everest twice this year and Shishapangma once," she wrote, adding that their mother seemed particularly content. "She is more relaxed than I have ever seen her. Of course, the fact that Jumik and Pemba are now doing well must be an enormous relief as the family is so big and money has been such a worry." Jumik celebrated his newfound prosperity as any Nepali male would: He went and bought a black Yamaha bike.

One day in December Virginia happened to overhear a conversation between Pemba Bhote and a Nepali colleague named Binay. Both Jumik and Pemba had girlfriends, Virginia knew, though she spent little time with them. Marriage is a different institution in Tibetan culture than it is the West. Traditionally, two distinct ceremonies take place to mark separate milestones. A formal betrothal happens when a couple enters into a public relationship and begins to have children. Most often they continue living with one set of parents, however; a couple isn't considered to be formally married until they have established their own household and achieved financial independence. As Virginia tells the story:

"Binay asked Pemba how old he was. And Pemba answered that he was thirty-five years old. And Binay's next question was: 'Are you married?' And Pemba said no. I looked up and said to Binay, who's Brahmin,

'You don't know this because you are from the [Kathmandu] valley but—it's very typical for people to not marry until they are old.' Binay at the time was under extraordinary pressure to marry—marriage is extremely important in Hindi society. . . . So, I explain to Binay that the custom of the Bhote people—they have a betrothal ceremony. There is an expectation that they will get married—but it doesn't happen until they economically can be independent.

"And so I tell it to him, and Binay's next question is: 'Do you have children?' And I saw an expression on his face. I knew. I knew that this was not true. I knew he had lied to me. Later, when we were in my apartment, I asked him, and he broke down and told me."

Virginia had known Pemba Bhote for ten years. She had been over to his home to eat dinner more times than she could count; she had raised money for four of his siblings' education; she had flown him to the United States to visit her and work. "He told me he was a terrible person, but he had lied to me so long ago.

"His first child had been born weeks before I met him—at the time he spoke little English, and was very young. He told me that a Westerner had told him that other Westerners did not approve of people having children if they were not married. I said, 'How could you imagine that I wouldn't love your children if I love you?'"

She forgave him.

"As those of you who know Pemba would expect, he is a kind and devoted father," Virginia wrote the next week after spending the afternoon with the three children. "He was clearly thrilled that the children took to me right away and had such a good time. As they left they called out, 'Good-bye, Grandma. See you on Friday!'"

By the spring of 2008, three of the four Bhote brothers had at last found profitable employment in Kathmandu. Jumik would be climbing Lhotse with Go Mi-yeong and Kim Jae-su, and Tsering, who had begun his college studies, decided to take some time off from school to work with him. Pemba went into business with a friend and started a formal company: a real trekking agency with business cards and a logo and Xeroxed leaflets they could hand out to Western tourists advertising treks and expeditions in the majestic Himalayas. They made a sign, designed a Web site and rented an office in downtown Thamel. The company was named Mountain Footprints. The future looked bright for the family, and Pemba Bhote took out a loan to build a house near Boudha, on a small piece of land he had purchased several years before.

But that spring Pasang, the second-oldest brother, got sick. Pasang had always struggled with things like money and keeping a steady job. Then he stopped working altogether, and began to have stomach pains and cough up blood. The same thing happened to other men in Hungong. In May, he died.

Jumik returned from summiting Lhotse at the end of the month. He had only a few days in Kathmandu with Dawasangmu, his partner, before leaving again for K2. The sorrow over losing his brother was smothered under the pressures of preparing to leave for Pakistan. As the lead climbing-Sherpa, Jumik had hired Pasang Lama, a friend from Hungong who had worked that spring on Lhotse with him, and Tsering, his little brother, who left school again to go on the expedition. But then one day Go Mi-yeong bumped into Pasang Bhote, another strong climbing-Sherpa from Hungong whom they had met on the South Face of Shishapangma the previous autumn. Stocky and powerfully built, Pasang Bhote was four years younger than Jumik, but in his short career he had been on several particularly challenging expeditions, like the South Face of Lhotse and an attempt on Makalu in the winter. Go Mi-yeong immediately offered him a spot on their team bound for K2.

Pasang's last-minute inclusion caused a brief crisis in leadership: Jumik had already promised the spot to Tsering. Kim Jae-su vacillated and Jumik suggested that if his brother lost the spot, he wouldn't go either—a monumental step, considering the financial security Jumik and his family had riding on the relationship. Finally, Kim relented and agreed to pay both their travel costs and salaries.

And so it was four Bhote men from the upper Arun Valley, exceptionally strong by any standards, but young, still in their twenties and with only a few years of serious eight-thousand-meter work under their belts, who served as Kim Jae-su's climbing-Sherpa team. Jumik, their leader, had just turned thirty, and he and his girlfriend were expecting their first child.

Ger McDonnell loved being in base camp almost as much as he loved standing on top of a mountain. A contemporary eight-thousand-meter base camp is not only a geographical location and organizational hub, but a social institution. During peak climbing season, one can expect to find a half dozen or more teams, dozens of climbers, dozens more climbing-Sherpas and cook staff, all housed in a multicolored tent village nestled into the folds of glacial moraine—to Ger, the base camp community must have borne more than a passing resemblance to his childhood home of Kilcornan.

"It's just the gorgeous place to hang out," Gerard said in an interview, reflecting on Everest base camp. "The whole nature of climbing an eight-thousand-meter peak is you have to relax. Sit down and chat with the lads, play cards. Some people complain about it. . . . However, the bustle of base camp on these popular mountains—I actually love it; you get to meet a lot of people, different cultures, and everyone is in the same mind-set. . . . That's what a lot of eight-thousand-meter climbing seems to have been like for me: socializing with climbing in between." After the 2003 season, an end-of-the-year report noted of Pat Falvey's expedition: "This Irish team is known for their camaraderie with their Sherpas; treating them as equals. The team is also well regarded by other climbers, who voted the Irish the most entertaining team in BC." That was the year Gerard summited with Pemba Gyalje.

Five years later, in K2 base camp, the affable Irishman whiled away the weeks of bad weather in much the same fashion, making friends, playing cards, telling stories for days on end. Nick Rice, who occasionally clashed with Wilco van Rooijen over shared responsibilities on the SSE Spur, remembers Gerard as the peacemaker. "Everybody at base camp liked him. If there was friction between the teams, he would be the diplomat sent out to talk to everyone. He had a very likable personality."

Despite the hostile environment, Gerard even found an outlet for his perpetual love of animals. "There's a mouse in the house!" he reported soon after arriving in base camp.

It was called Fred initially but Fred looks very pregnant (much to the kitchen staff's chagrin). Fred's increasingly evident pregancy has caused an increased need for a name change. "Sheena" has stuck (much to Sheeny's chagrin). At 5000m we're not too sure whether to admire its ability to survive this altitude year-round or to sympathize with the poor misfortunate for its decision to hop into an Askole crate and inadvertently relocate.

Updates on Sheena's status would punctuate subsequent reports.

Some of the last video footage taken of Gerard McDonnell captures an impromptu after-hours concert. The lighting is poor and the camera work shaky. Long shadows catch against a nylon tent wall behind him as Gerard bellows out a Gaelic verse; the pitch of his voice slides between harmonizing octaves with surprising ease. His eyes are closed, his head upturned, his thick beard quivering with power and focus.

Gerard sits in the center of the frame, surrounded by a captivated audience of Pakistani men. He is, in fact, the only Westerner in view. As the last note of the solo begins to fade, there is a sudden fury of motion. His thick forearms rise and his hands slam down on an upturned plastic tub. The drumbeat—an infectious, untamed tempo—instantly fills the tent. Everyone around him is nodding their heads, clapping their hands in perfect rhythm.

At ten p.m. on July 29, Dawasangmu gave birth to a healthy baby son. The boy was named Jen-Jen, after Jumik's late father. Three days later, at nearly the same time that Annie Starkey spoke to Gerard for the last time, Dawasangmu's cell phone rang. It was Jumik, calling from the summit of

K2. Their conversation was short. But for Go Mi-yeong, handing her sat phone off to Jumik and then watching him learn that he was a father became her single lasting memory of the summit. Jumik's eyes brightened, a smile lighting across his face as he stared out at the curvature of the earth's horizon from 8,611 meters, and thought about his healthy newborn son.

August 3 was Go Mi-yeong's birthday. The team was planning a celebratory party once everyone was safely down in base camp.

12

IDENTITY CRISIS

*A*s long as mankind—and the vast majority of them were men—have *ventured into the high mountains, there have been family and loved ones waiting anxiously for their safe return. And from the very beginning, some of them didn't return. What's changed is the time, the speed at which the news is transmitted back home. When Dick Renshaw knocked on the front door of thirty-year-old Maria Coffey's house to inform her that her boyfriend, Joe, was killed somewhere on Mount Everest's serpentine Northeast Ridge, the news was over three weeks old. That was in 1982. Within forty-eight hours of Gerard's passing, Annie Starkey was on a plane to Ireland.*

According to Coffey, who wrote a groundbreaking book about her experience, the climbing community regularly hangs a No Trespassing sign in front of any discussion of the loss experienced by the families of lost climbers. The schism is partly to respect the privacy of those grieving and partly, Coffey suggests, a convenient excuse for others to avoid confronting the true extent of the damage that can be inflicted by their choices. Most always, the silence is a well-intended shield. But sometimes, it becomes a barrier.

From Ireland, Annie, Damien O'Brien, JJ McDonnell, and their partners flew to Islamabad for a private meeting with the Norit team. "When
we got on the plane for Pakistan," JJ recalls, "there was still a glimmer
of hope. Just a glimmer. Even then we didn't know anything more than
what we had read on the Internet."

In an emotional encounter, Gerard's teammates tried to answer questions and give as much information as they could; Pemba and Cas pieced
together their best recollection of what happened on August second.
Because Cas and Wilco had been evacuated by helicopter, while the rest
of the team returned from the mountain by foot and ground transportation, it was in fact the first and only time the entire team would gather
together in one room and attempt to assimilate everyone's memories into
a single cohesive narrative. According to the standards of investigation,
this meeting would provide the most reliable testimony of what happened. A partial transcript of the conversation was later released by the
McDonnell family.

> **Cas:** Did you see something, Pemba? Because you also saw
> something or the boots or something?
>
> **Pemba:** Yeah. The Sherpa, before Sherpa rolling down because
> of the serac, he talk with me by the walkie-talkie. "Okay,
> Pemba, there is one member fall down from the traverse,
> the lower section of the traverse, because hit by serac." Then
> the visibility was very poor. You cannot see even three, four
> meters. . . .
>
> **Cas:** . . . sometimes it was little bit more clear; sometimes it
> was totally with the clouds . . .
>
> **Pemba:** Very poor visibility. Then I ask immediately with the
> Sherpas, "Can you identify him?" He told me, "He has a
> red-and-black down suit." A red-and-black down suit, I say,
> definitely Gerard.

After returning to Ireland for Gerard's funeral, Annie flew back to
home with pieces of Pemba's story lingering in her mind.

A man in a red suit with black patches was hit by serac fall. . . .
He was descending behind them. . . .

During the first few weeks back home in Anchorage, Annie felt as though she were being forced to sit through a movie she was only vaguely interested in watching. "No one can teach you to mourn. Like climbing a mountain, you can try to prepare for it, but it's impossible to know what will happen once you are on its steep slopes," Coffey writes. Annie concurs. "People always think they can imagine what it would be like, but you can't imagine," she says simply. Her friends were unceasingly caring and patient. Several encouraged her to try something new, perhaps find a new apartment. Annie demurred. She wanted to keep close to her life with Ger. "You feel like one of those parents of kidnapped kids who stay in the same house, keep the same phone number, just in case." The sun ebbed lower in the sky each day, the air redolent with autumn frosts and rotting salmon.

But grief can do curious things. It certainly did not consume Annie, dragging her down into apathy. "Some people don't want to know what happened," Annie would later muse. "I suppose they can't bear to even think about it." Annie's impulse was exactly the opposite. She wanted to know everything. "My friends Jo and Nora told me to stop," Annie remembers. "But I just kept researching. It felt like time was of the essence; I had to find out what happened and get his story out. . . ."

As time went by, losing Gerard began to draw out other unique aspects of her personality. Ever since she was a child, Annie possessed a sharp memory, paid acute attention to detail, and was unfailingly curious about the world around her. "On my second-grade report card, the teacher wrote that I was always the kid asking, 'Why?'" Describing her best friend, Jo Fortier immediately says this: "She's definitely a details person, but she's not interested in things, but people. Annie has this incredible capacity for memories, for pieces of the human story. She's always been fascinated trying to figure out the social parts of things." And having climbed Aconcagua and Denali, Annie herself knew a few things about mountaineering. She had also spent most of her adulthood living in Alaska, and Alaskans always try to keep their wits about them, especially in any situation concerning the wilderness.

After Islamabad, Annie and the McDonnell family expected Pemba's full story to be included in the final report that would be posted on the Norit Web site. It took until October, but when the report appeared it read:

Eventually Marco, after trying to help the Koreans, also descended, exhausted. Ger meanwhile spent some more time trying to help the Koreans and ascended 20m to try and make some further adjustment to free the Koreans from the ropes.

There was no mention of the final radio call between Pemba and Big Pasang, and instead the report described Gerard's death in the following quote, which was attributed to Marco: "I turned and four hundred meters above I can see a waterfall of ice coming from the serac pinnacle. I see the three Koreans and I also recognize two shoes; they are Ger's going pass me." The yellow boots.

"I was devastated when the report came out," Annie later said. "But to be fair, I think everyone was just having their own traumas. Wilco was in the hospital. The other survivors were exhausted. I don't know if they even really understood Pemba." The same month, *Men's Journal* and Outside.com ran features, and my own story was published in *Rock and Ice*. Pretty much every article acknowledged some degree of confusion in Marco Confortola's account, and expressed uncertainty as to what really happened to Gerard McDonnell. Several authors resolved the issue by stating that his friends and family concluded that he went back to help the Koreans, or some similar turn of phrase. That was especially maddening. "They just said we believed it, but they didn't say why," Annie says. "It was patronizing. There was a reason. We had evidence."

By then, because she had personally debriefed the Norit team in Islamabad, and corresponded via e-mail with many of the other survivors, Annie had likely accumulated the most firsthand information and documentation of anyone, anywhere, on the tragedy. Each subtle nuance to the story, the little changes and deflections and blank spots, every fragment of the story registered somewhere in her mind. Every word mattered.

All the way into November, Annie bit her tongue. There were many hours of long-distance phone calls with Ger's family in Ireland, who were equally tortured by the accounts of their brother, cousin, and son disappearing in a hypoxic stupor. "We initially thought if it comes from us, they'll never believe it," Annie says. "It felt as though it would be unseemly for me or the McDonnells to speak publicly. But then, all the media had come out, and none of it was true. I felt lost at sea. How do you fight the media machine?"

It all coalesced into a single purpose.

"We had to get Ger's story out, because nobody else was doing it."

"The widows are impossible to deal with," Andy Selters told me when I phoned to ask about K2. If there was one person present in K2 base camp during the first week of August 2008 with the mountain experience and journalistic talent to chronicle the disaster as a base-camp witness, much as Englishman Jim Curran did during the 1986 season, it was Andy. Selters spent a lot of time with Marco, helping him as they thawed his toes, and recorded some on-the-spot interviews with the Italian and other members of the summit push. But the media pounced so quickly that the magazine feature assignments were gobbled up almost immediately, before Andy, who was ironically on the scene in base camp, had the chance to communicate with potential editors and pitch the story. He returned home a little jaded, immediately jumped back into life as a busy middle-aged parent, and decided to work on a photo essay of the Sierra Mountains instead.

"A bunch of writers who don't know anything about climbing in the Himalayas, who haven't even been to Pakistan, got the story before I had arrived back home," Andy told me. I was quiet, since on none of my former expeditions to Asia had I ever visited the country. "Anyway, trust me, it's not an *Into Thin Air* kind of story," he said. "It just doesn't add up the same way. And no matter what you write, the families of the deceased aren't going to be happy."

The week after Annie commented on my blog, I received a phone call from Daryl Miller. Daryl was recently retired as head mountaineering ranger in Denali National Park. As the guy ultimately responsible for all search-and-rescue missions on North America's highest peak, he probably knows as much as anyone about the intricacies of high-altitude mountaineering rescue. I first met him when I was a junior guide on Denali, and it took me a little while to figure out Daryl wasn't just the highest-ranking officer in the Alaska Range but also the unofficial anchor of the climbing community for several generations. "Freddie, sounds like you know a lot about this horrible mess on K2. Would you want to talk to my friend Annie Starkey?" he asked. I knew there was sound wisdom in Andy Selters's decision to avoid writing about the tragedy, and there were good reasons too for keeping a respectful distance from the bereaved families. It would have been tempting to blow off Annie's criticisms if it weren't for Daryl.

I wrote Annie an e-mail and told her I believed Pemba's story.

"I too am one hundred percent sure that Gerard helped the Koreans," she replied a few days later. "Just think, if they had all lived it would have been one of the great survival/rescue stories of the century. Sadly, after so much effort put forth by all of them, they perish in serac falls. The story is now a true tragedy. . . ." We started exchanging e-mails, going back and forth on different theories and explanations.

Annie did not hold back her criticism when I suggested something she didn't agree with. "The agreement was for the strongest climbers from each team to participate in the advanced rope-fixing team on summit day, right?" I wrote her once, explaining why I was suspicious about equality on the mountain. "But look at Pemba's final list of who was on the advanced party—it was four Sherpas, three Pakistanis, and two Koreans. Not a single white boy, not one. I can't help but think that there is something going on there. . . ."

"It seems to me, Freddie, that from the beginning you have been looking at this whole situation as white Western climbers taking advantage of the Nepalese Sherpas," she replied, "and you have been painting it that way. Knowing what I know about Ger McDonnell *nothing* could be farther from the truth."

She had a point: "Heroes in Fine Print" was intended as a short, upbeat reminder to the climbing community that everyone in contemporary high-altitude mountaineering wasn't on a self-serving ego trip, as the layperson might have concluded after reading the op-ed section of the *New York Times*. But when I casually bestowed the mantle of hero on Chhiring and Pemba, it posed a silent question that hung unanswered: If the climbing-Sherpas were the heroes of K2, who were the villains?

"I do find it interesting that the white climbers are being closely scrutinized, even criticized, for their decisions that night and the next day," Annie wrote. "I would challenge you to try to flip the scenarios and see what that feels like—put Wilco, Ger, and Cas in place of Pemba, Chhiring, and Pasang. How does that feel?" She had a point: From the beginning, I was pretty certain the Pakistanis and climbing-Sherpas were somehow exploited on summit day. Yet it was three climbing-Sherpas who descended the fastest, making it into Camp IV while the rest of the summiteers inexplicably ground to a halt and bivouacked. Who abandoned whom?

Marco Confortola was the last man reported to have seen Gerard McDonnell alive. In November, three months after the accident, he publicly released a comprehensive account of the disaster, posting versions in both English and Italian on his Web site. "The Testimony of Marco Confortola," as it was titled, was apparently written to clarify past statements. It was a remarkable document. Whereas before, his published quotes about the time he and Gerard McDonnell spent with the stricken Koreans on the morning of August 2 were vague in the extreme, his testimony went into considerable detail to describe his efforts.

The first thing I noticed was that while in all previous accounts, both Wilco and Marco recalled encountering three Korean climbers, now he said it was two Koreans and one Nepali. It was the first time, in myriad interviews and articles, that Jumik Bhote was positively identified as one of the stricken party at the top of the fixed lines that morning. It's an understandable mistake, confusing two men of similar physique and features under those circumstances. Marco invested a thorough half page of writing to explain what happened next.

All three of them were in very bad positions, hanging head down. While Gerard holds the head of the expedition leader, who is in the vertically highest position on the serac, I descend toward the other two climbers. I see oxygen cylinders in their backpacks and look for their oxygen masks to help them breathe, but unfortunately I cannot find them. I take a knife from the climbing harness of the climber in the middle and find a small yellow "Grivel-Evo model" ice ax in the snow, then climb back up on the serac near Gerard. I start ascending to the right above them all and use the knife to cut about ten meters of rope. I return on the vertical side with Gerard and the Korean leader, then use the yellow ice ax to anchor the rope and descend toward the Korean leader. I tie the rope around his waist using another small rope. While I am doing this, Gerard leaves his position and starts to climb toward the top of the serac. I call him many times but he doesn't respond. Assuming he went to take a picture of rescue operations, lowering the Korean leader about ten meters closer to his teammates . . .

The technical operation Marco describes in the above passage is called transferring the load. With an ice ax and a spare hunk of rope, he built a new anchor system, tied the Korean leader into it, then released him from the old rope that pinned him to the mountain, and lowered him using some kind of a belay—quite possibly a munter mule knot like the one Pemba Gyalje used to lower me the first time we went climbing together. There was, however, another mistaken identity: the Korean team's leader, Kim Jae-su, was resting down in Camp IV by this time. The man Marco is referring to is most likely his chief deputy, Hwang Dong-jin, who commonly was introduced as the climbing leader of the expedition.

After securing Hwang, Marco wrote that he tried to stabilize the other two, including placing his glove over the left foot of one of the men who had somehow lost his boot. Then came a peculiar passage: "I see a radio microphone hanging from the Sherpa's jacket so I descend about fifty meters in the couloir to find the radio. I climb back up, turn it on and call the Koreans, asking for help. I think it is two Sherpas who answer and say they will come to help. I inform them about the injured climbers and myself. I am very tired and, after securing the three climbers, I start down." Every person I had interviewed who spoke English as their primary language agreed that Marco's command of the language was challenged under the best of circumstances. If it was two Sherpas he did indeed speak to, English would have been their second language as well. It's easy to see how the contents of such a radio call, made under such dire conditions, could be misunderstood.

What caught my attention was his description of finding the radio. Marco apparently saw it lying fifty meters below them, down-climbed to get it, and then rejoined the group. Fifty meters is a good amount of terrain. It's 165 linear feet, tilted at a forty-five- to fifty-degree angle: the same distance as standing on the forty-five-yard line of a football field and spotting a brick-size object lying on the opposite goal line. The sheer effort of losing and then gaining that amount of vertical struck me as daunting, though not impossible, and one might even assume he overestimated the distance by as much as a third. But if this terrain was fall line beneath the location of the team in Pemba's morning photo, where the radio would have gone, Marco would have been climbing down to the radio untethered, while the Diagonal traverses at nearly a forty-five-degree angle across the slope.

The path Marco followed to the radio would have been close to the same one Wilco took earlier when he lost the fixed lines and climbed straight down the hanging snowfield, only to reach the top of the cliff band that is its lower border, and have to climb back up to regain the ropes. It was at this point that Wilco, in his own account, recalls looking back and seeing Marco and Gerard with the Koreans, yelling at them, and not getting any response. According to Marco, the radio tumbled down more than a hundred feet of this same terrain, terrain steep enough to warrant technical systems to keep the victims attached to the mountain—then suddenly stopped. Everything in my own mountain experience as an alpine climber told me something was missing from this part of the story, but it seemed too bizarre in a way, too unexpected, for Marco to have just made it up.

According to Marco's testimony, the ropes had been avalanched *before* the start of the Bottleneck. Turning to leave the three (now stabilized) climbers, he wrote, "After a few meters, I notice that the traverse ropes are gone. I continue the very dangerous traverse toward the Bottleneck, reaching it with enormous physical and psychological effort. There I find some fixed ropes and descend the couloir." All the other climbers I'd spoken to who had descended the fixed lines—Pemba Gyalje, Chhiring Dorje, Pasang Lama, Cas van de Gevel, and Lars Nessa—recalled a continuous line of ropes to the top of the Bottleneck that ended in the emergency five-millimeter line the Norwegians had fixed over the top of the Bottleneck, and then no ropes below that. There were no gaps such as the one Marco described; one theory is that a secondary serac fall had occurred somewhere on the lower traverse, a little left of the top of the couloir.

In any case, as he neared the bottom of the Bottleneck, Marco later wrote this passage: "I hear another rumble from above and see a small avalanche on top of the ice cliff, cascading over the rocks. I see human body parts and other material emerge from the cascading snow and recognize the yellow 'La Sportiva' boots that Gerard was wearing. The avalanche continues toward me, leaving pieces of human remains and climbing material in its wake. It stops just below me to the right. . . ."

According to this description, Marco's identification of Gerard Mc-

Donnell's yellow boots happened as the avalanche was sweeping past; he makes no mention of identifying any body after it stopped. When asked to further clarify his ID of Gerard, Marco responded: "I am absolutely certain that Gerard remained involved in the avalanche, also because on the mountain above me there remained only Gerard, the two Koreans, and the Sherpa. I cannot know what happened to Gerard as at a certain point I could no longer see him and despite that I called him repeatedly he did not stop and began to ascend."

Marco continued his descent, and then fell asleep a short distance farther below. This is how he described Pemba's rescue of him:

> Dejected and fatigued, I sit down, then lay down, and soon fall asleep. Pemba Girgi [sic], Sherpa from the Dutch expedition, wakes me up. He insists that I put on an oxygen mask, even if I don't want to, and urges me to descend quickly with him. After descending about 200 meters, something hits my neck. I realize that it is an oxygen cylinder and that Pemba is trying to protect me with his body as another avalanche passes to our right, stopping not far from where we are. . . . I make out more human remains in the snow.

The pointed remark that Pemba forced him to breathe bottled oxygen is significant, as Marco had already publicly asserted on his Web site that his K2 climb was accomplished without supplementary gas.* But the details that were left out of the Italian's testimony are just as important as what was included.

Marco's description of involuntarily "falling asleep" gives no inkling of the desperate condition Pemba claims he found him in—down suit unzipped, gloves removed, harness hanging below his knees. Nor did he have any recollection of seeing Big Pasang and Tsering Bhote, though

---

* There's no governing body in high-altitude mountaineering that might officially define such a claim, but the rough consensus in the mountaineering community is that one should not have used oxygen at any point in the climb—going up and coming back down—to merit a true "oxygenless" ascent.

they had found him first and then radioed the news to Pemba. Moreover, Pemba Gyalje and Pasang Lama, both of whom were searching the Shoulder most of the day with their radios on, have absolutely no memory of any radio communications with Marco, Jumik Bhote, or any other members of the stricken party before Big Pasang reached them. And Marco's hypothesis that Gerard might have "left his position" to take photos of the rescue is demonstrably false. His camera, a high-quality Canon PowerShot G9 point-and-shoot favored by many alpinists, was with Pemba Gyalje—and the photos he would capture with it provide the best physical clues for what happened that day.

On the summit, Gerard, Pemba Gyalje, and their teammates posed with one another, passing cameras back and forth as they hurried to capture the moment. Minutes were slipping past, and they all must have been aware of the impending sunset and darkness to come. When the time came to begin the descent, Pemba Gyalje was holding Ger's camera, getting a few shots of his teammates. The Sherpa quietly packed it away, and moments later he left the summit a few steps in front of Gerard.

The next morning, August 2, dawned clear. A cluster of dots, unmistakably human, appeared to be stationary near the top of the fixed lines. Simultaneously, a lone person was also visible directly on top of the serac. Eric Meyer recalls that the climber paced back and forth, as if he were looking for a way down, and Pemba distinctly remembers counting eight climbers in total. With Gerard's camera, he took two photographs of the scene: the first at the camera's widest angle, thirty-five millimeters, the second zoomed in to maximum capacity.

The digital files of each photo produced by the G9 have a resolution of 3000 x 4000 pixels. When the image is blown up, the cluster of dots, lifeless and inanimate from afar, transforms into a searing portrait of struggle. The highest form morphs into a human body hanging prone, legs and arms splayed out and clearly visible. There are two more dots a few meters below, each apparently human as well—though it is impossible to tell whether each dot is one person or two lying next to each other. And leaning over the left dot, one can make out the unmistakable sliver of profile of a fourth person—someone who appears to be standing and mobile, giving care. A backpack hangs just below. The unidentified person on top of the serac is also clearly visible in the same shot, sitting in the snow approximately a hundred meters right of the cluster. He is almost directly above the Bottleneck couloir.

The wider shot captures the exact same scene, though in less detail, and two more climbers are visible in the frame. They are near its bottom margin, below the Bottleneck couloir, nearing the upper edge of the Shoulder at approximately eight thousand meters. It is the Korean rescue team: Pasang Bhote and Tsering Bhote. Just above them, even with the rocks that form the lower entrance to the couloir, is one final perplexing dot, possibly another climber sitting in the snow. Even with the lens zoomed in to maximum capacity, you can't tell for certain. The time imprint is eight fifty-nine a.m.

Not long after Pemba took these two shots, the cloud cap began to form and the view was obscured. The next photo documents the two lifeless bodies after the final serac fall. The time it was recorded was two-oh-eight p.m.

Pemba took a final shot of the view from Camp IV that evening. The upper mountain is entirely in shadows. The photo is not taken with quite the same zoom power as the morning close-up, but the cluster of dots at the top of the Diagonal has visibly changed. Now, only three dots are discernible. Two of the three are quite small, one of them likely a backpack, but the third looks to be the size of a body. The unidentified person on top of the serac is gone, and so is the dot at the bottom of the couloir. The photo was taken at six sixteen p.m. Darkness was less than an hour away.

Before the teams had even left base camp for the summit push, there was a discussion about synchronizing time. Besides the obvious language barriers, the teams on the Abruzzi Ridge and the SSE Spur were not even operating on the same time zones at the beginning of the season. The problem began with the inconsistent use of daylight saving time in Pakistan. From 2003 to 2007, the government did not implement any official seasonal changing of the clock. But effective on Saturday, May 31, 2008, at 11:59:59 p.m., for the first time in six years, Pakistani officials decreed a one-hour leap forward. Many of the teams who arrived later in the season on K2 automatically changed the time on their watches to the new daylight saving time. But the Norit team, who had arrived in May, before the change occurred, did not. And so, through June and July, the climbers on the SSE Spur and the Abruzzi Spur were unaware that many of their watches were an hour askew. The discrepancy was realized only during the final base camp meetings to plan the summit push. Everyone agreed to synchronize their watches to the new daylight saving time, one hour ahead of the old time Norit had been using.

Though the problem was apparently solved, the survivors' accounts afterward would systematically be plagued by one-hour time differences. Marco Confortola, for instance, the last man to reach the summit, claimed in his testimony to have topped out at six forty-five. But Cas and Wilco recall that they themselves didn't reach the top until seven p.m. and that Marco was a good half an hour to forty-five minutes behind them. Likewise, Marco said that he and Gerard decided to bivouac around eight thirty; Pemba is certain the whole group was still continuing down using the fixed hand line at nine p.m. Minor discrepancies like this are common in any high-altitude mountaineering situation, especially on K2. But it is worth asking: Could Marco's times, and perhaps others' as well, be off because they were relying on clocks set to the old pre–daylight saving time?

Maarten van Eck offers this theory: "They reset the watches, but did they remember to reset the clocks on their cameras as well? I think they did not. So you have to be very careful with the times the photographs give, and the actual time." Indeed, there is persuasive evidence supporting this argument, in the case of Gerard's camera, that the photos were actually taken an hour later than the time the machine recorded. Ger's summit photo was recorded at six-oh-three, but when he called Annie from the summit, it was seven p.m., local time.

Either way, the *increment* of time that passed between when the photos were taken is the same. Time-stamped at eight fifty-nine a.m., but most likely taken an hour later, at nine fifty-nine a.m., the morning photographs provide the last documented glimpse of the upper mountain. From them, one can reasonably conclude that someone was attending to the Koreans at the same time another person was off route, sitting on top of the serac, and Big Pasang Bhote, who would later rendezvous with Jumik and two of the Koreans, was approaching the start of the Bottleneck couloir. The next undisputed piece of information is that Pemba, Marco, and Pasang Lama all agree that two Sherpas and two Koreans were struck by icefall and fell out of the Bottleneck that afternoon. According to the next photo on Gerard's camera of the victims' remains, taken at either two-oh-eight p.m. or three-oh-eight p.m., it was all over in five hours or less.

Several theoretical scenarios have been proposed to explain how Jumik Bhote and his two clients became free. It's possible they managed to pull it off on their own after Marco descended. But taking Wilco's and Marco's descriptions of their dire condition at face value, it seems unlikely they would suddenly get up and start moving without additional help. It was suggested that Big Pasang could have climbed all the way up to their location—but in Islamabad, Pemba and Cas were convinced that Jumik and the Koreans were already descending when they rendezvoused with Big Pasang.

> **Pemba:** Two Koreans, one Sherpa keep descending slowly, slowly, slowly, very slowly toward the couloir. At the same time two Sherpas, two fresh Sherpas, they are also forcing by the Korean leader to reach them. Then finally they reach. They meet each other just top section of the couloir and then they are descending together.
>
> **Cas:** I thought they were already dead, the three who were hanging, but probably they'd been moving. . . .

The time line also supports Pemba's belief that Big Pasang and Jumik met at the top of the Bottleneck. Otherwise, from his location in the morning photograph, Big Pasang would have had to climb all the way to the top of the Diagonal (a vertical gain of nearly four hundred meters), do whatever it took to rescue his teammates from their predicament, and descend with them back down to the Bottleneck in no more than five hours. The pace is just within the realm of possibility for the fittest K2 climbers. Big Pasang was certainly fit, but he had also spent the entire night searching the Shoulder, and he wasn't using supplemental oxygen.

But neither of these solutions, that Big Pasang climbed all the way up to his stranded teammates or that they independently began moving down, explains Big Pasang's final radio call. "Okay, Pemba," he reported, according to Pemba's account of their conversation in Islamabad: "'There is one member fall down from the traverse, the lower section of the traverse, because hit by serac.' Then I ask immediately with the Sherpas, 'Can you identify him?' He told me, 'He has a red-and-black down suit.' A red-and-black down suit, I say, definitely Gerard."

A very short amount of time later—probably five minutes or less—Big Pasang and Jumik were killed as well; Pemba never had the chance to ask them more questions about the climber in the red-and-black suit. But the answer was obvious to Pemba himself: It was Gerard McDonnell helping them down.

The only problem with Pemba's version of the story was that Marco Confortola was convinced he saw Gerard die in an earlier avalanche.

One day it came to Annie.

She was looking at photos of the climb, and there in a magazine article was a picture of Hugues D'Aubarède and Karim Meherban hugging each other in triumph. The photo was vertically oriented, and the two men were lit in alpine glow. Karim was wearing a red suit—and yellow La Sportiva boots. Other than the boots, Marco had never mentioned any details specifically identifying Gerard's body. The lone person sitting on top of the serac, photographed at the same time someone was still helping the Koreans . . . the yellow boots. "I just knew," Annie says of the moment.

K2 August 2 2008

1. 5:30 AM (EST): MARCO, GERARD, & WILCO LEAVE BIVY
2. 9:59 AM: RESCUER PHOTOGRAPHED WITH KOREAN TEAM
3. UNIDENTIFIED CLIMBER SITTING ON TOP OF THE SERAC
4. 3 PM (EST) PASANG BHOTE MEETS JUMIC & 2 KOREANS,
   MAKES RADIO CALL
5. TSERING BHOTE'S APPROXIMATE POSITION
6. 3 PM (EST) PEMBA GYALJE & MARCO'S POSITION
7. 3:08 PM: JUMIK BHOTE, PASANG BHOTE & TWO
   UNIDENTIFIED KOREAN BODIES PHOTOGRAPHED
8. DREN MANDIC

positions based on the
recollections of
Pemba Gyalje Sherpa

ELee 2010

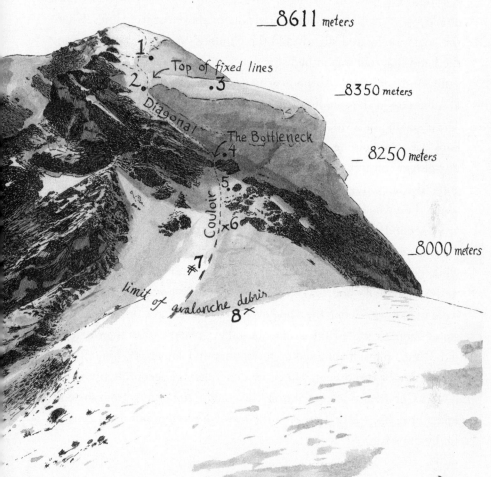

_8611 meters

1.
2. Top of fixed lines
   .3

_8350 meters

Diagonal

The Bottleneck
.4

_ 8250 meters

.5

Couloir x6

_8000 meters

7

limit of avalanche debris
8 x

view from camp IV at 7,800 meters on the

shoulder of the Abruzzi ridge

Marco saw Karim getting avalanched off the top of the serac.

It made sense based on what the Sherpas had told me. Pemba was certain he accounted for everyone except Gerard, Karim, and one of the Koreans. Pasang Lama, the last person to definitely remember seeing Karim on the descent the night before, recalls that Hugues's Pakistani employee was with them at the final anchor above the fixed lines, where the angle moderated slightly and the climbing-Sherpas stopped rigging the hand line. He was in bad shape, according to Pasang, losing motor skills, and very tired. An hour or two later, when Cas passed Hugues D'Aubarède in the middle of the Diagonal, the Frenchman was alone. The photographic evidence was also supportive—at the same time somebody was still helping Jumik and the Koreans, an unidentified climber was already on top of the serac. In the evening picture, that person is gone. If Marco did see Gerard falling in an avalanche off the top of the serac, then what happened to this person, believed to be Karim?

A second possibility, less likely but worth considering, is that Big Pasang, seeing the man in the red-and-black suit get hit by serac ice while descending the lower part of the traverse, and Marco, seeing Gerard McDonnell's body sweep past him near the bottom of the couloir, were in fact witnessing the same event. Perhaps Marco, in his confused state, simply recalled the avalanche taking place earlier than it really did. Pemba himself summed up his opinion in Islamabad. "Majorities of conclusions, even though Marco he don't like . . . according to the evidence, Gerard also fell down from the couloir; not exactly from the couloir, a little bit, a little bit . . . in the traverse section, but main cause is hit by the serac."

Sherpas are loath to publicly criticize others. I had noticed throughout my interviews and conversations with Pasang, Chhiring, and Pemba that they studiously avoided saying anything disparaging of other climbers. The closest they came to anything negative was vague assertions to the effect that everyone must always remember their limits. And that was as far as any public criticisms went. One of the more perplexing questions of the K2 tragedy is why Pemba Gyalje himself didn't speak out more forcefully to tell his full story. A handful of journalists interviewed him in Islamabad, but neither the final radio communication nor the Sherpa's well-reasoned explanation about what happened to Gerard was mentioned in print until months afterward.

One partial explanation is that Pemba himself wasn't aware of the alternative theory that Gerard was hypoxic and confused when he and Marco Confortola separated. Indeed, it's difficult to trace back to Confortola at all the specific claim that Gerard was not functioning rationally. In his testimony he wrote that: "Gerard leaves his position and starts to climb toward the top of the serac. I call him many times but he doesn't respond." Marco said basically the same thing in other interviews— Gerard did not seem to hear him. What's interesting is how this passage mirrors the testimony of Wilco van Rooijen, who, after leaving the Koreans to continue down, looked back up to see both Marco and Gerard stopped with them. As the Norit final report explained: "He looks up and sees the three Koreans AND Ger and Marco. He shouts and tries to ask them if they can see which way he has to continue. They cannot hear him and do not see him." Communication was a persistent problem that day; to assume that because Gerard did not respond to Marco he was no longer lucid is a weak argument, and one that Marco himself doesn't seem eager to publicly suggest. Pressed about what happened to Gerard, he says only that "I cannot know what happened to Gerard as at a certain point I could no longer see him and despite that I called him repeatedly he did not stop and began to ascend."

From the very beginning, it was Pemba's understanding that Gerard had gone up to the top anchor to add more slack into the rope that the Koreans and Jumik were tangled in. His reticence to delve into the details of what happened, and the absence of public criticism, was part of a larger dynamic. Sherpas are culturally taught to control their emotions around others, especially Westerners. Their "discipline of feelings," as Sherry Ortner describes it, concerning death is frequently attributed by Western mountaineers to a sense of Oriental fatalism. Among the many examples of this kind of thinking, Ortner points out the following passage, written by an Everest climber in 1978: "It's easy for the Sherpas. They simply believe everything is ordained from above. If one of them dies, then it must be meant to happen."

It's a different situation from the Sherpas' point of view. For one, if they are working as a formal employee of an expedition, they are conscious of maintaining an air of professionalism at all costs—an instinct that is universal with mountain guides the world over who must deal with a fatality in the mountains while responsible for clients. Additionally, Sherpas are probably aware that any showing of emotion would risk exposing themselves to a worse Asian stereotype: that Sherpas are immature and childlike.

Underpinning these two practical considerations is their religious belief system, which provides Buddhist practitioners with private mechanisms for dealing with emotion. Watching the memorial puja ceremonies at base camp after the 1996 Everest disaster, Jamling Norgay observed:

> Despite the crying and carrying on, I didn't sense a deeply sincere feeling of loss in many of the mourners. . . .After a death, Westerners tend to openly share remembrances and emotions as a form of catharsis. This is not an entirely satisfactory way to resolve a transition such as death, I believe. The Sherpas are as emotional about the death of loved ones as anyone else, but much of our grief and guilt are expressed through rituals and offerings, religious practice, and prayer. . . .

In another case, Sherry Ortner once witnessed the family of a Sherpa recently killed on Everest arriving in tears at Tengboche Monastery to seek the rinpoche lama's guidance. The lama, to Ortner's surprise, coolly greeted them and admonished the father of the slain young man to pull himself together. Only later did the anthropologist realize that the lama was modeling the correct behavior for a bereaved family within Buddhist teachings, in effect trying to lead by example. Several religious justifications are offered for this suppression. It is believed that the sounds of crying make it more difficult for the spirit of the dead to depart to the next life; too much crying might also cause blood to rain from the sky.

Historically, Sherpas have strong reasons, both theological and pragmatic, for maintaining emotional composure in the face of tragedy. It's likely that Pemba Gyalje felt similar emotions to those expressed by Jamling Norgay as he watched the media circus in Islamabad. All of which made the letter Pemba Gyalje wrote in the late fall of 2008 that much more remarkable.

The statement, which was distributed by e-mail but written as a formal letter, was not so much a direct comment on what happened, but focused more on the media's portrayal of what happened, both his own role and that of others. He carefully avoided naming any names, and it may have been a coincidence that Pemba distributed it only a few weeks after "The Testimony of Marco Confortola" appeared. But the deep-seated emotion it expressed was plainly felt.

Pemba explained that he had been forced to cancel his autumn work season. He admitted that climbing K2, and surviving the subsequent tragedy, had left him both mentally and physically exhausted, and also depressed after losing his good friend Gerard McDonnell. Meanwhile, he felt obligated to remain in Kathmandu to monitor the "filthy news broadcasting" after the tragedy.

As Pemba clearly struggled to express himself in written English, one also sensed a deeper conflict within him, a rift between the desire to speak out and set the record straight, and the more cautious instinct to not cause controversy by directly contradicting Wilco's and Marco's stories. "Already I was . . . worried in base camp because majority of survive person they cannot tell 100 percent truth about the tragedy because they don't remember well overall scenario on that day," he wrote. "I agreed 65 percent with them." In Pemba's estimation, his vast experience at high altitude gave him better judgment. In his own words, he wrote:

Because I reach more then 50 times 8000m. altitude during my 7 Everest expedition, 6 times on summit of Everest, 3 times on summit of Cho-Oyu, and I have a good experience how people work physically, mentally and why people became mad in extreme high altitude zone, and how capable human brain to remember the scenario around them in death zone. I did a couple of time rescue on Everest, Cho-Oyu for western people in death zone, That was my third rescue in death zone for others on K2 this year, I don't care whatever they said who survive after rescue, self rescue, self descent whatever, but they don't understand well and don't evaluation, about how much they increase the risk and other problem for others in extremely objective danger location and death zone.

In Pemba's view, some of the summiteers recklessly endangered others by pushing themselves to exhaustion, thereby creating a situation where rescuers would have to face extreme peril to save them. He seemed to be still coming to terms with what he had done. "When I came back home and see my family then my mind said I took unnecessary risk myself on mountain," he wrote. "But when I was there in mountain always my mind saying we have to help each other in mountain as much as possible when people into the problem that is the proud of mountaineering." The letter ended with a burning indicament of the collective judgement of many of the climbers on K2, and the public accounts given to the media:

> I understand well about the nature and attitude of
> climbers on K2 2008 from different team, because I
> watching carefully them during the expedition, I know
> how they work, what is the their intension, what is the
> their performance, and experience in high altitude also
> what they want to from K2, and what they did on moun-
> tain even second of August when situation was most
> critical, I have seen more clear scenario then other be-
> cause physically I was more good condition,
>   Personally I don't want to talk too much with media
> about the K2 tragedy, because Gerard was not media

lover also I don't want to disturb the people sentiment, even I know very well actually what happened on K2, but very few media company forced me to tell some thing about the K2 tragedy 2008 from Sherpa point of view and they said you are the only one eyewitness, then I gave them some interview but still they forced me to tell more, I don't care also people whatever they said about K2 tragedy, but always we have to pray and respect to casualties, and don't disturb the people sentiment,

—*Pemba Gyalje Sherpa*
Kathmandu Nepal

13

LIFE RIGHTS

*I*t *turned out Annie was not just talking to me.*

She wrote to the authors of both the *Men's Journal* and *Outside* stories. She talked to several writers involved in book projects, and others who were working on documentary films. She was willing talk to just about anyone if it would help get Gerard's story out there. "The funny thing is, they should have expected some mistakes to be made in the first round of reporting," Annie says. "Real journalism takes time." Then, at the end of December, Tom and Tina Sjogren at ExplorersWeb stepped back into the fray with their own comprehensive account of what happened on August 2. " 'Who is helping the stranded climbers?' we asked on August 2nd," the story began. "Now we know." The centerpiece of the story was a close analysis of the photos from Gerard's camera, which were published for the first time with permission from the McDonnell family. The article concluded by giving Gerard McDonnell the "Best of the Year" award for heroism.

Annie got a thoughtful response from the author of the *Men's Journal* article; the magazine later published an update agreeing with Explorers-Web. "Marco had reported seeing McDonnell's body that morning, but evidence now points to him having seen the body of Karim Meherban, a Pakistani porter," it read. "It's now clear that McDonnell had performed a selfless and heroic feat: a successful rescue attempt above 8,000 meters. He could have proceeded down and saved himself, but he sacrificed his life in order to try to save others."

The replies from other journalists were more mixed. One wrote that he had tried to contact Pemba, but heard he had signed a contract and was no longer giving interviews. Others expressed doubt about the quality of ExplorersWeb's journalism based on their reputation for controversy. There were more disappointments than successes. "It felt like coming up against the power of the first story. Everyone knew Marco's version of what happened. To change the story, the onus was on us." Annie was, in a sense, on the losing end of a contemporary adventure media race. Still, millions of people unquestioningly believed in Gerard.

In his home country of Ireland, for instance, the newspapers universally reported that he stayed to help the Koreans, dubbing him a national hero. "Eventually, Marco also descended, exhausted. Ger meanwhile again ascended 20m to try and make some further adjustment to free the Koreans from the ropes," the *Irish Independent* reported, echoing Pemba's version of the story, first published in the Norit final report. "We are extremely proud of the many heroic and brave achievements of our son and brother," Gerard's brother-in-law Damien said in a statement on behalf of the McDonnell family. "He brought honour, not only to us, his family, but the whole country. . . ."

And among those who knew him, there was absolutely no doubt. Twice before while descending on summit day—with the two Taiwanese women on Denali and Pat Falvey on Everest—Gerard had tied himself to failing climbers to help guide them down. Gerard's teammates from the Norit team immediately agreed when they belatedly heard the full story. "Of course we believed it as soon as we heard it," Wilco van Rooijen told me. "It is just that we never heard the full story; we never understood it, until now."

The climbing community in Alaska rallied as well. Matt Szundy, owner of Anchorage-based Ascending Path Guides, was hired as a technical consultant by the production company that made the documentary on the accident for the Discovery Channel. Szundy organized what is, that I know of, the only full-scale attempt to actually reenact what might have happened. Five guides participated in rigging possible scenarios Gerard might have faced, several of whom knew from personal experience Gerard's skill set and training. "My guides all agreed that Ger had the moral breadth, knowledge, equipment (minimal needed) and skills (even at altitude) to '*transfer the load*,'" he writes. Szundy notes that Alaskan climbers are generally well practiced in this kind of procedure, a fundamental skill in any crevasse rescue situation, because of the intensive glacier travel mountaineers encounter on Denali and other peaks. "I know for a fact that Ger had trained for crevasse rescue (with these specific skills) in order to climb Denali. . . . Every responsible Alaska Range climber must have these basic crevasse rescue skills."

Once I asked Annie why she kept fighting the media machine, why it mattered so much. She said she'd have to think about it. "This is how much I love Ger," she told me the next time we spoke. "I know who he was. He would never abandon another person. I know it sounds like we're just saying things because he's gone, but he really was that special; he really, really was."

"Thank you! I sold my life rights; now they want to write my life story! Thank you, Freddie!" Chhiring Dorje spoke so fast it was hard for me to follow his heavily accented words. But his excitement was written all over his face: a wide smile cracked across his broad chin, and his eyes sparkled like those of a kid on Christmas morning. He glowed.

It was late March, and I had returned to Kathmandu to spend some more time with the climbing-Sherpas and see if Tsering Bhote would be willing to speak. The load shedding had increased to sixteen hours a day without electricity, and Thamel felt empty except for the Everest expeditions that were preparing to leave. Chhiring Dorje and I met for coffee and it was cold sitting at a table outside in the shade. He immediately brought me up to speed on what had happened over the winter.

In the four months since my last visit, the Sherpas had been discovered. Chhiring had signed deals with both a film and a book project that would—he told me again—tell his life story.

There wasn't a trace of bravado or boasting in his demeanor. Chhiring was just plain *psyched*, and it occurred to me that his break was a long time coming. The first wave of coverage of the accident had not reported his rescue of Pasang Lama; the feature-length articles that came out two months after the disaster mentioned his feat, but only in passing. Most accounts focused instead on Pemba as the token Sherpa in the K2 story—Pemba had, after all, played the key role in rescuing Marco and Wilco on August 2 and 3, while Chhiring descended the Abruzzi with his American teammates. Still, I had to wonder: Pemba rescued two Europeans, while Chhiring Dorje saved the life of another Sherpa. Would Chhiring's exposure have been different if Pasang Lama had been a white guy with a satellite phone handy?

In any case, the Sherpas were beginning to get the recognition they deserved. Despite Chhiring's extrovert personality, I suspected his excitement wasn't about getting public attention, but the new professional opportunities and financial security for his family that it could provide. The publicity might even give him the chance to mount more expeditions as a sponsored professional, climbing alongside Western mountaineers as a peer instead of guiding paying clients.

Chhiring thanked me for helping get his story into the public eye, but I wasn't sure if my own writing made a difference. It didn't really matter. What amazed me, as I tried to find Tsering Bhote to help piece together the final story of what happened on August 2, was how the aftermath stripped away so many of my own preconceptions. It wasn't until the climbing-Sherpas stepped into the limelight that I could see, for all their cultural differences, how human nature is really the same.

Ngawang Tashi, Chhiring Dorje's little brother, and I went to Kopan Monastery a few days later. The monastery sits on a hill a few kilometers from Boudha, northeast of Kathmandu center, on the fringe of the urban sprawl where fields and rice patties intermingle with dirt lots and rusting rebar. The bike's engine strained as it carried both of us up the final section of road to reach the walled compound. We parked the bike and passed through a sturdy iron gate, which was open. A sign hung near the corner of the first building we came to:

WHILE IN KOPAN MONASTERY PLEASE REFRAIN FROM:
KILLING
STEALING
SEXUAL CONDUCT

The list went on. We walked up the paved walkway, climbed several flights of stairs, removed our shoes, and entered the monastery's main meditation hall. Its doors were open.

Incense burned in the cavern darkness; it took my eyes several minutes to adjust to the light. We walked around the room clockwise, stopping at several altars as Ngawang politely whispered the theological significance of each display. I tried to follow everything he was saying, but mostly I thought about how this was the quietest space in Kathmandu Valley. I shuffled around in my socks, made an offering in a tactfully positioned jar, and we stepped back into daylight. A saffron-robed monk glided toward us, and Ngawang waved. Songbu, a cousin by marriage from Chhiring's wife, Dawa, was from Namche. Young, soft-spoken, and smiling, he seemed at first glance the perfect manifestation of Buddhist values. We spoke for a few minutes, and then Songbu suggested we have lunch together.

Just inside the gated entrance was a snack bar owned and operated by the monastery. A wall of large windows provided a commanding view south over the cacophonous urban landscape toward the Boudha Stupa and the runway at Tribhuvan airport beyond.

I wanted to gain more perspective on the Sherpas' spiritual practices and beliefs. When the subject turns to the religion practiced by the Buddhists of the high Himalayas, most mountaineers conjure up an image of prayer flags and snow-clad mountains, the air resonating with the unceasing baritone chants of indecipherable Tibetan texts and laced with the acerbic smell of juniper. Utter serenity. Intuitively, I understood this popular image was an Orientalist construction, built in part on the very same misunderstood perceptions that also created the Sherpas' powerful reputation as guides. And I had to admit it: At first glance, Kopan certainly fit well into that image.

Buddhism first came to Tibet in the seventh century, and the original Sherpa clans brought it with them over the Nangpa La when they arrived in the Solu Khumbu. The Sherpas followed the Nyingmapa sect of Tibetan Buddhism, which teaches that for a prosperous life one must always entreat the protection of the good through regular ritual, prayer, and good behavior. There were no monasteries and no monks back then. Rather each village had a lama—a religious specialist who, unlike monks, were allowed to marry, have children, and participate in everyday life. Neighbors would turn to their local lama for blessings and rituals that should be performed, not only seasonal events, but also baptisms, marriages, and funerals. Sherpa villages were generally poor, and nobody could afford to devote himself exclusively to religious practice, nor was there much money available in the community that could be donated to public works such as constructing a monastery.

That began to change toward the end of the nineteenth century. "The founding of the monasteries emerged from essentially the same trends that produced the move to mountaineering," Sherry Ortner writes, "although in this case from the effects of those trends on the big people, rather than the non-big." After the Ranas took power, several of Namche's traders benefited enormously from exclusive trading rights they negotiated with the Kathmandu government. By the turn of the century, a few Sherpas had also struck it rich in Darjeeling. For the first time, significant monetary wealth began to accumulate at the top level of Sherpa society. Those wealthy families, however, still faced the same issues that had driven many of the children of poorer families to run away: namely, the cultural and practical reasons not to dilute the family wealth through a system of shared inheritance. Just like the sons of poor families, the sons of the wealthy had to find someplace to go. In 1916 and 1924, the first two monasteries were built in Solu Khumbu.

We ordered two plates of chili-cheese fries and Songbu began to describe life at the monastery. Though there was a palpable sense of time-lessness to the place, I was surprised to learn Kopan was a modern institution. It was founded in only 1971, roughly the same era that the first generation of climbing-Sherpas began living in Kathmandu full-time. Today, there are approximately three hundred and sixty monks in residence. Room and board is free—the monastery pays its costs from the revenues earned by donations and a lucrative side business running spiritual retreats for Westerners.

Songbu's grandfather had been a climbing-Sherpa; his parents operated a successful teahouse lodge. He became a monk. This generational lineage tells a story: Ever since the original Everest expeditions of the 1920s, as more Sherpas found economic prosperity through mountain-eering and the trekking industry, donating money to support monasteries and supplying children to become monks was viewed as an important obligation necessary to accrue good karma and be a well-regarded member of society.

Songbu asked where I was from. "New Hampshire," I answered. "It's maybe six hundred kilometers north of New York."

"Of course," Songbu replied. "I enjoy Boston very much." The electronic chimes of a cellular phone interrupted our conversation. Songbu reached underneath his robes and pulled out a state-of-the-art iPhone.

Life as a Buddhist monk, I was discovering, could be a little more sophisticated than I imagined. Songbu was an assistant to one of the head lamas. He made several international trips each year; in addition to seeing a half dozen American cities, he had also been to Europe, Singapore, and Malaysia to attend conferences and visit other monastic institutions that were all part of an international federation of Buddhist centers. In a sense, Kopan Monastery was a monument to the success of the Sherpa people—to the hard work of generations of Khumbu climbing-Sherpas, teahouse proprietors, and trekking guides. Songbu finished a brief conversation and the iPhone disappeared back under his robes.

I asked Ngawang and Songbu what they would prefer to be: a monk or a climbing-Sherpa. They giggled and looked at each other. "Monk, it is better to be a monk, I believe," Ngawang responded. On a practical level, I knew religion for most climbing-Sherpas and their families has less to do with fancy institutions like Kopan, and more to do with a daily spiritual routine. Almost every Sherpa home has a small prayer altar; it's considered important practice to try to spend at least a few minutes giving thanks and making offers to the gods to accrue good karma and future success in life. Ngawang told me that he lit incense and prayed every day that his older brother was climbing on K2. The week of the summit push, he visited a temple in Boudha each afternoon to pray for Chhiring's success and safety.

Though most Buddhist climbing-Sherpas believe prayer and other pious behavior—such as not killing animals, not drinking too much, and not engaging in sex while in base camp—make a difference, they aren't afraid to hedge their bets. As the office manager of his brother's company, Ngawang earnestly makes sure that Chhiring Dorje is covered with rescue insurance, a health-care plan, workman's comp, and life insurance for every expedition. The three months' coverage for Chhiring's K2 expedition cost five thousand rupees, about seventy dollars, with a payout of six hundred thousand rupees should Chhiring die.

That was a bargain, really, considering that one in ten K2 summiteers don't make it down alive.

A couple of days later I went climbing with Pemba. On the way back into town, we stopped for lunch. As we slurped on thick Tibetan-style noodle soup, he filled me in on the other side of the story. Pemba had declined to participate in this latest media project. "It's good for them," he said. "But they are thinking money first. We should be thinking more . . . long-term. We could do something, and have the money go to help the families from these tragedies." Pemba shrugged passively.

I pointed out that there were several different funds that had been started to help the families of the four men—two Pakistani and two Nepali—who had been the professional casualties of K2.

"The charities are okay—but when you give them the money, in two, three months, it is spent, gone." He flicked his hand in a low cut across the table. Pemba had a point. Most widows of climbing-Sherpas are young women in their twenties or even their teens. They still have long, potentially hugely productive lives in front of them. What they need is a better education, a helping hand to get some start in a new direction—not just a monthly stipend.

A colossal SUV with the United Nations emblem barged along the road outside the restaurant, dwarfing the stream of motorbikes and hatchback cabs. Pemba's boots-on-the-ground critique echoed a raging global debate among economists, policy makers, and aid donors about how best to help the millions of people throughout Asia and Africa born into poverty. "Doing good is harder than it looks," *New York Times* columnist Nicholas Kristof recently wrote. "For example, abundant evidence suggests that education can be transformative in a poor country, so donors often pay for schools. But building a school is expensive and can line the pockets of corrupt officials. And in my reporting, I've found that the big truancy problem in poor countries typically involves not students but teachers: I remember one rural Indian school where the teachers appeared only once or twice a year to administer standardized tests." Several controversial studies have found that the billions of dollars recently invested in aid to Africa produced zero change in the economic realities for the continent's poor. Most often, the missing ingredient in failed programs is accountability. Conversely, many of the efforts that are most effective, like the Khumbu Climbing Center, are smaller, more tightly focused, and more adaptable to changing conditions.

Pemba also seemed a little cynical about whether future climbing-Sherpas would learn from what happened on K2. "No one has even read *Into Thin Air*," he said, shaking his head. "I say to them, 'You are climbing-Sherpa, you should understand this.' But they don't listen. Do you think any Nepalis will read your book?"

"This winter, things got a little crazy," Tshering Pande told me. We were riding out to Hattiban, another small sport climbing area on the rim of the Kathmandu Valley. Halfway into the forty-minute trip, raindrops began falling on the discontinuously paved thoroughfare, and two guys plus the weight of a rucksack of cragging gear on one dirt bike called for caution. We pulled over at a roadside café, drank coffees that were really made of Nescafé and powdered milk, and waited for the squall to pass.

Tshering is another Bhote from the Arun Valley. Big Pasang Bhote had married Tshering's sister, Lhamu, and they had two children, Dawa and Nima. Tshering Pande first made a name for himself back when he was a kitchen hand. On one trip to Island Peak, he stayed behind to make breakfast for a resting client, left camp, scrambled up a new route, solo, to reach the summit, and was back in time to serve a late lunch. His career as a climbing-Sherpa and guide began to take off after that. The summer of 2008, Tshering was guiding in Norway when he got an urgent e-mail from family back home. The Internet newspapers were saying two Nepalis were killed on K2. But no one knew the names. A couple of weeks later, Tshering flew home to help his sister deal with the insurance.

Over the winter, it got worse. "Everyone wanted to talk to the family. There was no rest. They were offering contracts and money; they even wanted to use interpreters. Hey, we all speak English!" The language barrier was an interesting issue—it had never occurred to me to use an interpreter, mostly because one was out of my budget. There had been plenty of instances when I had to go over a question several times before feeling like I understood the answer. It felt awkward enough hanging out with Sherpas one-on-one; introducing another person to the situation seemed like it would completely destroy any chance of catching an authentic glimpse into their lives.

I asked if Tsering Bhote, Jumik's little brother, would be willing to talk. I saw Tshering Pande wince for a moment, almost like he was embarrassed by something, and then he shook his head.

It was the Flying Jump expedition's cook, Nawang, who called from base camp. The call came on Monday, August 4. Virginia O'Leary spent that evening at the Bhote home in Boudha. Virginia had always been slightly in awe of Jumik and Pemba's mother, a slightly built woman with a wrinkled face and toothy smile who dressed in chubas—traditional Tibetan jumper-gowns—and spoke no English. Outwardly, she appeared frail, and yet Virginia knew she had to possess immense strength to have raised so many children in an undeveloped Himalayan village.

That night, Virginia held her for half an hour. Maybe longer. Gumu cried and called out for her sons: for Tsering in Pakistan, who was soon coming home, and Pemba, who was working in the United States for the summer. She called for them and she cried for Pasang and for Jumik. It seemed as though the indomitable woman had surrendered herself to the darkest thoughts:

> She has it in her head that if she had been a better mother Pasang, Pemba's brother who died a few months ago from the ravages of alcohol, and Jumik would not have died. . . . The idea that the death of a child is the fault of the mother is a common one in the Bhote (mountain) culture of eastern Nepal. Beliefs can save and destroy. . . .

But for Virginia, looking Dawasangmu in the face was maybe the hardest task. It was all too familiar. An unexpected phone call. A newborn baby. The hollow eyes.

In another week Tsering did come home, and soon after he arrived in Kathmandu he and his mother left for Hungong. Then Pemba Bhote returned from the United States just as the situation with the life insurance got complicated. On paper, Jumik and Pasang Bhote were covered through a policy in Nepal with Himalayan Guides. But they were killed in Pakistan and their bodies had not been recovered. With no physical proof of their deaths, a death certificate, incident report, police report, and official statement from Kim Jae-su were needed to file a claim. Even the photocopied death certificate that was originally sent from Islamabad was not enough; it required a proper seal. Virginia and Pemba spent a full day waiting in line at the Pakistan embassy before being told that they would have to send their request to the Nepalese embassy in Islamabad.

Then Kim Jae-su turned up in Kathmandu. Only three weeks after K2, he and Go Mi-yeong were sticking to their plans to climb Manaslu that autumn, their third eight-thousander of the year. The Korean leader requested a meeting with Jumik's and Big Pasang's families, and Virginia came along to help facilitate. When they arrived at the Hotel Annapurna, Kim was waiting with an interpreter from the Korean embassy. In a lengthy statement he told the families he was sorry for Jumik's and Pasang's deaths, that they had been well aware of the risks of K2 and made their own decisions accordingly, and that there was little he could do to provide long-term support for the two fatherless families. After he was finished speaking, he presented each widow with an envelope.

Although there were no official laws governing compensation in the event of a fatality in the nineteen-thirties, expeditions typically paid two thousand rupees for the loss of a married man, and one thousand rupees for a bachelor. For frostbite injuries, climbing-Sherpas were given ten rupees for each amputated digit. Inside the envelopes Kim Jae-su gave Dawasangmu and Lhamu was five thousand dollars. Cash. Combined with the insurance settlement, if the claim was ever processed, Jumik's and Pasang Bhote's wives each stood to receive thirteen thousand five hundred dollars from their husbands' deaths.

A discussion followed about whether additional support would be available, and if Kim's sponsor, Kolon Sports, might be able to help. Kim indicated that the five thousand dollars was all they could expect from him. Then Virginia heard Pemba ask if the Bara Sahib, as Jumik had called Kim Jae-su, would consider using his company, Mountain Footprints, for future expeditions.

Kim said he'd think about it.

A couple of weeks later Tsering and his mother returned from Hungong after presiding over a puja for Jumik there. Gumu looked as though she had aged a lifetime from that festive night a year ago when Jumik returned from Shishapangma and took them all out to dinner in celebration. When Virginia saw her, the old woman pulled at the neck of her chuba. The burn marks were black and round, the size of quarters. There were several, and she did not hide them. In fact, it seemed as if she wanted to show them to Virginia and wanted her to understand. As if the burns were a secret badge that could be shared only between mothers.

They held one more puja for Jumik at the Boudha Stupa. Virginia went to this one and after it was over she got a ride home with another friend from Hungong named Ngang Dorchi. "No matter what happens," he told her as she climbed off his motorbike in front of her apartment, "we must never let them call the baby a father-eater."

I asked Virginia when she knew that Pemba Bhote was lying to her.

It was December now, sixteen months after the disaster on K2, and Tsering's account of what happened in the Bottleneck still hadn't surfaced. It was my third trip to Nepal in year. Virginia O'Leary and I were having lunch in the courtyard of a restaurant in Patan, near the Kathmandu University School of Management, where she teaches. The semester was almost over, and her cell phone rang several times during our meal together as students frantically called to consult her before their semester projects were due to be turned in at the end of the week. "I assigned them this project back in October," she said with a sigh after fielding one call, "and they wait until three days before it is due to arrange to meet with me? Everyone here wants the diploma, but I don't know if they really want to learn.

"It took me unraveling the first lie to discover all the other lies," she said, returning to my question. "After Jumik died, I spent a lot of time with his family that fall. I noticed that Pemba and Jumik's sisters were spending a lot of time around the house when they were supposed to be in boarding school." It slowly dawned on Virginia that the girls weren't in boarding school.

"All that money we raised for their education . . . Pemba Bhote took me for thousands and thousands of dollars. He's one of the best liars I've ever met in my life. Over eleven years, he lied and lied and lied. I used to introduce him as my Nepali son. I was devastated when I figured it all out."

I steered the conversation back to K2. "There's no way Tsering will talk to you—there's just no way," she told me point-blank. "The last journalist who tried to contact the family, Pemba Bhote demanded ten thousand dollars to talk to his brother."

I tried to explain why it was important. Tsering was the highest person to survive the Bottleneck and so far no one knew his account of what happened. He could verify where Jumik, Big Pasang, and the Koreans were when they got hit. And Tsering was the one person on the planet who might also be able to explain to Annie Starkey and Gerard Mc-Donnell's family what had really happened.

Virginia only shook her head. "You think that they care about appeals to journalistic truth? They had their pujas for Jumik. He was put to rest their way. If Pemba Bhote says Tsering is forbidden from talking, then he won't talk."

Virginia was still haunted by the extent of Pemba's deceptions. The girls were complicit, having pretended to be going to private boarding school. She wasn't sure about who else had been involved. She preferred not to think about it. Virginia had not seen or spoken to Pemba Bhote since December 20, 2008. But she heard through the grapevine that the house finally got finished. "The insurance money, the money from the memorial funds . . . I'd bet it all went to finishing that house. Oh!" she exclaimed. "I will never know if the young man I met in 1997 changed or that's who he always was."

"I don't know why I signed the contract," Pasang Lama told me. He was staring into the middle distance somewhere beyond the surface of the café table we sat at. "Pemba Bhote told me not to sign anything."

Of all the climbing-Sherpas, the line between professional success and personal tragedy cut the closest to Pasang Lama. By accepting a modest payment and signing his nonexclusive life rights to tell his and Chhiring's stories, he immediately alienated himself from some of his own family. Pemba Bhote threatened him and they almost had a physical confrontation. Things got very bad. Yet simultaneously, after the tragedy, Pasang Lama's career began to take off. 2009 was his busiest year of high-altitude work: With Chhiring Dorje and Fredrik Sträng, he climbed Makalu and Lhotse in the spring, then traveled back to Pakistan to work on a commercial expedition attempting Gasherbrum II in the summer, and finally attempted Annapurna with Kim Jae-su in the fall.

"There were so many avalanches," Pasang Lama told me of his last expedition with the Koreans. "We were trying to descend but the lines we had fixed in one couloir were gone." In a situation unerringly similar to the one they faced on K2 the year before, Pasang, Kim, and their team were stranded. Eventually they turned around, climbed back up the mountain to a higher section of fixed ropes, removed them, and used them to escape the mountain. After four consecutive eight-thousand-meter expeditions in one year, I asked Pasang Lama, how long did he think he could get away with taking chances like that? He didn't have much of an answer.

"Please," he said instead, "don't try to talk to the family. That is my request. In the family now, for Tsering, it is like . . . remote control. It will only make things worse." Pasang Lama frowned and pitched his head back and forth in dismay. "We will see who is right, Pemba Bhote or the writers."

"He's a super-nice kid," says Phil Crampton, the leader of the Gasherbrum II expedition Pasang went on the summer after K2. "He's young and learning. We got a lot of older, more experienced Sherpas teaching him. We had him fix a lot of the ropes." One magazine article even went so far as to call Pasang Lama a climbing prodigy. But when I looked at him I saw only a shy young man, caught between a promising career that could elevate him to first-world wealth and the uncompromising patterns of poverty and family that tied him down.

I asked why Pemba Bhote would not let Tsering speak. "He loved Jumik too much." Pasang Lama shook his head.

More than a year after K2, it would be an overstatement to say that Chhiring Dorje and Pemba Gyalje, the first two Sherpas to climb K2 without bottled oxygen, were estranged. But at the same time, it was hard to believe that they, or any of the surviving four climbing-Sherpas, had emerged from the experience as closer friends. As one of Chhiring's teammates put it to me in a moment of unguarded bluntness: "Pemba's gotten too much media attention. Now it should be Chhiring's turn." Did the magazine articles, documentary films, and book contracts change anything fundamental in their relationship with each other, or did the tragedy simply illuminate a world that generations of climbing-Sherpas had kept carefully hidden? I wondered if they had been friends to begin with.

There was no mistaking that Pemba and Chhiring each had his own distinct personal style, and since climbing K2, their careers had gone in different directions. Chhiring Dorje seemed to redouble his efforts at the eight-thousand-meter game. In the race to become the first Nepali to climb all fourteen of them, Chhiring is a definite underdog, with only seven summits; the leader, Serap Jangbu Sherpa, had eleven summits. But there was always a chance, and Chhiring Dorje and Pasang Lama were fishing for sponsors to pay for them to spend the summer of 2010 in Pakistan climbing Nanga Parbat and the Gasherbrums.

Pemba Gyalje, on the other hand, has not been on a single eight-thousand-meter expedition since K2, nor did he have any immediate plans to return to high altitude. Instead, he landed a well-paying job working for an American company, Mountain Madness, leading mostly short treks and easy climbs of six-thousand-meter peaks. Pemba's real energy is devoted to building the Nepali National Mountain Guide Association, an organization dedicated to educating the climbing-Sherpa community to the standards of European guides.

"Nobody wants to do the background work," he told me one afternoon in the NNMGA office. The sign on his desk said, GENERAL SEC-RETARY. "They are all thinking about becoming guides and making big money, but to build the organization it will take time. I am doing this for the future generations." A barrage of laughter tricked from the next room, where a half dozen young climbing-Sherpas were looking at photos of frozen waterfalls and planning the monthlong ice-climbing course they would take that winter. The good-natured teasing, the excitement, all the talk about mountains and climbing: It reminded me of the guide service I worked in when I graduated from college.

I understood Pemba's frustration with the pace of change, but change was happening. The next year, the first class of Nepali-educated guides will take their final exams. If they pass, they will be in a sense completing a process that began a century ago, when Alex Kellas hired a few Sherpa men from the labor pool in Darjeeling to accompany him into the mountains.* Over the years their job description changed, from coolie to porter to Sherpa to climbing-Sherpa. Pemba's dream was to help his people, with proper training and international recognition, take the final step and legitimately become what they should have been called all along: guides.

My last day in Kathmandu I found myself in Thamel with several hours to kill before my next appointment. I had arranged to meet that evening with another member of the Hungong Bhote clan who was familiar with Tsering's plight. After idly window-shopping for a while, I ducked into a surprisingly modern-looking equipment store. Inside, brand-name American technical apparel hung in clean display cases. Most of the prices, given in Nepali rupees, had four zeros at the end. I struck up a conversation with

---

* To date, one Nepali citizen, Sunar Bahadur Gurung, has successfully completed the UIAGM certification process through the National School of Ski and Alpinism (ENSA) located in Chamonix, France. He is the only native of a Himalayan state to achieve that distinction. The Nepali National Mountain Guide Association's mission is to build a program offering the same education Sunar received at ENSA in Nepal.

one of the store's proprietors, a middle-aged Sherpa man well dressed in Western corporate-casual attire. "Have you ever heard of Sherpas climbing just for the fun of it?" I asked.

"I only know of two," he replied. "The first was my dad, and the second was me." Jamling Norgay still lived in Ghang La, in the house his father built after he climbed Everest in Darjeeling. But all the money in the trekking business is in Kathmandu these days, he told me, and so that was where he had opened shop as an importer of climbing equipment. It wasn't easy for Jamling, selling the best-made Western gear in a city chock-full of cheap rip-offs. "Everyone wants to bargain," he said, rolling his eyes.

He handed me a glass of tea, and I asked about the difference between a Bhote and a Sherpa in the first place. "These days, there's so much intermarriage and everyone is living in the city. There's not much difference. I guess we're all Sherpas, now," he said with a chuckle.

Jamling had taken Edmund Hillary's original photo of his dad standing on the summit of Everest, and had blown it up into an eight-foot-high poster. The poster hung by the entranceway and a cheesy merchandizing slogan was printed across the bottom: *Radical Thinking*. "See the photo of Dad?" He pointed it out to me. "I just got it printed. I like how it came out." He was looking up, nodding his head.

I looked at the iconic image. Tenzing Norgay was a small man, but his posture cut the perfect profile of a successful mountaineer. You can't see his face, but somehow he managed to look both elated and exhausted, triumphant and humble. It was radical thinking—that mountaineering could bring so many different people from so many different backgrounds together, that they would so often be led by men born into one of the poorest, most poverty-stricken regions on earth, that men like that could rise to become the elite players of such an arcane and useless activity. When people from different cultures meet on a mountain, I suppose, what happens next has the capacity to bring out the best and the worst that both cultures have to offer.

I returned to my hostel late that night, still not knowing what Tsering had seen in the Bottleneck couloir on August second. I checked my e-mail account and found I had just received a new message. The subject read: *Transcription.*

The next morning, Chhiring got up early to drive me to the airport on his bike—a Honda Hero, same as Pemba's. He walked me to the gate at the entrance to the building where they checked everyone's passport, presented me with a Kharta scarf, and then turned to leave.

When I first met Chhiring and Pemba a year ago, each man spoke admiringly of the other. Pemba seemed pleased to learn that I was interested in speaking to all the Sherpas involved. "It has been just me, telling the Sherpa perspective," he told me in November. As Chhiring had first told me, they climbed together for most of the final stretch on summit day—and afterward, both seemed content to share the title of being the first Sherpa to summit K2 without using supplemental oxygen. Now, the subtle rivalry between Pemba and Chhiring had crystallized into the debate over what happened on August 2. Whereas Pemba Gyalje was certain Gerard McDonnell freed the Koreans, Chhiring was beginning to express doubts. Toward the end of my last discussion with him, I asked if he had any parting comments.

"I want to say this," Chhiring told me. "Wilco and Marco, they weren't heroes. Gerard is not the hero. Pemba Gyalje is not the hero. . . ." For a moment I wanted to interject, to say that I was pretty certain Pemba Gyalje didn't think of himself as any sort of hero. But I swallowed my words. If K2 had taught me anything, it was that being a hero had nothing to do with how a person feels about himself, and everything to do with what the rest of the world thinks. ". . . Big Pasang, he was the hero," Chhiring finished. "He went back up the Bottleneck to help."

After passing the third security checkpoint, I boarded the plane. It was funny, in a way. I had flown halfway around the world to try to talk to Tsering Bhote, only to receive an e-mail. Shuffling toward my seat assignment, I was surprised for a moment to see that well over 80 percent of the economy passengers were young Nepali men. They wore nylon jackets, New York Yankees caps, and casual street clothes that smelled like cigarettes. They bantered back and forth between aisles, cracking jokes and laughing as the airplane taxied toward the runway. Several ordered alcoholic drinks once the plane was airborne. Most were Hindi, but I thought I glimpsed a few broad faces and flat noses, vague features of Tibetan ancestry melted in among the rows and rows of seat-belted migrants.

I couldn't understand a word any of them said.

When we touched down in Qatar five hours later, the mood seemed a little more sober. I saw them once more after we had disembarked and cleared immigrations. They stood in a line, shuffling toward a waiting bus and a burnished oil field.

14

BELIEF

"*W*hat do you believe?"

I tried to dodge that question more than once. It wasn't about belief; it was about a clear-eyed analysis of the facts. My job was simply to present both sides of the debate and let the reader decide. Annie persisted. She knew better.

"With all due respect," she wrote, "it does come down to what you truly believe, Freddie. No matter how you think you can write your book, your beliefs will be evident to your readers." I felt a little exposed when I read that, and poorly equipped to be writing about the K2 disaster in the first place. Any judgment rendered on another human being says as much about how you feel about yourself as it does about how you feel about them.

Fundamentally, that's what the story of K2 was all about. It's a question that everyone, at some point in their lives, probably asks themselves: *What would you do in that situation? Would you give your own life to help another person? Would you make that sacrifice?* Regardless of the answer, there is no way to be sure it is correct until you've actually been there. The answer is why we celebrate firemen, soldiers, mothers, and religious leaders. It occurred to me that what the world believed happened to Gerard McDonnell was a litmus test, an indicator of mountaineering's self-esteem as a community and what we believe our own answers might be to the question.

Author Jim Curran understood this when he wrote about the media scrutiny Willi Bauer and Kurt Diemberger faced after the 1986 tragedy. "The anger was . . ." he wrote, "a subconscious resentment that when put into the ultimate survival experience, Kurt and Willi in the end had to fight for their own lives, not save others. Could this anger be a deep-rooted admission that, put in those circumstances, most of us would do the same? I felt that question was really addressed to the questioner."

I wasn't there. I'd never climbed the mountain. I never knew Gerard McDonnell, Jumik Bhote, or Big Pasang Bhote. For that matter, I did not know anyone on the mountain prior to the accident. I was a twenty-nine-year-old blogger sitting halfway around the world. But every word I wrote mattered—it mattered immeasurably. "The only drama and suffering that exists in the world exists in human relations," Saint-Exupéry wrote. My one qualification, I realized, came from those times I had actually sat down with somebody, shared a cup of coffee, and listened to his or her side of it. I saw the tragedy playing out in them, in the impact K2 had on their lives—not in the eleven names listed on the Internet. I saw the pain through their eyes, and also heard the unexpected laughter.

Once I asked Annie what she thought Gerard would think of this— the tragedy, all the stories in the news, him being at the center of so much fuss. Annie let out a startling snort, a sort of nasal convulsion that was loud and genuine, and momentarily irrepressible. "He'd hate it!" she answered after her laughter subsided. "You know, he didn't even like getting asked questions about Everest. He always changed the conversation. . . . We're both really private people. He told me once that if he could stand on top of K2, and never have another person know about it, that would be his wish. I wish I never had to talk to the media, either," Annie continued. "The most important thing isn't my story, or the family's. It's just for everyone to know how sad we are, and how much we miss him, every single day."

"He'd be the first one saying, 'Now, lads, don't go making me into Saint Gerard,'" bandmate Dan Possumato agrees. "Of course, that kind of humility was what made him so special in the first place."

I visited Alaska, Ireland, Nepal, the Netherlands, and Colorado, among other places, and exchanged hundreds of phone calls and e-mail messages—but of all the people I spoke to and all the different perspectives I heard, I tied into a rope and went climbing with only two of the K2 survivors: Cas van de Gevel and Pemba Gyalje Sherpa. Both were Gerard McDonnell's teammates, both went above Camp IV on August 2 to try to help others down, and both struck me as exceptionally solid all-around mountaineers, and not just in the eight-thousand-meter game.* I never knew Gerard, but I did get to know his teammates enough to realize I'd trust them with my own life in the mountains—and both of them are convinced that Gerard freed the Korean party, and was descending behind them when he was hit by serac fall.

Because of the contradictory nature of the eyewitness accounts, there will always be potential for future debate. It's also possible that new information might surface. But after eighteen months of travel and correspondence, given Pemba's story, there is no reason for everyone to not at least reconsider the evidence. "That's one thing that hurts," Annie confided. "Why won't Marco at least admit the possibility that it was Karim he saw; why can't he admit that he might have been confused?"

Many climbers will tell you that it's pointless to try to rescue anyone above eight thousand meters, that it's every man for himself up there and that's the way it should be. But ultimately, I kept coming back to one thing: the character of the man in question. Again and again, everyone I spoke to told me of Gerard's unique ability to see people, to focus on them as individual beings and his unwavering commitment to help those in need, regardless of who they were. If you don't believe in Gerard

---

* After K2, Cas attempted the seriously steep north face of Kalanka, in India, while Pemba and Tshering Pande Bhote climbed the Namche Waterfall, a fifteen-pitch grade-six technical monster, in two days' round-trip from Kathmandu.

McDonnell—or if you don't even believe a guy like him could exist in the first place—then I don't see much future for this sport I love.

I'm not willing to admit that.

The accident did spark a well-informed and constructive dialogue in a few circles, though those conversations weren't given as much public attention as they deserved. What lessons did the accident have to offer future K2 climbers regarding strategy and tactics? Thoughtful arguments were voiced on all sides of the debates over the use of bottled oxygen, fixed lines, climbing-Sherpas, and overall strategy and cooperation on the mountain. There was no universal consensus, no easy answers, but it was certainly productive to listen.

At a panel discussion on the accident that was held at the Banff Centre in Alberta, Canada, in November 2008, moderator Geoff Powter had the following exchange with leading French alpinist Christian Trommsdorff (who attempted K2 alpine-style in July 2008 and shared a permit with Hugues D'Aubarède):

> **Powter:** It was said in several of the media reports that these people were guided . . . and I wonder when people then started saying in response, 'No, no, they're not being guided; there are no commercial expeditions on the peak,' and so on, whether we're kind of mislabeling the term. In a sense it seems like people are getting guided on this mountain, in that camps are prefixed, ropes are fixed. . . .
>
> **Trommsdorff:** On K2, what's happening is what I would call totally supported climbing. Like the Korean team was totally supported. They didn't have to do anything themselves other than pull up the fixed ropes.
>
> **Powter:** Do you have the sense that they could have done it if they didn't have the fixed ropes there, or the high-altitude porters?

Trommsdorff: No, as I said earlier I think only two people this year were really qualified to go up K2, out of all those who chose the normal route—Pemba [Gyalje] and Alberto [Zerain].

Trommsdorff spoke adamantly in defense of a minimalist lightweight style, without heavy fixed lines, and even suggested the most qualified teams were limited by the false sense of safety the lines provide. "For example, the Dutch team, even though they had strong technical climbers, none of them would go one meter beyond the fixed line. . . . We were very surprised to see that."

American mountaineer Chris Warner, who summited K2 in 2007, agrees in part with Trommsdorff's diagnosis of the problem, but doesn't assign the blame on the use of fixed lines, per se. "When I summited last year, there were two guys who were making their ninth eight-K summit (Portuguese and Italian), without ever having led any part of a route. One of the guys took off with the radio; the other guy died. . . . These are the guys who dominate the sport these days. They like to show up late and don't want to leave Camp Four early." According to Warner, the problem is essentially a question of leadership. "When we had this problem last year, we took control of the summit-day strategy and we made sure it was personally us that got assigned the most difficult part of the job, fixing the Bottleneck and the start of the traverse. Wouldn't you want to be in charge on the most dangerous day of your life?" he asks.

Certainly, there *were* strong leaders up there, but due to a variety of complex dynamics and fate, no one—Asian or Westerner—properly took control and coordinated everyone's effort on summit day. Shaheen Baig's food poisoning and Qudrat Ali's early departure from base camp to lead another trip stripped the advance team of the two most able Pakistanis on the mountain. Not only did they lose skilled manpower, but also their leadership abilities at effectively organizing the other Pakistani professionals. Many of the climbers going for the summit without supplemental oxygen, meanwhile, calculated that it would be better to let the teams using bottled oxygen fix line. And those teams, particularly the Korean and Serbian expeditions, detailed the job to their employees.

In fairness, it should be said that properly applied, either strategy—the lightweight, independent sprints of Trommsdorff or the well-coordinated collective efforts suggested by Chris Warner—can work successfully on K2. But the collective summit team of August 1, 2008, by a devastating combination of cumulative errors and bad luck, found themselves in a situation that combined the disadvantages of both with the benefits of neither.

Austrian Peter Habeler, who with Reinhold Messner was the first person to climb Everest without supplemental oxygen, spoke at the same panel discussion as Trommsdorff about the dangers of relying on bottled gas. "It's an illusion—you have oxygen, you go up. . . . Because then, of course, if you run out of oxygen, then you have a problem; then it's really hard." According to Raymond Huey, a biology professor and oxygen statistician, the use of bottled oxygen on K2 has steadily increased, from 10.2 percent in the 1980s, to 32.7 percent in the 1990s, to 50.8 percent in the last decade. In 2008, eight of the eleven dead were using bottled oxygen.

A vocal opponent of Habeler's perspective is Kim Jae-su himself, who said in a taped debrief of the accident in base camp: "I think climbing K2 without supplemental oxygen is suicide, especially in bad weather. I would like to ask refrain climb K2 without supplement oxygen. If one has to climb without it, I would like to recommend solo climbing or climbing with less than three members. When too many people climbing without oxygen if one have a problem all the people behind him could be affected and encounter great danger."

Meanwhile, all of the climbing-Sherpas I spoke to at one point or another voiced the same clear criticism: There needed to be more climbing-Sherpas up there. "Many people, they did not respect the mountaineering expedition philosophy, also they did not hire enough Sherpas, that was the mistake," Pemba Gyalje wrote in one e-mail. "K2 is not dangerous by itself," Pasang Lama said during an interview. "But at least eight or nine

Sherpas should prepare the entire route the previous day. . . . First, fix the Bottleneck, come down to Camp Four, then take the group the next day." On Everest, reputable commercial operators typically provide for a one-to-one climbing-Sherpa-to-client ratio on summit day. Common sense dictates that it would be prudent for any "fully supported" K2 expedition, where professional Pakistani or Nepali employees are given responsibility to fix lines, porter loads, and carry oxygen, to adhere to at least that same ratio as a minimum guideline.

If future expeditions are to follow this advice, it will mean plenty of employment opportunities for future generations of climbing-Sherpas in Pakistan and Nepal, and it would also undoubtedly expose them to roles in future calamities as well. Despite existing national organizations and largely unenforced laws in Pakistan, India, and Nepal, abuses and fundamentally exploitative relationships are common throughout the trekking and climbing industry in the Himalayas. Most often the worst abuses occur at the fringes of the job market. Established cooks and climbing-Sherpas who are respected and sought after for their services are consequently also well compensated, enjoy strong relationships with good employers, and have the luxury of accepting only the best jobs. Those with less experience must content themselves with more demanding work at less pay, frequently on more challenging mountains and with hard-driving employers—and the hungrier they are, the harder they'll work.

In this regard, perhaps no group has it harder than the Pakistani climbing-Sherpas. After the 2008 season, the Singaporean team of Robert Goh and Edwin Siew posted a lengthy report on the performance of their three employees, whom they paid four thousand dollars each to ferry loads and set up camps.

On 14 July 2008, Mr Mehraban Shah and the other 2 HAP (Mr Zulfiqar and Mr Jhan Baig) load-carried with our team up to Camp 1 (6,000m). The guys noted that Mr Zulfiqar was very slow and did not know how to use the figure-of-8 descender for abseiling.

Mr Jhan Baig had to loop the descender for him. Mr Jhan himself abseiled off a fixed rope tied to the opened gate of the karabinar. Robert had to yell to him to stop and retie the anchor.

Jehan Baig, whose technical skills were clearly lacking, was eventually dismissed from the expedition. A few days later, Robert spotted Baig in the Serbian base camp, and then the Serbian liaison officer confronted them for having unfairly dismissed him. "We were thus known in BC as the 'HAPS sackers,'" Robert wrote in an e-mail. When Jehan Baig ultimately wound up employed by Hugues D'Aubarède, Robert decided not to take issue with the arrangement. "I had previously spoken with Nick Rice [Hugues's climbing partner] about our disappointing HAPs. Also, I did not want to ruin Jehan's opportunity in finding employment as our opinion of his incompetency was ours alone. Maybe other climbers had different ethics and style and threshold for risks and mistakes. In other climbers' eyes, maybe we were being too inflexible."

Sadly, Jehan Baig's misfortunes continued. As Nick Rice wrote in his blog for August 1, the summit day:

> . . . there [were] a number of others who were not feeling well in Camp IV. One of these, I believe, although he wouldn't admit it, was Baig, one of Hugues' high altitude porters, who in Camp 3.5 (7,800 meters) had a headache and an apparent problem, according to Karim, in vocalizing his symptoms of AMS. Hugues gave him an aspirin and Diamox (acetazolamide) which apparently helped him feel better. His symptoms, in my opinion, resurfaced at Camp IV in the morning, as it took him around 30 minutes with the help of another to get his crampons on, and he also was having trouble with his headlamp.

Were Jehan Baig a Western climber, it is unfathomable that his teammates would not—at the very least—express concern for a friend who took half an hour to strap on his crampons. But according to Rice: "Hugues was extremely frustrated by the delay that this caused, as he was quite cold, and knew from the last few years that he needed an early start in order to secure the summit." The Frenchman evidently decided that Baig was still capable enough to carry a load of oxygen tanks to the top of the Bottleneck, and then descend on his own. On his way down, Baig slipped and fell in the ensuing body recovery of Dren Mandic.

Though there were several other complaints about the abilities of the Pakistanis on K2 in 2008, many seasoned Karakoram climbers are quick to speak in their defense. "People are so used to treating people in an 'Asian mentality,' treating them like servants," says Jamie McGuinness, who regularly guides other eight-thousand-meter peaks in Pakistan. "That doesn't work with Pakistanis, trust me." McGuinness suggests one reason for the Pakistanis' perceived lack of motivation is that they typically earn a set day rate or fixed salary for the entire expedition, whereas in Nepal, significant bonuses are more frequently offered as rewards for carries to high camp and summiting.

"Pakistani climbers are exactly as strong as Sherpas, but they have less of a tradition in guiding and organizing climbs," Italian climber Simone Moro writes. Noting that the mountains of Pakistan are more remote and less explored than other regions of the Himalayas, and that the country was closed to expeditions for many years, Moro doesn't think the Pakistanis are any different from the climbing-Sherpas of Nepal—they just got a later start. As he explains it: "The problem is not the Pakistani high-altitude porters, but the mountaineers that need someone to fix completely the route for them, because they are not able to be self-sufficient and independent in their climb."

Many others echoed these comments, including American K2 summiteer Chris Warner, who says bluntly: "It's immoral to ask anyone to go through the Bottleneck for money." As Pakistan's most famous mountaineer, Nazir Sabir, wrote in a public letter after debriefing many of the survivors in Islamabad:

The Sherpas and the high-altitude porters can't be expected to play the role of fixing lines and camps on higher ground on K2. Most often the local crew is part of the route making team and not left on their own to decide where to place the ropes and most importantly around the most crucial section of the Abruzzi Spur. . . . Commercial climbing has no place on K2 like on comparatively easier mountains and normal routes of Cho Oyu, Shishapangma, Broad Peak or even Everest.

Sabir recently proposed abolishing the term "high-altitude porter," or "HAP," and suggested instead that Pakistanis working in the high mountains be called high-altitude crew (HAC).

What can be done to prevent similar situations in the future, when blatantly unqualified men still find enough financial incentive to go high on the one of the world's most dangerous peaks, despite the obvious and severe risks involved? Though the governments of Pakistan and Nepal require basic insurance for those working in the trekking industry, it's doubtful they will institute a skills-based certification program anytime in the immediate future. One bright spot is that training and certification are slowly being voluntarily adopted, through such programs as the Khumbu Climbing Center, the Nepali National Mountain Guide Association, and a new mountaineering school founded in the village of Shimshal in Hunza, Pakistan.

But the real paradox, the thing that makes the K2 disaster an incalculable affair, is this: If the climbers had been more coordinated, if the advance rope-fixing team had worked more efficiently, if there were more climbing-Sherpas or the summit party left earlier or climbed faster, or more had turned around before the top—it's likely that more would be dead with Rolf Bae, in the initial serac fall, who was descending several hours in front of the rest of the group. As it turned out, at least six, and maybe as many as eight, of the fatalities were directly the result of climbers being struck by ice. And the 2008 K2 season would certainly be a different story if not for the mountain's final spasms, which swept five men down the Bottleneck inside of half an hour.

"We were discussing in the base camp about this serac, because the main risk on K2, on the last day . . . the main risk was this serac," Christian Trommsdorff reflected, noting that there was evidence from climbers who had already been high on K2 earlier that season that suggested the serac had avalanched several times in the weeks leading up to the accident. "What we found was that people were simply not interested. . . . It's a risk that people didn't analyze; they just accept a fairly significant risk, which is totally random, and which is related to the amount of time spent in this section. . . ." Some climbers, including Kim Jae-su, theorized that global warming was to blame for the serac's instability. Chris Klinke remembers the face of the serac was sweating. "I can't recall if I had the conscious thought that it could avalanche, but on some level, it definitely factored into my decision to turn around," he says. Andy Selters, on the other hand, is one of the few who doubts that daytime heat had much to do with it. "Above eight thousand meters, even on the best days, the ambient air temp is still minus twenty Celsius in the shade," he says. "I can't imagine global warming makes a real difference up there."

In retrospect, it's easy to say that all the signs were there. But before 2008, not a single fatality in seventy years of human history on K2 is confirmed as being caused by icefall from the serac. Cognitive scientists have a formal name for this phenomenon: "Hindsight bias" is defined as the inclination to see events that have occurred as more predictable than they in fact were before they took place. Though it's tempting to agree with Christian Trommsdorff, to point out all the errors and failures with clear-eyed perspective afterward, the fact is—at least thirty people, all acting more or less rationally when they left Camp IV, chose to place themselves under the serac on August 1. The weather was perfect, and there appears to have been nothing obvious, nothing overt that suggested such a massive loss of life was in the offing.

My own research into K2 has now stretched from August 2008, to January 2010. During multiple conversations with the same contacts, stretching over a period of months and sometimes lasting more than a year, I noticed that opinions rarely changed. Instead they seemed to harden, congealing into thorny, self-evident truths that were impossible to debate. Psychologists have a term for this, too: It's called "motivated reasoning." "When the facts get in the way of our beliefs, our brains are marvelously adept at dispensing with the facts," a September 2009 *New York Times* article explained. Comparing everything from partisan politics to Cook and Peary's original adventure-media showdown, research suggests that our brains function in qualitatively different ways when considering two sides of an argument:

> When we contemplate contradictions in the rhetoric of the opposition party's candidate, the rational centers of our brains are active, but contradictions from our own party's candidate set off a different reaction: the emotional centers light up and levels of feel-good dopamine surge.

A century after the polar feud, and despite the fact that current evidence persuasively argues that neither Peary nor Cook reached ninety degrees north, there are still adamant believers in both camps. Was this the root cause of all the derisive disputes in exploratory history: the imperceptible secretions of the right chemicals inside our own heads? All the debates and evidence might suddenly seem so trivial, except that, somewhere in the process, personal lives are lost and broken.

But if our beliefs don't change, what about our conduct, our actions? One reason the 2008 K2 disaster struck such a lasting note in the media is that it was taken as evidence of the modern degradation of the sport, a sign. Have modern mountaineers fundamentally changed in ethics and moral standards from a half century ago? Maurice Isserman thinks so. "It strikes me that the real contrast here is that, in the thirties, the fifties, and into the early sixties, there was a real expeditionary culture, and that culture emphasized collective achievement as opposed to individual achievement, and it emphasized mutual responsibility," he told the audience at the Banff Centre while sitting on the same panel as Trommsdorff and Habeler.

"That's unfair coverage, trying to compare K2 in 2008 to K2 in 1953," Andy Selters responds. "Sure, technology has changed, circumstances have changed . . . but people are the same. In base camp throughout the tragedy, I saw people struggling—only to a very small degree were people not helping each other, doing everything they could. People aren't angels, but they are not villains either."

After all I had learned about K2, I had to agree.

On an overcast April day, I left early from Cas van de Gevel's apartment in Utrecht and boarded a train heading east, out into the countryside. I changed lines at a small suburban station, boarding a second, smaller rail that rattled farther into the flat, verdant landscape. A well-used expedition Land Cruiser with sponsor stickers puttered to a stop in front of the station steps. Wilco van Rooijen drove me two miles back to his home—the partially converted barn he had purchased a year ago, right before he left for K2. He led me inside, walking with a stiff, uncomfortable gait, and we sat down in two chairs side by side in his living room and talked about the accident for three hours.

"After a while, people want to say, 'Hey, listen, this is the explanation . . .'" Wilco told me, clearly chagrined at the intense media scrutiny in the wake of the disaster. "Finally there was one American, I think; he said, 'Hey, listen, stop the whole discussion; let's be proud and have respect for all those climbers who had the guts to go there and climb to the summit'—and that's the thing you have to remember, not the climbers comparing and saying this and that about each other. . . ."

Heleen, Wilco's wife, and Teun, now a year and a half old, walked in from the kitchen and played quietly on the other side of the room. "The majority thinks that a lot of climbers are adrenaline junkies, not on the safe side—but Rolf, he was a hell of a climber, Rolf Bae. Gerard, he was always on the safe side. If there was something which was not safe, he was the first one who would have turned around. And Pemba as well. It's nothing to do with safety, nothing to do with the capabilities of the climbers. If you had bad luck, if you were in the wrong place at the wrong time, you were finished. Why I survived and others didn't . . . I talked with Cas about it, you'll never get an answer. It's just bad luck."

Wilco thinks of Gerard often, he told me. "He was so warm; he was always helping . . . he was a very special guy."

Toward the end of the interview, Wilco bent down and untied his shoes. "The surgeries were successful," he said, and he was already able to jog and begin training. Just beyond the balls of his feet, in place of his toes, two flaps of skin curled in toward each other in a long incision. Wilco was receiving help from the government lab helping soldiers wounded in Iraq; with the help of special supporting insoles, he could walk and even run without a cane.

Marco Confortola also suffered through months of surgery, amputations, and recovery. He is convinced to this day that the three climbers he met at the top were beyond saving. "I think that all three were not in shape to descend. But I decided to try to help them because they were still alive and in grave condition. My choice was dictated more by a sense of compassion than that a real chance existed to get them down," he wrote in an e-mail, explaining that his decision to stop and help may have cost him the front of his feet. "Having stopped at that altitude and after a night of bivying at that altitude it probably caused the serious congealing in my feet and consequently in September 2008 I had to amputate ALL of my toes on both of my feet. But I think that I would do it all over again."

"Marco is not being dishonest," Wilco said in another interview. "Based on his memory of the events, his explanation is his truth. How could anyone be lucid and analytical right before he became unconscious?" Looking down at the fleshy lips of Wilco's wound, and knowing that Marco had endured even worse injuries, I found it hard not to believe that both men really had done everything they could and that the mountain had permanently taken something away from them, too. Wilco preferred not to dwell on the past, and instead he directed the conversation toward future aspirations.

"My recovery is good," he told me, "and of course I would like to climb more eight-thousand-meter peaks."

Evoking the lost men of a different tragedy on a different mountain, Norman Maclean wrote: "A storyteller, unlike a historian, must follow compassion wherever it leads him. He must be able to accompany his characters, even into smoke and fire, and bear witness to what they thought and felt even when they themselves no longer knew." There are blank spots as to what happened on K2 on August 2, 2008—but that should not stop us from following the story to its final end. For what happened on K2 on August 2, 2008, to change from disaster to tragedy, as Maclean might say, it must become a story, and to tell this story as best we can we have first listened to as many voices as possible. There is one final voice we must listen to: the voice of Gerard McDonnell himself, offering a fitting requiem and cautionary note for all those who can no longer speak.

"Oftentimes, when an incident like that happens when somebody does lose a life, what went on is held up under the microscope, and all these people start criticizing, and some people might say, 'Well, they did this wrong, or she did that wrong . . .'" Gerard told an interviewer a year before his death. "I think there's a lot of people that are still alive today and might be people less inclined to criticize. . . . They don't realize how close they might have come themselves; they very well could have been in that situation had some little thing gone wrong. Just because you survive a mountain doesn't make you an expert—and I don't think it gives you any right to say that somebody made a mistake. When you weren't there, you don't know. Only the mountain knows the full story."

On August 2, 1939, another Tshering left what was then called Camp VI, and now is closer to Camp II, and was seen descending the lower slopes of the Abruzzi Ridge. He was frightened and hurried down the mountain as fast as he could. He was alone. When Tshering reached base camp, he told his companions that Pasang Kikuli, Pasang Kitar, and Phinsoo, who had tried to rescue Dudley Wolfe, were gone. All four had perished. Why did Pasang Kikuli, the first Sherpa sirdar on K2, give his life to try to rescue one of his clients? "We can only guess," Jonathan Neale wrote of his sacrifice, "but I don't think his decision arose out of loyalty to sahibs. It was a matter of *nyingje*—love." Sixty-nine years later,

Big Pasang and Gerard McDonnell's sacrifices to help Jumik and his clients, and Tsering Bhote's act of witness, echoes with history.

The two climbing-Sherpas, who were assigned to the Korean "B" team, met Pemba Gyalje, Pasang Lama, and Chhiring Dorje below the Bottleneck sometime after eleven p.m., on August 1. They stopped for a moment to share a hot drink and Big Pasang admonished them for leaving the others behind. Tsering and Big Pasang went up, while the other three, exhausted from the summit, continued down to Camp IV. Another headlamp was soon visible, trudging down to meet them in the darkness. Tsering and Big Pasang climbed toward it, ascending the steepening slope that led into the bottom of the couloir. It was Kim Jae-su. Tsering and Big Pasang gave the Bara Sahib hot water and they rested. There was no sign of Go Mi-yeong.

"Didi is coming down behind me," Kim told them.

Tsering and Big Pasang went higher. They could not find her. Near the top of the couloir they could see more headlamps coming down. Suddenly, two of the headlamps fell.

Tsering saw one bounce to the right, over the east face, toward China. The other fell left, to the south. Big Pasang radioed base camp. He told them that they had seen two climbers falling down the couloir, and one of them might have been Didi. They didn't know who it was. Tsering and Big Pasang searched the east face for several hours. Tsering estimated they went as high as 8,200 meters, but that might be exaggerated. By four a.m. they were freezing and exhausted. They turned and began to descend the Shoulder, making their way down toward Camp IV. Then they saw a headlamp off the trail and heard someone's muted cries.

It was Didi.

She must have fallen off the crest of the Shoulder. It was hard to tell how far Go Mi-yeong had slid or if she was injured, but it was obvious that she needed help to get back to Camp IV. Tsering and Big Pasang did not have any real rope with them. They girth-hitched several slings and cordelettes together and began to drag her. By the lights of their headlamps they pulled and coaxed and pushed Go Mi-yeong all the way to her tent. Then Tsering and Big Pasang went back to their own tent and rested for half an hour.

It was nearly dawn, and four of their teammates were still missing.

It must have been very cold that night for all of them.

We will never know why Jumik, Kim Hyo-gyeong, Hwang Dong-jin, and Park Kyeong-hyo fell. In some interviews, Marco recalled seeing lights in front of him and Gerard. Those lights mysteriously dropped from view, and shortly thereafter they decided it would be safer to stop and wait until dawn, rather than continue looking for the top anchor in the dark. Later in the night, perhaps much later, Wilco joined them.

We can't even know for sure that all four men were together at the time of the fall. But the four were last seen together, connected to the anchor at the bottom end of the emergency rope that Jumik had carried to the summit and that was used as a fixed hand line to negotiate the summit slopes on the descent. It's reasonable to presume that after Pemba Gyalje, Pasang Lama, Chhiring Dorje, Kim Jae-su, Go Mi-yeong, and Cas van de Gevel descended, they stayed together, tied to the line for security.

If they were descending in such fashion, the first (lowest) man would have reached the top fixed line and continued down, by either clipping into the fixed line with a carabiner on a tether, putting a jumar on the rope, or employing a hand wrap to create friction. Possibly it was a combination of two of these techniques. But did that man make the added effort to disconnect from the separate line that still joined him to the three men behind?

Pasang Lama, who fixed the last section of line on the ascent, remembers running out of rope at the top of a section of exposed ice on the very edge of the serac, and, with no hardware with which to build an independent anchor, tying his line to an old section of rope that was exposed. The sun-bleached line was stretched tight by the glacial creep of the serac, and the only knot Pasang Lama could form was a simple clove hitch. It is possible that this line broke. It is also possible that one of the climbers fell on the patch of water-ice just below, where Chhiring Dorje and Pasang Lama each took short but heart-stopping falls, and yanked his other teammates off.

We do not know how it happened, but after the fall, Jumik could not move. The rope pinned him to the mountain and he must have heard noises, groaning in the darkness.

It takes a certain mind-set to run under a serac. You try to do most of the thinking beforehand. You figure what the safest route is, calculate the odds, estimate how long it will take. Then you make up your mind and commit. After that, it's only a matter of putting one leg in front of the other. You try not to think about it any more than you have to. Most of the time, you are doing it because the risk seems worth it. Because there is no other place in the world you would rather be than deep in one of the earth's untamed wildernesses, climbing a mountain, with nothing else to worry about than controlling the lactic acid in your legs and the pace of your breath.

Sometimes, you run under a serac because you have no other choice. One widespread rumor in base camp was that Kim Jae-su ordered Big Pasang and Tsering to go under the serac and rescue their teammates. Pemba recollects trying to talk them out of going up the Bottleneck several times, once in person at Camp IV that morning, and later via radio as they were ascending the Shoulder. At the very least, it's true that the Korean leader worked his employees very, very hard. But I'd prefer to believe that, like Pasang Kikuli before them, they did it for the nobler reason.

Light slowly seeped between the giants of the Baltoro Glacier.

As Big Pasang and Tsering gathered themselves to leave Camp IV and head up again, Wilco, Marco, and Gerard already stirred. They wandered down a little way from their bivouac. It was hard at first to regain coordination after such a difficult night, but with each step down, with more blood forced throughout their bodies, they might have felt a little better.

They stopped on top of the serac. They looked for the top anchor of the fixed rope but could not find it. Wilco began to down-climb alone. He was untethered, and guessed at the best route. Marco and Gerard lingered behind. Then Gerard traversed a little way to the south, onto steeper terrain, and he could look down and see the route below.

"Walk, Marco," Gerard called to him, indicating where the route went over the edge of the serac to the top of the Diagonal. Marco climbed to the edge and saw the fixed lines below them. And there were three human beings. They had fallen; they were alive, though badly tangled in rope and obviously injured.

We will never know what happened to the fourth member of their party. Kim Hyo-gyeong, or "Little Kim," as he was nicknamed, was thirty-three years old and probably the weakest member of the Korean "A" team. According to Kim Jae-su, the climb was his first major expedition. Little Kim was climbing slowly during the last few hours of the ascent; the rest of the team waited on the summit for more than an hour and a half for him to join them. His oxygen ran out just after they began to descend, and Pasang Lama gave him his own partially used oxygen bottle. Little Kim was, according to Pasang Lama, steadily losing motor coordination and strength during the rest of the descent. The other two missing members of the Korean team, Hwang Dong-jin and Park Kyeong-hyo, each had multiple eight-thousand-meter summits to his credit, and both were much stronger and more experienced, Kim Jae-su says. From this testimony, and Marco's descriptions of them, the three men found alive were likely Jumik Bhote, Hwang Dong-jin and Park Kyeong-hyo.

If you believe what Gerard McDonnell's friends and teammates say about him, it was probably preordained from the moment they found the distressed Korean team that Gerard would not leave them so long as he believed they could be saved. Marco's testimony describes lowering the "Korean leader," but he mentioned few precise details about the other two, who were presumably also tangled in rope. And in earlier statements, the Italian painted an even more desperate scene. "I tried everything and more, but I simply couldn't do it, could not take them back home. In my role of mountain rescuer I felt worthless . . . useless," one article in the *Guardian* quoted him as saying. Based on either version, it's clear that Jumik and the Koreans were not entirely freed from their entanglements when Marco decided he could do no more and continued his descent. Gerard McDonnell was by temperament a problem-solver and by training an engineer. He was also methodical, persistent and safety-conscious. His outgoing personality, his love of music, family, friends, and travel, were rooted in one more trait that was the bedrock of who he was: unfiltered empathy for all human beings. All of these elements of his character must have combined in what happened next.

There are myriad ways Gerard might have finished the job. Matt Szundy describes one simple step-by-step process by which Gerard could have transferred the load. First, he would have had to determine which rope within the tangle needed to be unloaded. Then he would have ascended to the anchor point above, and tied a three-wrap friction hitch around the taunt line. This would be connected to a spare section of rope, which in turn would be connected by a munter hitch to the anchor. With a new load-bearing system thus created, Gerard could then cut the tensioned line above the friction hitch, and lower the climbers using the munter hitch with the spare line.

Regardless of how he did it, there would have been few words exchanged between them as he worked. Neither Jumik or the Koreans spoke fluent English under the best of circumstances; after thirty hours above eight thousand meters communication would be reduced to all but the most basic messages. By then, very little needed to be said. There was only the persistent pull of gravity, the involuntary panting of each man as his body yearned for more oxygen and a parched dryness burned in his throat, and the taunt rope that bound them all together.

We know from Tsering Bhote's story that Big Pasang never went much higher than the top of the Bottleneck. Tsering was close below, still close enough that they could communicate by shouting. He waited on the right side of the couloir, just beneath the Bottleneck itself, and watched as an intermittent whiteout swirled around—the landscape awash in the snowless, colorless vapor of cloud.

Big Pasang never quite met Gerard McDonnell. But he also must have been close, close enough that through the openings in the whiteout Big Pasang could see another human form descending the lower section of the traverse, just to his left. He was coming down last, behind his teammates, in the traditional position of a guide or the strongest member of the team.

If Big Pasang could see Gerard, it is possible that Gerard saw Big Pasang. He probably wouldn't have recognized him; he would have noticed only another person, that someone had arrived to help them down. For a moment, he might have felt some shiver of warmth, knowing that they were not alone.

Minutes later, Tsering saw them climbing down in a row toward him. They were roped together and Jumik was in the lead, with Big Pasang behind him, and then the foreigners.

Tsering saw the accident with his own eyes.

He cried at the top of his lungs, but no sound came out.

ACKNOWLEDGMENTS

In 1998 and 2000, I did my first two expeditions to the Alaska Range. Beginning in 2003, I returned every year for six straight seasons. In all those trips I never met Gerard McDonnell, though later I learned we shared a handful of casual friends from the Anchorage climbing scene. Over the last two years, I've caught myself wondering if we ever did cross paths somewhere on the wide Kahiltna Glacier, or anonymously rubbed elbows at the West Rib Cafe and Pub in Talkeetna. I might have even poked my head into the Fairview Inn on a raucus late-spring evening, when the twilight lasts forever, and heard a few minutes of Last Night's Fun, Anchorage's own Irish band. If it happened that would have been Gerard McDonnell playing the bodhrán and singing.

Among one of Gerard's many future projects was to make a documentary about his friend and climbing partner Pemba Gyalje Sherpa that would tell something about his life and the Sherpas' perspective on the world. When I began writing about K2, I found myself fascinated with the climbing-Sherpas' experiences on the mountain, and I hope that their story is a reminder that different worldviews and alternative perspectives lurk beneath every human interaction. Some readers might feel that at times in this book I push too hard, belaboring an Orientalist "us and them" divide—a fair criticism to which I can only respond by saying that I believe part of a writer's job is to make his or her readers uncomfortable, to try to force them to at least question their own beliefs and values.

Early into my research, I realized that to do justice to the full scope of the tragedy, the story had to be told not only from the perspective of those on the mountain, but also the family and loved ones who were scattered around the globe waiting for news from K2. I would like to express my deep gratitude and respect to the family of Gerard McDonnell—including his brother, JJ, brother-in-law, Damien, and mother, Margaret—and to Annie Starkey, for not just allowing me to write not about their son, brother, and partner, but also for letting me include part of their own struggles in the aftermath of the disaster. Similarly, I would also like to express my thanks to Dawasangmu Bhote and Lhamu Bhote. Without them sharing parts of their personal stories, I strongly feel that it would be impossible to evaluate the full impact of the media and the consequences of how such events are publicly reported. While writing this book, I tried to constantly remind myself that eight more tragedies, each one of immeasurable impact, occurred in Korea, Pakistan, France, Norway, and Serbia. I would like to express my condolences to all the families and friends who lost a loved one during the disaster.

Heartfelt thanks go to everyone who was on K2 during the summer of 2008 who helped me by sharing their stories, perspectives, and opinions, either in direct person-to-person interviews, phone conversations, or e-mail correspondence. They are: Cas van de Gevel, Wilco van Rooijen, Roeland van Oss, Jelle Staleman, Pemba Gyalje, Marco Confortola, Lars Nessa, Kim Jae-su, Pasang Lama, Chhiring Dorje, Mike Farris, Chris Klinke, Eric Meyer, Fredrik Sträng, Nick Rice, Robert Goh, Chuck Boyd, Andy Selters, Christian Trommsdorff, and Milivoj Erdeljan.

Additionally I interviewed, corresponded with, or informally spoke to dozens of other people who were not present on the mountain, but experienced the disaster in other ways or could help lend perspective to different aspects of the narrative. Mountaineers with K2 experience or knowledge of modern eight-thousand-meter climbing who helped include Chris Warner, Steve Swenson, Thor Kieser, Charlie Mace, Barry Blanchard, Jamie McGuinness, Fabrizio Zangrilli, Steve House, Marko Prezelj, Eric Remza, Phil Powers, and Simon Moro.

I'm indebted not only to the climbing-Sherpas on K2 themselves, but also the kindness of their families and friends, and the hospitality of many more who helped me while I was in Kathmandu, or by sharing their knowledge of the country of Nepal, including Dawa and Ngawang Tashi Dorje, Jammu Gyalje, Tshering Pande Bhote, Pertemba Sherpa, Ang Tshering Sherpa, Jamling Tenzing Norgay, Virginia O'Leary, Sherry Ortner, John and Judy Aull, Mark LaMont, and Ian Wall. Nazir Sabir was invaluable in helping to explain the Pakistani mountaineering perspective. I also would like to acknowledge the help I received from Gerard McDonnell and Annie Starkey's friends in Alaska (and elsewhere), including Dan Possumato, Daryl Miller, Joe Reichert, Jeff Jessen, Hilka Korvola, Evie Whitten, Jo Fortier, Charlie Sassara, and Matt Szundy. My Korean contacts also deserve recognition for their support, including Jae Jung, Ryu Dong-il, Kyu Dam Lee, Sonia Knapp, and especially Jake Preston. I offer my sincere thanks and appreciation to you all.

Chris Klinke, Virginia O'Leary, and the family of Gerard McDonnell were extremely generous in granting permission for me to include their photographs in this book. Thank you. Special recognition goes to my longtime friend Emilie Lee for the exceptional illustrations.

Any rookie author brings far more enthusiasm than practiced skill to the job. I was incredibly lucky to have a string of talented editors working with me on the K2 story from the very beginning. Alison Osius and the rest of the editorial staff at *Rock and Ice* deserve special mention for collaborating with me on "Perfect Chaos," my original feature article on the disaster, which proved to be the crucial launchpad for the rest of this project. Katharine Zaleski (formerly of the *Huffington Post*, now of the *Washington Post*) and Katie Ives of *Alpinist* read early sections of the book and provided feedback and encouragement, as did two of my siblings, Posie and Ben Wilkinson. Tony Whittome and Marni Jackson, my editors at the Banff Mountain Writing Program, were wonderful at helping me get over a pivotal hump in the process, as were my fellow participants in the workshop. Other journalists and editors I spoke to or corresponded with about the story and who provided feedback, advice, or encouragement along the way are David Roberts, Brad Wieners, Ed Douglas, Michael Kennedy, Kelly Cordes, and Dougald McDonald.

Mark Chait at New American Library has been an unusually perceptive and forgiving editor to work with. I thank him for his shrewd feedback and suggestions, and for guiding me through the book-making process. Additionally, this book would not have happened in the first place without my exceptional team of agents, Bruce Ostler and Ian Kleinert. I'm grateful for Bruce's advice and cheerleading from the very beginning, and Ian's willingness to take me on despite being very green at a project of this scope.

I'd like to thank my friends and family for their support and love. My parents deserve special recognition for encouraging my passion for climbing and adventure from childhood. Lastly, this manuscript was almost entirely written and revised in the twelve-by-twelve cabin I share with my loving fiancée, Janet Bergman. How she was able to share such confined living quarters with a boyfriend and first-time author often in the throes of big-time stress is a mystery I will never understand. I couldn't have done any of this without her.

A NOTE ON SOURCES

Individual comments and notes are offered for each chapter below. However, I would like to offer one general comment on the use of Internet blogs as sources for reporting what happened. As is shown in the narrative, serious mistakes can be made when unsubstantiated reports on the Internet are repeated as verified news in the mainstream media. That said, personal blog reports from the high mountains are a new phenomenon that is only bound to increase in the coming years, and I think they do serve a valuable purpose to the climbing community, so long as everyone realizes their inherent flaws. Many of the teams and individual climbers on K2 during the 2008 season posted public dispatches, and after the tragedy, many wrote personal statements summarizing their recollections of what happened and posted them on the Internet, including Marco Confortola, Wilco van Rooijen, Milivoj Erdeljan, Chris Klinke, Nick Rice, and Fredrik Sträng. Though none of these reports can be considered authoritative, as primary documents, they provide a fascinating and important record of what each person saw, felt, and believed to be happening during the disaster. I have quoted and used such material accordingly throughout the narrative.

CHAPTER NOTES

PROLOGUE

These scenes are based primarily on a series of interviews and follow-up discussions I conducted with Chhiring Dorje, Pemba Gyalje, and Pasang Lama in Kathmandu that began in October 2008, and lasted until December 2009. See endnotes for chapter seven for a more detailed summary of accounts concerning the initial three hundred meters of the descent from the summit on the night of August 1, and the subsequent splintering of the summit party.

CHAPTER ONE

The Jim Curran quote is from "A Bad Season on K2," by Jon Krakauer and Greg Child, published in *Outside* magazine, 1987. See also: *K2, Triumph and Tragedy*, by Jim Curran (Mariner Books, 1989). Statistics on K2, Everest, and eight-thousand-meter climbing are available at 8000ers.com and adventurestats.com. In addition to Norit's public dispatches, much of the background information on the Norit team and their communications during the tragedy are based on interviews with Roeland van Oss and Maarten van Eck, as well as Norit's blog.

CHAPTER TWO

With Roeland van Oss, Chris Klinke was invaluable for helping sort out the narrative and time line in base camp as the disaster evolved. I spoke to Tom and Tina Sjogren for their recollections of the communications issues that occurred, and ExplorersWeb and Maarten van Eck agreed to release their personal e-mail correspondence during the disaster, which helped clarify the precise time line for certain events. Wilco van Rooijen also gave permission for Human Edge Technology to share details about the signals location of his sat phone with me.

CHAPTER THREE

For the original documentation on the disagreements over media reports, see "Swedish Climber In K2 Death Drama," Claudia Rodas for TT, August 2, 2008; "K2 Mountain Drama Over: 11 Dead," Claudia Rodas for TT, August 3, 2008; "K2 Expedition Dispatches," by Nick Rice on his Web site: http://www.nickrice.us/index_files/expeditiondispatches.htm; "The Dramatic Events on K2 and Other Reflections," by Fredrik Sträng on his Web site: http://web.strang.se/frmIndex.aspx; and "K2's Double Tragedy: Blowing out Candles for Scoops and Fame," editorial for Explorersweb.com, August 3, 2008.

CHAPTER FOUR

Eric Meyer was patient in explaining the medical issues he faced in treating Cas van de Gevel, Wilco van Rooijen, and Marco Confortola.

CHAPTER FIVE

For historical perspective on the race for the North Pole, I used "Who Discovered the North Pole?" by Bruce Henderson in *Smithsonian* magazine, April 2009; *The Trust: The Private and Powerful Family Behind the New York Times,* by Susan Tifft and Alex S. Jones; as well as numerous articles published in the *New York Times,* including: "London Applauds Peary's Exploit," September 7, 1909; "Peary Before Start Arraigned Cook," September 9, 1909; "Dr. Cook and the *Times*," December 13, 1909; "Copyright in News Reports," March 10, 1912; "Aurora at Hobart; Crew

Cheer *Fram*," March 13, 1912; "Waiting to Hear from Scott," March 13, 1912; "Amundsen Hearing Put Off," March 16, 1912; and "A Correction," August 23, 1988.

Accounts of the 2008 K2 disaster cited include: "11 Feared Dead in Mountaineering Disaster on K2," by Stephen Graham for the Associated Press, August 4, 2008; "Dutch Survivor of K2 Avalanche Describes Ordeal," by Stephen Graham for the Associated Press, August 4, 2008; "Death Toll on the World's Most Treacherous Peak Reaches 11," Randeep Ramesh for the *Guardian* (UK), August 5, 2008; "Chaos on the Mountain That Invites Death," Graham Bowley for the *New York Times*, August 5, 2008; "Italian Reaches Base Camp after Tragedy on K2," Matthew Pennington for the Associated Press, August 5, 2008; "K2 Survivor Wilco van Rooijen, in His Own Words," Kirkpatrick Reardon for National Geographic Adventure Online, August 7, 2008; "'I Was Desperate, Hopeless, But I Wasn't Going to Give Up,' says K2 survivor," Omar Wariach for the *Independent*, August 9, 2008; "Does Climbing Matter Anymore?" Graham Bowley for the *New York Times*, August 9, 2008; "The Descent of Men," Maurice Isserman for the *New York Times*, August 10, 2008; "Catastrophe on K2," Simon Hattenstone for the *Guardian*, August 23, 2008; "Death or Glory: The Truth about K2," Andrew Buncombe for the *Independent*, August 28, 2008; "The Killing Peak," Matthew Power for *Men's Journal*, October 2008; and "A Few False Moves," by Michael Kodas for Outside Online, October 2008.

CHAPTER SIX

Considering the essential role that climbing-Sherpas played in the history of mountaineering, I was surprised to learn that only a handful of books seriously attempt to document the expeditionary experience from their perspective. Two standout exceptions are Jonathan Neale's *Tigers of the Snow* (Saint Martin's Press, 2002) and Sherry Ortner's *Life and Death on Mt. Everest: Sherpas and Himalayan Mountaineering* (Princeton University Press, 1999). Each in its own distinctive style does an extraordinary job of documenting Himalayan climbing from the climbing-Sherpas' perspective, and I leaned on them both heavily. Two more titles that focus on the Sherpas from an anthropological perspective are James F. Fisher's *Sherpas: Reflections on Change in Himalayan Nepal* (University of California Press, 1990) and Christoph von Furer-Haimendorf's *The Sherpas Transformed* (Sterling Publishers, 1984). Lastly, I recommend a trio of books recently published dealing with Tenzing Norgay: *Tenzing: Hero of Everest*, by Ed Douglas (National Geographic, 2004); *Tenzing Norgay and the Sherpas of Everest*, by Tashi and Judy Tenzing (International Marine Publishing, 2001); and *Touching My Father's Soul*, by Jamling Tenzing Norgay and Broughton Coburn (HarperOne, 2001). Excellent accounts of the 1939 American expedition can be found in *K2: The 1939 Tragedy*, by Andrew Kaufman and William Putnam (The Mountaineers, 1992); *K2: Life and Death on the World's Most Dangerous Mountain*, by Ed Viesturs and David Roberts (Broadway, 2009); and *K2: The Story of the Savage Mountain*, by Jim Curran (The Mountaineers, 1995).

CHAPTER SEVEN

Additional information on life in the Rolwaling Valley was used from *The Sherpas of the Rolwaling*, by Janice Sacherer; "Letter from a Lama" at http://rolwaling.tripod.com/lama-letter.html; and "Interview with Tulku Ngawang Lapsum" at http://www.rolwaling.com/tulku.html.

CHAPTER EIGHT

The different perspectives on base camp meetings and summit day are based primarily on conversations and correspondence with Pemba Gyalje, Chhiring Dorje, Pasang Lama, Wilco van Rooijen, Cas van de Gevel, Mike Farris, Chris Klinke, Eric Meyer, Fredrik Sträng, Lars Nessa, Kim Jae-su, and Marco Confortola. I also relied on public statements and accounts many involved posted on their personal Web sites, or gave for other publications. Much of this material is widely known; however, one original source of note is a video deposition made by Kim Jae-su and Go Mi-yeong immediately after they arrived in base camp. A translation of these statements, originally given in Korean and filmed by Fred Sträng, confirmed many details, including the climbing-Sherpa's use of a temporarily fixed hand line to navigate the summit party down to the top of the fixed lines.

CHAPTER NINE

I was unaware of Pemba Gyalje's full story until, after several informal meetings and afternoons climbing together, we sat down at Himalayan Java, a popular coffee shop in Thamel, the second week in November for a long discussion about what happened. Months after that, the McDonnell family released the partial transcripts from their meeting in Islamabad. Comparing the two records of his experience, I found no significant changes or alterations to his story.

CHAPTER TEN

Virginia O'Leary, Tshering Pande Bhote, Pasang Lama, and Chhiring Dorje helped explain Jumik Bhote's personal history. Facts cited about Nepal's modern humanitarian struggles came from "The CIA World Factbook," https://www.cia.gov/library/publications/the-world-factbook/, and also the Amnesty International Web site, http://www.amnesty.org/. I found a series of interviews Gerard McDonnell gave to Irish Public Radio in 2007 to be particularly helpful in understanding his story, along with conversations with members of his family and Annie Starkey.

CHAPTER ELEVEN

Sonia Knapp and Jake Preston helped answer questions about the Korean "Flying Jump" expedition and Go Mi-yeong, and explained some of the dynamics of Korean climbing culture in general. Ryu Dong-il was very helpful in interviewing Kim Jae-su and translating his answers to my questions. I interviewed Jeff Jessen, Daryl Miller, Dan Possumato, Hilka Korvola, and Annie Starkey for information about Gerard McDonnell's life and climbing adventures in Alaska.

CHAPTER TWELVE

Maria Coffey's earth-shattering book *Where the Mountain Casts Its Shadow* (Saint Martin's Press, 2003) was both an important source and an inspiration in helping me tackle how to incorporate the struggles of the McDonnell family and Annie Starkey after the tragedy. Excerpts from the Islamabad transcripts, a recording made by Damien McDonnell of the original Norit team's debrief after the disaster, were made available to all journalists working on this story. "The Testimony of Marco Confortola" is posted on his Web site in Italian and English versions at: http://www.marcoconfortola.it. Sections of the November 2008 letter by Pemba Gyalje Sherpa are quoted with permission. The time line presented in the August 2nd illustration is my own synthesis of data, presented with the imput of Pemba Gyalje Sherpa. ExplorersWeb and others have presented a slightly different version of events.

CHAPTER THIRTEEN

Virginia O'Leary's blog is quoted throughout part three with permission. "How Can We Help the World's Poor," Nicholas Kristof for the *New York Times*, November 20, 2009.

CHAPTER FOURTEEN

Various quotes are from "K2: High Stakes on the Savage Summit," a panel discussion at the 2008 Banff Book Festival. To my knowledge, Tsering Bhote spoke publicly about his personal experiences on K2 during August 1 and 2, 2008, on only two separate occasions. Both were videotaped interviews for documentary projects in the fall of 2008 and both were conducted in Nepali. Unfortunately, as of March 1, 2010, neither project has been completed, and the information contained in the interviews has not been made available by any other means—posing the very real risk that Tsering's account might be erased from the history of the tragedy. A translated transcript of one of these interviews was provided to me with the permission of the filmmaker who conducted the interview.

INDEX

Freddie Wilkinson is a New England–based professional climber, mountain guide, and outdoor writer. He has made numerous first ascents on difficult peaks in Alaska, Patagonia, and the Himalaya. In 2007, the American Alpine Club awarded him the Robert Hicks Bates Award for outstanding accomplishment by a young climber. His writing frequently appears in the Huffington Post, *Climbing*, *Rock and Ice*, *Alpinist*, and the *American Alpine Journal*. Wilkinson lives in a twelve-by-twelve cabin with no running water and a "superfast" wireless Internet connection. Visit his Web site at www.huffingtonpost.com/freddie-wilkinson.